CORVETTE AND SUBMARINE

MAX SHEAN

To the men of His Majesty's Ship Bluebell
and
Submarines X4, X5, X7, X9, X22, X24,
XE 3, XE 5 and XE 6
who were lost on active service
and to those who loved them.

To Patrick,

With my compliments.

Max   May 1995

Max Shean

©1992 by Max Shean
Second edition 1994.
This book is copyright. Apart from any fair dealing for the purpose
of study,research,criticism, review,or as otherwise permitted under
the Copyright Act,no part may be reproduced by any process
without written permission.Inquiries should be made to the
publisher.

Published by
Max Shean
Unit 2, 6 Bindaring Parade
Claremont
Western Australia 6010

Printed by
Scott Four Colour Print
40 Short Street
Perth
Western Australia 6000

National Library of Australia Cataloguing-in-Publication entry
Shean,Max, 1918
   Corvette and Submarine

 ISBN 0 646 09171 9

 1.Bluebell(Corvette) and X-craft(Submarines).
 2.World War 1939-45 naval operations,British.
 3.World War 1939-45 campaign Atlantic and Pacific.

940.545

Back cover: Reproduction of painting by Geoffrey Mainwaring
commissioned by the Australian War Memorial, of Lieutenant
Commander Max Shean. Oil on hardboard 76.4 x 61 cm.
Transparency number 27531.

CONTENTS

FOREWORD

by

Vice Admiral Sir Ian McIntosh KBE CB DSO DSC Royal Navy (ret)

Max Shean was one of that small band of gallant young men who, volunteering for "special and hazardous service", manned X-craft and Chariots and by their coolly audacious attacks on shipping and installations in harbours and inshore areas carried the sea war into the enemy's closely guarded waters. That so small a body of men were awarded no less than four Victoria Crosses, 11 Distinguished Service Orders (two of them to Shean), six Conspicuous Gallantry Medals and over 40 other fighting decorations and medals reflects the hazard faced and the successes achieved despite those hazards.

Interrupting his engineering studies at University to join the RANVR his early training in Anti-Submarine Warfare focussed his interest not only on the operation of the equipment but also on its functioning. This served his corvette *Bluebell* well in the arduous battle protecting merchantmen against the U-boats in the Western Approaches in the often foul weather of the North Atlantic.

With his combination of engineering and seamanship skills, Max, probably without realising it, was ideally suited to submarines. He added to this the courage to volunteer for an unspecified but obviously perilous service. His engineering logical deductive approach shows clearly when you read how he tackled the problem of cutting nets effectively to allow X-craft to penetrate defences as those around *Tirpitz*.

The generation caught up in the great conflict of World War II is now dwindling and it is good when one of those involved directly records his experiences. These, though unique to each person, are stitches in the vast tapestry of that time and stitches make up the full picture. This over-modest account of an active and successful war is not only an enthralling story but it has the rare merit of being written in lucid and economical prose that is a delight to read. Do not be delayed further by me.

ALVERSTOKE
HAMPSHIRE
November 1993.

CHAPTER ONE

CHANGE IN STUDIES

The magnitude of World War II was such that all its significant details must be beyond the comprehension of any individual. It is, for good reason, the topic of much interest even now, fifty years after it started. Many people of younger generations than mine ask about it and suggest that I should record my own recollections before it is too late, so that is what I have done.

As a security measure, in the Royal Australian Navy, we were not permitted to keep a diary or any papers containing classified information. Therefore, I had little recorded fact around which to arrange my recollections of incidents. Nevertheless, there are some letters, photographs and publications by others from which I can extract key details. Research at the Public Record Office, Kew, England, has provided a factual framework. Above all, I am fortunate in still having the comradeship of my submarine crew, and long may they live. They correct me when I am wrong, which it seems is most of the time.

It was on Monday, the fourth of September, 1939 that it began for me in the Undergraduates' Common Room in the University of Western Australia. We second year Engineering students were listening to a radio report on developments in the Nazi invasion of Poland and learned that Britain had declared war. Such was the integrity of the British Empire, Australia followed suit.

Far from the fields of conflict, study carried on much the same, except that most of us had an uneasy feeling of obligation. At the dinner table at home the topic was discussed, of the Nazi spread across Europe.

"There's nothing you can do about it," my father said. On

the scale of things, he seemed to be right, I thought, but what a hopeless, fatalistic attitude. I did not say so, but continued to think about it.

Vague misgivings of students were brought into focus in May 1940 during the Allies' evacuation from Dunkirk. At the conclusion of one thermodynamics lecture, one student asked the lecturer, "Should we students join the Forces or continue with our studies?" The lecturer replied "Continue with your studies. Then, upon graduation, decide for yourselves where you should serve. Wherever it is, you'll make a greater contribution as qualified engineers." That, to me, seemed a sensible summary. At the same time, we had doubts because the war was going badly for us and could be lost before we were due to graduate in two years' time.

At the start of a hydraulics lecture soon after, another student asked the same question, quoting the advice already received. This lecturer, an Englishman of enormous loyalty to his mother country, spent the whole hour telling of how he thrilled at the marvellous rallying of the English people to rescue the retreating soldiers from the advancing Germans. He used emotional phrases like "shoulders to the wheel", "rallying to the colours" and so on, imploring us to join up forthwith. Well, that was the other point of view. Both had merit, though I thought that the former had more logic.

My good friend Peter Taylor had strong inclinations toward the Navy. Peter's father had a launch *Willana*, mine had *Medana* and we two spent our leisure in sailing dinghies. There must have been a trace of salt water in our blood, flowing down from our ancestors. Peter had two powerful sources of motivation toward the "Grey Funnel Line" (Navy). One was his loyalty to King and country and the other, a fear of final exams at University, only weeks away.

"Come on Slapsie," he said to me "We're off to join the Navy."

Came the next free period, we drove down to the RAN Headquarters in Cliff Street, Fremantle, and fronted up to the lieutenant commander recruiting officer. He advised "I could enlist you as stokers, but why not go back to University, complete your course and qualify? You would then be eligible to be commissioned as engineer officers; better for the Navy, better for you." There was another consideration. We were all subject to manpower regulations and were obliged, as third year students, to continue with studies, which we did, as best we could, with the ever present call of the sea and the conflict thereon.

Mercifully for Peter, there appeared in the West Australian newspaper on 25th June 1940, a notice inviting applications from gentlemen with yachting experience to be commissioned as Temporary Acting Sub Lieutenants in the Royal Australian Naval Volunteer Reserve and to be trained in anti-submarine duties. "Come on Slapsie, off to Fremantle," said Peter.

This time the enlistment process got underway with application forms, interview, tests, medical and hearing examinations. There followed a wait, as final examinations at University came dangerously close. Jubilation erupted as a letter for each of us came, dated 14th August 1940, from Captain C Farquhar-Smith, District Naval Officer, Naval Staff Office, Fremantle, saying:

"Dear Sir,

I beg to inform you that the marks obtained by you in the tests you underwent for qualification for a commission in the Anti-Submarine Branch of the Royal Australian Naval Volunteer Reserve are satisfactory. Your papers are being forwarded to Naval Board with a recommendation that you shall be gazetted as Acting Sub-Lieutenant (On Probation) R.A.N.V.R. It is not anticipated that you will be mobilised for a period of approximately two months.

I am,

Yours faithfully".

The only worry for Peter was that he would not be mobilised until University examinations were over. He could not settle down to study with the adventure of his life about to start. I looked beyond this to the eventual day when I might return to my books, and studied as best I could. The exams came; Peter did not do very well and I had difficulty in one subject; Design. However, the Faculty must have taken a broad view of the position and accorded me a clear pass, which was to be of great value five years later.

28th October 1940 was our first day in the Navy; a significant day for any officer as it determines his seniority, or position, in the pecking order. Romney Moran and Colin May were appointed on the same day as Peter and I. We were fitted out with uniforms with one narrow, wavy, bright gold stripe on each sleeve, and a week later, sent off by rail to Flinders Naval Depot (FND) in Victoria. At Adelaide we were joined by five more and in Melbourne, another three. Thus we became twelve, of "R" Class, presumably the eighteenth batch to go through the anti submarine (A/S) school. There had to be one in charge when necessary, so as we were all mobilised on 28th October, the senior among us had to be E.J. Adams, decided by the alphabet.

At Flinders, on the Mornington Peninsula, there came four weeks of disciplinary training, including squad drill with rifle or sword, instruction on gunnery, torpedoes, signals, seamanship and ship administration. Also, we had our introduction to the sick bay, or "ship's" hospital, for immunisation in preparation for travelling the globe and for influenza which struck all arrivals to that miserable rain soaked district, described by Peter as "The last place God made, and He threw His shovel at it."

All the same, it was new and exciting. The strict timetable and the frequent scurry to get it all in was in direct contrast to self regulated University life. Here was a naval tradition of high expectation and no evasion. The quality and cost of defence equipment amazed me. All the superb engineering of torpedo propulsion and guidance equipment, to be used once only and to be destroyed as the result of its own success, was different from anything I had known. From a human point of view, it was utter waste, but for its purpose nothing was too good; it must be better than the enemy's.

Model "war games" in battle fleet manoeuvres were fascinating; games that anyone could make and play. Part of the drill hall floor was marked out to a scale with squares representing miles of ocean. There were wooden models of battleships, cruisers, destroyers and submarines to the same scale with information on the weapon range and speed of each. Our class was divided in two, each "manning" one fleet. The fleets were initially deployed at opposite sides of the "ocean". Each team, under a selected Flag Officer, decided on individual ship course and speed to intercept the enemy and at two minute intervals, the models would be moved, to scale. As each two minute period passed, so the sea battle developed, weapons being fired also at the two minute time.

I found this absorbing, especially as the components were so simple. Sophisticated simulators were not always essential it seemed. In contrast to this technical and tactical training, we also did some "square bashing" on the large parade ground. Marching to and from places of instruction, each of us taking charge for a day, was useful experience and did improve our bearing. The officer in charge addressed the squad as "R Subs" but it came to sound as if we were inverted! Joining with the entire ship's company on the parade ground, all under the shouted commands of one man, became an ordeal of confusion. "On the right, at the halt, form squad" I will not try to describe because we never mastered it, neither would the course of the war have changed if we had.

One thing that was of value on the parade ground was the FND Brass band. When they had finished one piece of march music, a drum and bugle band often would take over and keep the march in step. Even now, after many years, I fancy that I can hear the tunes they used to play while we were trying to keep in time, erect and dressed by the right all at once. I confess to being stirred by a good band, especially a navy band and when it accompanies the colour party in white uniform and bearing the white ensign, the emotional effect is profound. To many of us it says "Navy" and symbolises all that is good, or ought to be good, about our chosen service.

Another inspiring experience was my first mess dining night in the fine dining hall, with its panelled walls, paintings of battle fleets under sail at each end, the polished cedar tables and the small table lamps with shades made from sections of naval charts treated with oil to resemble parchment. Although mess dress should have been worn, we reserve people did not have it so we wore our uniforms with a black hand-tied bow tie and a stiff collar. The dinner was conducted with discipline and dignity, the President of the Mess at the centre of the table and the Vice President opposite. Stewards, also smart in their white jackets, moved with precision.

After the various courses, prior to the port, all tables were cleared and crumbs removed with silver backed brushes and silver pans, leaving the cedar polished tables immaculate. Decanters and glasses were then placed, after which, at the same moment, each of the presidents removed the stopper and passed the decanter to his left. When all had filled their glasses and the decanters had returned, the Vice President raised his glass and said "Mister President, the King." to which the President replied "Gentlemen, the King." All present, still seated as in Nelson's day, raised their glasses saying "The King," and sipped their port.

Conduct from this point relaxed a little. Smoking commenced, previously taboo topics like women and politics could be discussed and more frivolity was indulged in, just so long as the President did not call some over-jubilant officer to order. That put the brakes on for a while, but there were a few players, as there always were and will be. During all of this, members of the FND band were playing in the small gallery midway along one wall. I have since attended many mess dinners, but this first occasion always remains foremost in my memory.

Instruction was crammed, with little free time. Instructors no doubt were repeating verbatim what they had done many times, performing a recitation. It is claimed that if a gunnery instructor (GI) is asked a question while in full flight, he must start at the beginning again. Phrases like "cut away for lightness and built up for strength" of a ship's gun seemed contradictory, but it did not do to say so. We practised gun drill on a four inch breech loading, that is to say, not muzzle loading, gun mounted on a concrete pad at the side of the parade ground. There were seven in the gun crew. After completing the loading, training, laying and firing procedure, we all changed positions and did it again.

Wooden replicas of projectiles and propelling charges were used. Of course, after each loading and firing exercise, there was no bang and the wood pieces remained within the barrel, which, by the time we had done a turn in every position, was becoming full.

Eventually, on loading a replica projectile, the first loaded would reach the mouth of the barrel and fall out onto the concrete. This struck me as amusing but I had enough understanding of the situation and the determination of the G.I. to keep tight control, to know that it was best not to laugh.

Then came the misfire procedure. Gunnery instructors are to be obeyed and not questioned, so if something is not understood, one carries on regardless, hoping it will all come clear before disaster strikes. "Upon a misfire occurring, the captain of the gun will shout 'Still. Misfire. Carry on.' whereupon the breechworker will say 'Striker gone forward'..." and so on. On our first run through this part of the drill, our breechworker said 'Strike a gong forward.'

Having achieved proficiency at loading and firing wooden projectiles, R Class were taken to sea on Port Phillip Bay for a day in *HMAS Orara*, a trawler converted into His Majesty's service by the installation of a four inch gun on her forecastle. There was a target comprising two floats with cloth covered vertical frames, towed one behind the other. We manned the gun with instructions to aim between the targets. It would have been safer for the targets if we had aimed at them, but then we might have hit the tug.

I learned two things from that morning's practice.

1. If you stand close to the gun and watch in the same direction as the barrel, you can see the projectile as it leaves and quickly shrinks to nothing before it hits the water, and

...

2. If you do not protect your ears, the detonation of the gun causes pain.

Ear protection was not provided in those times and I believe that I started going deaf that day, a process which was to be given a boost in my first operational appointment, the following year.

At the end of the month, we knew a little about many things. But there was no time for more. "There is a war on" was a frequent remark. We had to get on with it. So twelve R Subs, with Sub Lieutenant Adams in charge, left Flinders by rail for Sydney to join another shore establishment, *HMAS Rushcutter*, one of the most efficient training schools that I was to enter in the period of hostilities.

The RAN anti-submarine school was sited on the shore of Rushcutter Bay in Sydney Harbour. Commander Newcomb, RN, was commanding officer and our instructor was Chief Petty Officer Bill Beer. We lived in digs close by and started each day by falling in in front of the school with a different Sub in charge. As well as classes under training, there were the instructional and maintenance personnel. These had to be reported correct by their divisional officer, and the Lord's Prayer read by the officer in charge, who would then order "Sweepers stand fast. Remainder carry on to instruction." Humble duties like cleaning were beneath our recognition it seems, because on our first morning, we heard "Mine sweepers stand fast...."

Our instruction was on the asdic, the then secret device for detecting submarines by transmitting a sonar signal through the water and listening for the return echo. The name asdic was an acronym for "Anti Submarine Detection Investigation Committee". Every detail of the equipment, circuits, components, testing, repairing and operating had to be memorised. Notes taken during class had to be destroyed. There were several variations in design, according to the class of ship to be fitted. Several of us had come from universities and were familiar with study, but here the intensity of instruction and the examination standard required were of a high order. My friend Peter, who did not always work to capacity at UWA, certainly worked long and hard at *Rushcutter*. A compelling factor was that failure could mean discharge from the Navy.

It impressed me that a chief petty officer (CPO) could be such an effective instructor, but then I would be subconsciously comparing him with university professors who are lecturing, not instructing, in the same way. One morning, toward the end of our course, we were given the circuit for raising and lowering the asdic transmitting oscillator and its protective dome through the keel of a destroyer; a requirement whenever steaming at high speed. It was a complex circuit which we doubted we could ever memorise. CPO Beer gave us the incentive.

"You will all put threepence in the kitty now. First thing

after lunch, you will all draw the circuit from memory. The most accurate diagram wins the kitty." Nobody had lunch. Brains were exercised as never before. Upon reassembly, the Chief said, "Draw the circuit for a destroyer's asdic dome raising gear set to lower." We all did it, though not all to perfection. Bill Mitchell, an engineering student from Adelaide, got it right. I had the circuit correct except that the contacts were shown in the open position as per the morning instruction, whereas some should have been closed as for lowering.

Attack technique and strategy was a major part of the course. There was an attack teacher or simulator which was a valuable tool, as we had no ship or submarine to practise with. Time on this was precious and all too brief. Once again we all took turns in the various roles: commanding officer, anti-submarine control officer, asdic operator, helmsman and signalman. The remainder of the class watched the automatic "plot" where ship, submarine and asdic beam were represented by lights projected onto a ground glass screen and moved strictly to scale. We were all in a highly nervous state, trying to apply new-found knowledge on a strange process with an audience of instructors and trainees. At the final examination in the presence of the Commander, the submarine would take evasive action, there would be reports of simultaneous attacks by enemy aircraft and surface ships, fires in magazines and other distractions, as if an attack on a hidden submarine were not difficult enough.

Training at *Rushcutter* was in two periods, separated by a month at sea in *HMAS Kybra*, formerly of the Western Australian State Shipping Service. Here we learned seamanship, navigation, watchkeeping, fire drill, boat handling, and more discipline. *Kybra* had two boats, a navy whaler and a ship's lifeboat. Every morning in harbour we would lower these, man and pull (row) them for a mile or two before hoisting and breakfast. The whaler was a delight; five oars and a lively speed, but the lifeboat was designed to hold lots of people and was a log to row. Good for her designed purpose, but not for going places.

The navigation training was quite realistic, with the ship in constant motion. I was, and still am, prone to sea-sickness.

Aboard *Kybra* I became accustomed to navigating while not feeling like it, an ability which has been useful many times since. There is a difference between learning in the Navy where there is no excuse, and learning for pleasure, which stops when displeasure sets in.

One of our instructors was Lt Eric Barron, a Western Australian who, after the war, served as I did in Legacy, an ex-serviceman's organisation dedicated to the care of dependants of servicemen who have died. He, and indeed all instructors, persevered until we did learn. This training was "for real", as the term now goes. Thorough, it was, if sometimes exhausting, and I loved it. It all seemed to be directly relevant to the essential task of stopping the Nazi idiocy.

By April 1941 the A/S course was finished, and those who qualified were given the opportunity to state a preference of appointment; an Australian station or overseas. Most opted for a posting where the action was. It was not hard to be brave at a distance, but all the same, there was always a deep sense of fear. As a small boy I had visited the Guildford home of the Bessell-Browne family and was impressed, albeit with horror, by the display of swords and bayonets in the hall, trophies of the Great War. My resolution then was that I would avoid such exposure at all costs. Perhaps that is why, subconsciously, I chose the Navy, where hand to hand fighting is rare.

Two weeks' leave followed, and what excitement, to board the Trans Continental train for Perth. The five months had been an eye-opener for me, apart from the technical training. Melbourne and Sydney were so large, with substantial engineering works all around. What a lot to tell family and friends. Many nights I had nightmares about being so far from home with no hope of getting back. But by day it had been all go and interest; no regrets, but still looking forward to leave. We were still growing up. Homesickness is not all bad. At least it indicated that there was happiness at home, which not all enjoy. My first taste of it was my first day at school; Forrest Street, South Perth, at age six, when I sat in the lunch shed after the first half, unwrapped my sandwiches and thought "My Mum made these." Perhaps everybody goes through this slow maturing and gradual gaining of self-confidence.

In wartime the process must accelerate.

Leave was a great morale booster because we were all made a fuss of. There was a gang of Perth lasses and lads of my age who used to spend leisure together. Half of them were now in service training, but we managed to arrange a camping holiday at Careening Bay, Garden Island, going by my father's launch. I had a particular friend, a girl whose parents came from Sussex, England. Elsie was there and we had some discussion on the future, which we knew little about, and reached no conclusions. Looking back, that appears to have been a very sensible arrangement. Elsie gave me her aunt's address in Burwash, Sussex and a leather writing case.

My mother had continued to pack my lunch through university days. On any day of an examination, out of the package would appear a celluloid Mickey Mouse; for luck, Mum said. My embarrassment was such that I threatened to destroy it. But you know how it is with mothers; all of us had one, and they know best. So Mickey Mouse was in my kit when we gathered at Perth Station in May 1941. My brother-in-law to be, Harvey Morrish, was there, travelling on the same train to finish his course as Wireless Air Gunner in the R.A.A.F. So were all our families and The Gang. My older sister Beryl and younger sister Yvonne had combined to knit me a black sweater, one the front and one sleeve, and the other the back and other sleeve. It was not until later that the sleeves established their individuality by taking up differing stations along my arms; one long, the other short.

Fond farewells all round, and the puffer drew us out to the east. Sitting back in solemn contemplation, I was brought back to realism by Harvey.

"Did you mug 'em all?" he asked.

"Yes, I kissed every woman and girl in our group, and a few in the next group."

He seemed slightly shocked at my departure from customary conservatism.

"Was that your pre-em (pre-embarkation) leave then?"

"Yes" I said, "but that is classified information."

In Melbourne, members of R Class re-assembled to learn their destinies. Seven of us were to sail for England aboard *M.V.*

Coptic with a load of chilled lamb. The date of departure was confidential. We had to report each morning prepared to sail. I was staying with Jack Blanshard's family and witnessed the daily distress of his mother bidding her son farewell, and I felt for her. The third time was it. On 8th May 1941, *Coptic* motored out of Port Melbourne and Port Phillip Bay, turned east to pass Wilson's Promontory, our last view of Australia for four years, and headed for Panama.

CHAPTER TWO

ATLANTIC

The voyage to the Panama Canal was a pleasure cruise. The Pacific was indeed peaceful at that time. The ship was loaded to the degree of being tender; that is to say, she had much weight high up in her hold and would roll slowly. With a strong wind on the beam, she would take up a list and hold it for days. On arrival at the Canal the authorities were not certain about her safety in transit. Nevertheless, she got through all right, and made a short stop at Bermuda on 10th June to refuel.

Not being needed as watchkeepers or lookouts, we had spent some time practising stripping and re-assembling the ships' Hotchkiss guns, her only defence against aircraft attack. That mastered, Jack and I were taken into the engine room to do odd jobs and to get some experience with the Sulzer two-stroke diesels. These engines were given to breaking piston rings as they passed the cylinder ports, making quite a racket in the process. The watchkeeper, on hearing the familiar sound, would record a chalk mark on the side of the offending cylinder. When a cylinder had scored four, that engine would be shut down, the cylinder head and piston removed, and new rings fitted. No great worry in the Pacific, far from Hitler's U-boats, but while the replacement was going on in the North Atlantic, and *Coptic* was reduced to the speed that one engine could maintain, the Captain would be suffering agonies of anxiety on the bridge. Of course, all were subject to the risk of being torpedoed, especially we in the engine room, but it was the Captain's responsibility so why should we worry? Within a few hours, both engines would be running, speed regained, the defensive zig-zag resumed, and the Captain restored to his normal state of anxiety.

Approaching the British Isles around the top of the Hebrides was quite a spectacle. In the Atlantic we seven had kept daylight lookout while manning the Hotchkiss guns, port and starboard. All we had seen was one Allied ship at a distance, until approaching the Island of Lewis, the most northerly of the Outer Hebrides. It was in the long twilight of mid summer and a fishing fleet covered the ocean. Picking her way between trawlers and nets, *Coptic* moved carefully toward that land about which we had read throughout our youth. It was hard not to expect Fairyland, and the fishing fleet did seem to have a magical quality. No doubt the trawlermen saw it differently.

Dawn on 22nd June 1941 found us hove-to near the Bar Light Vessel, which marks the approach channel to the River Mersey. The Captain came up to the gun positions to say that there would be a delay because of a recent blitz of Liverpool. Eventually we proceeded slowly up-channel, searching through the haze for the first sight of Fairyland. First sight was the remains of a merchant ship resting in the shallows next to the channel. Her stern was missing, affording a direct view into the engine room. She had probably been mined in the channel and steered for the bank for her last rest. Next to appear were barrage balloons, floating above the smog. Then we were in the river, steering to clear masts standing out of the swirling tide; more mine casualties. Soon *Coptic* was tugged and pushed in through lock gates and alongside a wharf where unloading ten thousand tons of meat began; one meal for everybody in Britain.

The blitz obviously had taken place some weeks earlier and cleaning up was progressing. It did not look, or smell, like Fairyland. We went ashore for a drink at a dockside pub and found the beer weak, warm and flat, as British beer seems to any Aussie. Sub Lt Adams did his duty and off we went to London by train. I hoped that I would not be returning to Liverpool. A quick drive in a Service truck through that great city and we were on a train again to Hove, on the south coast, for further training.

Arriving at digs very late in the day, with the sun still above the horizon, some RNVR sub lieutenants greeted us with the news that we must be bound for *HMS King Alfred* for basic training. We had heard of being bumbled, to use a polite word, around by experts, and now it was happening to us. But S/Lt Adams, to his credit, spoke to the authorities first thing next morning, convinced them that basically trained we already were, and had us sent on a week's leave while they re-arranged the manning of the Royal Navy to accommodate us.

Back in London, we made our first visit to the serviceman's mecca, Australia House. In the basement was the legendary Boomerang Club, where lady volunteers, many of them wives of Australian service and civilian officers, operated a canteen and leave billeting service. Ross James and I asked if we could visit Devon, and Hey Presto, it was all arranged. Guests of Mr and Mrs Gundry at Broadhembry we would be, and so we were, enjoying every minute.

This was an estate in the country, where strawberries were grown, and a small sawmill operated. The hospitality was marvellous. Ross and I tried to do such work as we could to justify our accommodation, but it was really a holiday. Mr Gundry gave me a brief as a student of engineering. As a national security measure, food had been distributed into the country for storage against any emergency, as if there were not an emergency already. On the first floor of one of his store buildings he had some fifty tons of bagged sugar. The building was stone with timber floor and beams. These were obviously overloaded, and he asked my opinion as to their safety. I knew what to say but went through the process of calculating the stress in the beams. It was, of course, excessive, so I advised him to place stout props at intervals under certain beams. He did this and thanked me. Perhaps he wanted to build my confidence for the task ahead.

Next, he asked us to show how to make and throw boomerangs. Neither Ross nor I had ever handled one, but we had taken note of the fine library in the hall. At first opportunity we stole in and consulted Encyclopedia Britannica on the subject. It was a revelation. There were killer boomerangs with unequal arms, and the popular even-armed model which is a plaything. With copied sketches, to the mill we went, to select our timber. Here was a difficulty. Not a stick of mulga in the stack. Taking the hardest and densest of a soft lot, we sawed, rasped and whittled, in a most untraditional manner, until it looked right to us, then repaired to a lonely field for trials. At first throw, our boomerang soared in a graceful circle, swooped low past us, hit a tree, and disintegrated. A matter of back to the mill with stouter timber, rather than back to the drawing board. Our next prototype had more timber on it to compensate for the lower density and strength compared with the Australian hardwoods. With care to avoid impact, this later model survived, and our reputation as dinkum Aussies was established. Thankful was I that our host did not ask for a didgeridoo.

This was the England that fulfilled our romantic expectations, but the week passed and back to London we went. Reporting to the branch of Admiralty that dealt with appointments, I filled out a small form which is before me now, having shaped my fortunes for the succeeding fourteen months:

"Rank, name and initials
in BLOCK LETTERS   M.H. SHEAN   Sub Lieut   RANVR
Present or Last Appointment   HMAS Rushcutter
Address for Official Communications c/- Australia House, London
Nature of Enquiry   re Appointment
Date   7th July 1941."

It was one day after my 23rd birthday, but I didn't record that. While awaiting my fate, I took in the notices on display. Quite symbolic of the times was a cartoon by Fougasse with the comment **"Argument thrives where facts are scarce. Keep your mouth shut."** Promptly, my paper was returned, endorsed under "Office Remarks:" *"Bluebell.* **Report Commander D. (Destroyers) Liverpool."**

There it was, back to Liverpool. Homesickness started to set in. Now I was on my own, no E.J. Adams, no R.W. James. I was not to see a familiar person for the rest of 1941. On to the train for another night-sitting on the way to Liverpool, then alighting next morning with all my possessions in one suitcase and my study briefcase, I was directed by the Rail Transport Officer to the Royal Liver Building.

"What does it look like?"

"It has two liver birds on two towers. You can't miss it."

This last common phrase gave me no confidence whatever. It is usually employed in lieu of a detailed description; an easy way out. But in this case, as everybody now knows from television, it was adequate description. It was fortunate for me that Hitler had been, and always was, unsuccessful in making good his threat **"to make the birds fly from the Liver Building."** At the Navy office in that famous building, I was directed to Clarence Dock, by following the elevated railway by the River Mersey.

The railway was a sad sight, having been put out of service in the blitz. A policeman gave me further guidance: "Just a short walk down river past the stink". Not wishing to stick my neck out with a constable any more than with a gunnery instructor, I contained my curiosity and marched off toward the sea, sniffing all the while. It did not take long. As they say, you can't miss it. On the city side of the riverside road was the shell of a bombed building that had been a cold-store. Mechanical shovels were digging into a mountain of rotting food and loading it onto trucks. Shortly after, on the river side, came Clarence Dock Power Station. Through the gate, past the dockside police, and there she lay, my first ship, and lifetime inspiration, *HMS Bluebell.*

CHAPTER THREE

H M S BLUEBELL

Most people's impression of a warship is of one visiting their port and "Showing the Flag". This is usually a major war vessel like a cruiser or destroyer, smartly painted, officer of the day on the quarterdeck and sentry at the foot of the gangway. *Bluebell* was a minor war vessel. Her two-tone grey camouflage bore the rust streaks that said "seatime". Nobody at the gangway, but there was a rating on deck. I hobbled up the narrow gangway with my cases, dropped them on deck and saluted the "quarterdeck". Not the scrubbed teak and bright brass of the Flagship, but bare steel, busy with depth charges on rails and throwers.

I was escorted to the wardroom where I met the first lieutenant (No 1), Lieut G.H. Walker RNVR. As one might expect, he had no knowledge of my appointment, but accepted my advice that this was so and also that I was to replace S/Lt Moxley, a popular Canadian who was due for re-appointment. We then sought out "Mox" and gave him the news. As I met the other officers, each responded with dismay and disappointment that Mox was to leave them.

No 1 took me on a tour of the ship. First the 4 inch gun on the foredeck, his pride and joy as a gunnery specialist. It was similar to our FND practice gun, a relic from the great war. But it worked all right as I would see and hear. Then back aft to the depth charges, duplicate rails leading to the stern, one for heavy and one for light charges. Heavy charges sink faster than the light, thus giving a vertical dimension to a pattern of charges. Linear spread was achieved by releasing three, four or five pairs at intervals as the ship moved forward. Two pairs of throwers port and starboard propelled charges to the side giving a transverse dimension. Thus a full pattern comprised five, six or seven charges distributed over an area set to explode at one depth, and an identical pattern set deeper. The aim was to have the target submarine in the centre. A voice pipe ran from the bridge to the control position aft. Alongside each thrower was a davit with which to hoist reload charges into place. This was always done in a hurry in readiness for a second attack, while the ship was manoeuvring at high speed with the sea washing over the low deck. This was to be my action station, so I got to know it well.

The anti-aircraft guns comprised a quadruple point five inch mounted abaft the funnel, and twin Lewis guns on the wings of the bridge. These were point 303 inch bore and had short range. In fact, none of these guns was "state of the art" to use today's expression, but they were better than nothing. Flower Class Corvettes were ships modelled on ocean going trawlers, built in a hurry at the rising of the emergency just pre-war, and armed with what was available. Asdic was their only modern equipment, initially. More powerful weapons and RDF (radar) were fitted later, progressively as the war continued. Convoy escort was their purpose.

We walked the upper deck, saw the two sixteen foot skiffs and four Carley rafts, then to the bridge where my asdic control was located, in a cubical house with windows all round, and voice pipe to the forebridge, that is to say, the very front exposed walk where the officer of the watch or the captain directed operations. At each side was space for lookouts, steel protection against bullets and shrapnel, and to the rear, the signal flag lockers and halliards. On top of the asdic house were the PAC rockets, of which more anon. On the starboard side aft there was a small covered table for the log book, charts and other papers and instructions. The canvas cover would enclose the user and prevent the escape of light at night. Blackout was an essential technique in remaining undetected. No lights were shown at sea except by hospital ships, and shaded stern lights by ships in convoy.

Next we descended to the wharf and walked the length of the ship, all two hundred and five feet of her, so it did not take long. At the bow I remarked on one steel plate which was more rusty than others, but No 1 made no comment. The engine room was left to me to explore, later, guided by our Chief Mechanician Hyde, a pleasant, dedicated, man. Propulsion was by one triple expansion steam engine, supplied by two cylindrical fire tube boilers, in which fire goes through steel tubes set in a drum part filled with water. Those glamour ships, the destroyers and larger, have water tube boilers which produce more power for their weight and push along at thirty knots. Our top speed was sixteen. Never mind, direction is more important than speed I say, and we usually knew where we were going.

Until Mox departed, I had nowhere to move into so my cases stayed in the wardroom flat, the lobby serving wardroom, officers' galley and cabins. I had joined ship on the first anniversary of her commissioning. There was to be a wardroom party that night, but I confess to not having been in a party mood. I was to sleep in the wardroom until my own bunk became available, so, tired as I was, having sat up the previous night on the train, there would be no rest till after the party.

Bluebell's Commanding Officer, Lt Commander Sherwood, RNR, lived ashore when in Liverpool. He possibly went home to Wales where he had worked pre-war as captain of a Belfast-Holyhead ferry. We met as he returned for the party. Wilfred Stiff, who had joined the previous April, was the Sub Lt next senior to me, which meant that upon my joining, he was no longer junior officer; I was. Sub Lt Isted, RNR, was navigator, very competent and covetous of his domain. Nobody else could use the ship's sextant. I had a sextant at home and then wished that I had brought it, but eventually changed my mind. Later, when I was to command a submarine, encouragement was given to anybody with enough initiative and interest to want to try.

Guests at the party were mostly WRNS personnel from Royal Liver Building. No doubt they already knew about this Australian who was the cause of their Mox departing their area of influence. In the small wardroom it was quite cosy and chummy. One of the lovelies had been sitting on the settee, with her arms folded behind her. Two of our officers, who shall not be identified, were beside her, each with one arm around her, holding a hand. When, at length, she arose to circulate, they discovered that they were holding each other's hand. They were not that sort normally.

By the end of festivities, the empty room had the usual after party look. I tidied up enough to have a length of settee to stretch out on, and decided to try a whisky and soda for the first time. It tasted awful. I *must* have been unhappy.

One of the Wrens had invited me to visit her home in a suburb of Liverpool on the following evening. We met at the Royal Liver Building and took the tram. I enjoyed a pleasant evening, typical of many that all dominion servicemen enjoyed throughout the war. As yet, the long twilights and double summer time were strange to me. By the time dusk was becoming evident, it was quite late and the last tram had departed. So the long walk back started, guided by the distant barrage balloons. That was one way to see Liverpool, and to ensure a sound sleep on a strange settee.

Bluebell had been on the Halifax run, escorting merchant ships half way across the Atlantic and bringing others back. Sometimes she went right across and the crew had an interesting run ashore in Canada. They had not recently encountered U-boats, so the atmosphere was comparatively relaxed. On 11th July the Captain went to a briefing in the headquarters of the Commander-in-Chief, Western Approaches. On returning to the ship, he called an immediate meeting in the wardroom, to brief his officers.

The U-boat offensive in the Atlantic was escalating. They were now operating in packs, guided by reconnaissance aircraft. Escorts were to be formed into Groups, with one destroyer, sloop or frigate, as Senior ship, and five corvettes. *Bluebell* was to be junior ship in the 5th Escort Group. We were to escort convoys to and from Gibraltar, starting the next day. Action was expected to be intense.

The officers expressed disappointment that their Halifax run had ceased, and were unhappy with the prospect of further action. On the contrary, I was feeling so homesick, nothing mattered except to get on with the fighting and to get home again. This view was not popular, but we all settled down to preparation. Next day, Mox left the ship amid sad farewells, while I was happy to see him go;

not that he was anything but a splendid fellow, but now I had a place where I could live and unpack my bags. My bunk was against the ship's starboard side, below water level where the asdic dome recovery cable up to the deck lay and rattled whenever she was underway, which was most of the time.

At 1000 on Saturday 12th July 1941, for the first time I heard *Bluebell's* quartermaster's shrill pipe from his bosun's call, or whistle, to attract attention and "Special sea duty men to your stations." This brought the captain, navigator, signalman and lookouts to the bridge, quartermaster and messenger to the wheelhouse, chief mechanician and stokers to engine and boiler rooms, sub lieut and forecastle party to the forecastle, and sub lieut (me) and after party, to the main deck aft.

Lt Cdr Sherwood appeared on the port wing of the bridge. I heard the merry ringing of the engine room telegraph signalling to the wheelhouse that they were ready to obey orders.

"Let go aft" called the Captain. The seamen around me unwound the mooring wires from the ship's bollards, and the shore party lifted theirs and dropped them into the polluted, stagnant waters of Clarence Dock, while "my" men heaved them aboard and stowed them.

"All gone aft, Sir." I called to the captain.

Then the telegraph sounded "Ding. Ding. Ding." followed by a slow vibration as engine, shaft and propeller turned and a swirl of water and flotsam (floating rubbish) flowed astern. Our stern swung slowly away from the wharf.

"Ding. Ding. Ding." and the engine stopped.

"Let go forward," from the captain, and Wilfred Stiff, S/Lt RNVR, smart in his uniform and cable handling gloves, got his party busy retrieving lines. More chimes from the telegraph, and we were moving astern. We stopped and, swinging to starboard, headed for the open lock gate. My crew stood with fenders as we negotiated the narrow exit. We entered the River Mersey at the top of the flood tide, and swung to starboard down river, as the seamen stowed wires and fenders, past the masts of sunken ships, and into the dredged channel toward the Bar Light Vessel.

The convoy assembled in the Irish Sea and headed north of

Ireland into the Atlantic. Until I gained experience watchkeeping, I doubled with Wilf or the First Lt. Learning was interesting and enjoyable, but seasickness took the pleasure out of it. For the first three days I kept watch with a bucket as well as with Wilf or No 1, and at the end of my watch crawled miserably into my bunk. Meals did not interest me but Wardroom Steward Gawn, bless him, brought me a mug of Bovril during my watch below to keep me going, and it did.

First afternoon at sea I studied my given action station back aft on the depth charges so that I would know it in the dark. We would be leaving the long twilight as we ran down our latitude toward Gibraltar. I prepared lists of depth charge settings for different submarine depths, and fixed them adjacent to the rails and throwers. I was secretly disappointed to be stationed aft when I expected to be at the asdic control position alongside the operator as we had been trained to be at *Rushcutter*, but being green for lack of experience, besides seasickness, I accepted as the Captain's prerogative that this was where he wanted me.

The First Lt was a conscientious officer, and took every initiative to exercise every procedure, such as action stations for surface (gun) action, anti-submarine action, anti-aircraft action, fire drill, "Away sea boat", and so on. We ran through these soon after putting to sea, usually in the Dog Watches between 1600 and 2000. Such exercises, while vital, were not popular because watchkeepers standing four hours on and eight off, had little time for their "part of ship" duties, personal activities, and sleep. Harbour was a good place to exercise, but our Captain was usually ashore, and at the subsequent action we sometimes had slight misunderstandings. For example "for exercise" meant, to the crew, that they went through the motions of, say, dropping a depth charge, but made sure that securing bars were in place to prevent an explosion close to the ship.

On the first occasion when the captain was in charge of "For exercise, for exercise, drop one depth charge", my crew completed the motions and I reported "Exercise completed, Sir." After a period, the Captain's voice came down the voice pipe,
        "Shean, I don't hear any explosion."

"No, Sir," I replied, "it was for exercise, we went through the motions but did not actually drop it."

"Well, you bloody well should have."

"Aye, aye, Sir."

I instructed the depth charge crew to remove the retaining bar and drop one charge. This done, I reported to the Captain.

"Charge dropped, Sir."

"Bloody Hell. Full Ahead."

It seemed that he had reduced speed and way was falling off the ship. Thanks to her excellent Chief Mechanician Hyde, she picked up speed, and when the explosion did occur, the stern was not blown off.

This was the most serious case of a near accident, but I considered that *Bluebell*, efficient though she was, could have done with more practice, for this crew member at least. There was another factor in the above incident of misunderstanding. The occasion was of a group exercise involving the other ships. There was, therefore, an additional and unusual link in the chain of communication, that from the Senior Commanding Officer to *Bluebell's* C.O. I was to experience another small communication breakdown with significant consequences, but that was in another vessel which I will be telling you about later.

This first convoy, designated OG 68 (Outward to Gibraltar), could not have been located by the enemy, and no action as foretold at our briefing, came to pass; from U-boats there was no bother. The escort was led by *HMS Walker*, an old V&W Class destroyer. She took station ahead of the columns of merchant ships. These were about a sixth of a mile apart, some seven columns with four or five ships in each. Of course, some convoys were larger. We always had the slow convoys to escort, nominal speed 7½ knots which was not always achieved, under the direction of the Commodore who would operate from the leading merchant ship in a centre column. He was responsible for navigation while the escort kept station on the convoy, keeping their own navigation going as well. After noon each day, each ship in convoy would hoist flags indicating its noon position. That must have been a moment of truth and embarrassment.

We corvettes, including also *Campion, Mallow, Myosotis,* and *Stonecrop* took up station in order of seniority of C.O.; starboard front, port front, starboard rear, port rear, and the junior ship astern. This last was our position for some months, so I can report at first hand the particular attractions from the vantage point of Tail-end Charlie. To operate effectively, asdic needed non-turbulent water, not as found after the passage of thirty-one ships of 8,000 horsepower. Therefore, we were often reduced to listening only on asdic. Some of the thirty-one propellers could be heard clearly, and a submarine's propeller at reduced speed not at all. At night the screen would be close in where U-boats attacking on the surface might be seen.

While the convoy steered a steady course, the escort were constantly zig-zagging as a defence against torpedo attack. At the front of the convoy this was without hazard, but not so at the rear. Zigging across, behind each column at night, necessitated constant peering through binoculars to pick up the position of the rear ship of each column. If these were all on station and in line abreast, it would be easy and safe. Frequently, however, some ship in a column had difficulty maintaining correct speed all the time and fell back. The remaining ships had to steer out and pass, or drop back also. As a result, there was always likely to be an uneven line for the rear escort to zig behind. Sometimes the lookouts might not see a straggler at all, and collision was possible. If we were making a zig from left to right columns, searching intently ahead and on the port bow, any straggler would be steaming up from starboard. So a sharp lookout had to be kept all round, at all times.

The convoy was routed north of Ireland, westerly, until three hundred miles from the Irish coast, then south along the meridian of 21°30' west longitude, to pass five hundred miles west of the Spanish coast till on the latitude of Cape St Vincent, then east-south-east and east to Gibraltar. This 2400 mile long course, which was nearly twice the shortest route, was set to keep distant from the German aircraft bases on the south of France, and to make it more difficult for U-boats to intercept. The route was set out in our Sailing Instructions as a series of seven points, lettered J to Q, omitting letter O to avoid confusion with numeral 0.

On 15th July, CinCWA signalled to alter course to avoid U-boats known to be patrolling ahead of us. Similar alterations were also signalled on 16th and 21st. The intelligence was very good as we were later to find, when U-boats were reported to be shadowing the convoy, and were subsequently seen or engaged in action. But on this occasion, the strategy was successful, and although we were advised on 22nd that our convoy had probably been reported by an Italian submarine, there were no attacks.

On 18th, *HMS Walker* left us to augment the escort of another convoy. This was the pattern of movements as we approached or were becoming distant from Gibraltar. Additional escorts, mostly destroyers, would leave or join according to the perceived need. It impressed me to learn how the game of sea warfare was played out in two areas simultaneously, ours the slow moving assembly of merchant ships and naval escorts, directed from the remote Operations Room hundreds of miles away in London or Liverpool. As we approached Gibraltar, orders and directions would come from Flag Officer Commanding North Atlantic, who was based there.

OG68, my first convoy, arrived at the Straits of Gibraltar intact. However, there was one minor incident which aroused our suspicions that an enemy agent might be in our midst. On 24th, we saw that one of the ships in convoy had her navigation lights switched on, whereas complete blackout was the policy at all times. We closed her and signalled her by lamp to extinguish all lights, which she did. This was reported to the senior officer who instructed us to board the ship to see if there were any suspicious circumstances. The sea boat's crew were called away, and, in charge of the First Lieut, boarded what proved to be the *Monte Gorben*, registered in Bilboa. Her Master was most friendly and apologetic, so it appeared to have been an error on the part of his crew. Nevertheless, we still felt suspicious.

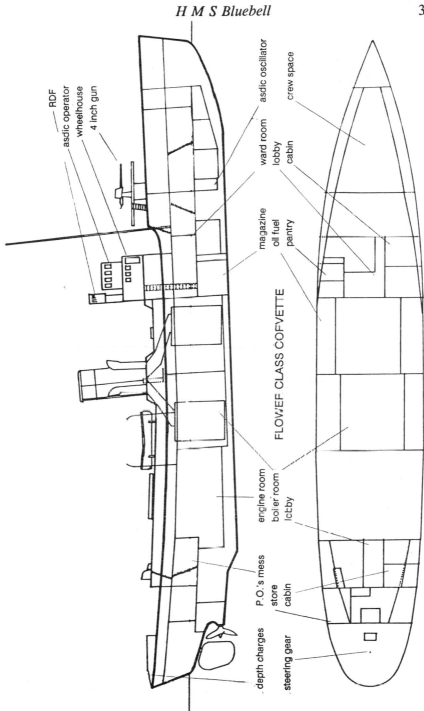

RDF

asdic operator

wheelhouse

4 inch gun

asdic oscillator

crew space

ward room

lobby

cabin

magazine

oil fuel

pantry

FLOWER CLASS CORVETTE

engine room

boiler room

lobby

P.O.'s mess

store

cabin

depth charges

steering gear

CHAPTER FOUR

GIBRALTAR

W e were approaching Gibraltar where U-boats could expect more escort ships. There was no further change in our escort group, but other ships were around. Our instructions were to stay with the convoy unless contact was made with a submarine. Then we could counter-attack so long as asdic contact was maintained. After a depth charge attack, the water was so disturbed that contact was often lost. Also, the submarine would take evasive action, like going deep, stopping, altering course, increasing speed for a minute then reducing again, hoping that we would hold contact with a patch of disturbed water, or some other technique. If contact were lost, we had to resume station. Our first duty was the safe and timely arrival of the convoy, not to hunt and destroy U-boats except for short periods.

This may seem a questionable strategy but an answer was evolving. Groups of destroyers and sloops were later formed to hunt and destroy, with considerable success. We in corvettes felt that we were largely ineffective, but this was not the case. Had we not been present, every ship in the convoy could be sunk. Mere presence was a deterrent, a fact which was not obvious to those maintaining the presence. If we all sped away searching for our attackers, they could detail one off to act as a decoy, while the rest of the pack picked off the merchant ships from close range, with impunity.

Entering the Straits of Gibraltar, the escorts took up station close to the ships because of the narrowing waters. This first arrival was after sunset. Without a moon, all was quite dark. Gibraltar and the Spanish coast were bright with lights. As we were no longer zig-zagging, engine revolutions per minute had to be regulated so that our speed was the same as the ships'. Otherwise we would have set revolutions for say ten knots, and varied the angle of zig to keep level. Now we called for "75 revolutions". This was an order to the quartermaster in the wheelhouse below the bridge, where the engine room telegraph and the voicepipe to the engine room were also located. The engine room would advise the boiler room through another voice pipe. This night was quite still; there was very little sound except for the boiler and engine murmurs reaching the upper deck, and the wail of the condenser air pump as it made each stroke.

We were gradually moving ahead on the convoy.

"70 revolutions."

"70 revolutions," from the quartermaster. We were able to hear the flap-flap of the boiler room voice pipe cover as the engine room attracted attention and passed on this speed reduction and heard their acknowledgment. The boiler room ventilators were turned to face forward and we on the bridge could hear the stokers' voices. Gradually, *Bluebell* started to slip back. We usually called for revolutions in increments of five. Now we needed a smaller change.

"72 revolutions." The quartermaster repeated, and relayed the order to the engine room who called the boiler room. Flap-flap,

"72 revolutions."

"What's wrong with the bridge? Can't they make up their bloody minds?"

I was keeping lookout on the starboard wing of the bridge while Wilf watched out to port where the convoy was. On my side, not too far away, were the North African coast and fishing boats. Suddenly a straight line of phosphorescence flashed into sight from our beam into the ship's side, immediately beneath the bridge.

"Torpedo," I thought, and my heart revolutions doubled. But there was no explosion. "Green eight oh. Phosphorescent track." I shouted. The Captain sprang across, stared at the fading line, and listened. All was quiet, except for the murmurs and the singing air pump; still, black night, dark ship outlines gliding smoothly into the Mediterranean. It must have been a fishing net rope that we ran into.

We arrived in Gibraltar Harbour on 26th July, and five corvettes secured side by side at the south breakwater wharf. This was our first opportunity to meet our fellow officers and crew in the other corvettes. The ships were all named after flowers. Indeed, my first reaction to the name *"Bluebell"* was, "What a name for a warship!". But, as Shakespeare said, "What's in a name?" That which we call *Bluebell* by any other name would fight as well.

We had *Campion, Mallow, Myosotis* and *Stonecrop*. Wardroom social sessions occurred frequently. Captains, of course, visited each other once they had called on the senior officer of our group, who in turn, reported ashore to the Commander in Chief's Office. Our ultimate chief, in Liverpool, was the Commander in Chief, Western Approaches, a grand title I thought. Here it was Flag Officer Commanding, North Atlantic.

Gib was an interesting place to go ashore. For all of us it was symbolic of British sea power. On my study wall, at home in South Perth, was a Frank Mason painting of "The Fleet at Gibraltar" which had everything! Battleships in line ahead, union flags and white ensigns prominent, foaming bow waves and the solid Rock in the background. Indeed, as we approached, the leading signalman on the bridge was inspired to start singing "Rock of Ages".

Our Captain and all officers took a walk next morning through a tunnel to the Mediterranean shore for a swim, my first since leaving Australia. It was a new experience, in clear, light blue water, and a prickling sensation around my neck from the moving shingle on shore. Aboard ship I missed the opportunity to escape to natural surroundings, so this was greatly enjoyed. A walk up the Rock was another novel activity. From the north end we looked down onto the airstrip which ran east-west across the only flat land in the British Territory. Just visible under water, on the west side, were the dark shapes of two aircraft which had overshot the short runway.

On 29th July, three days after our arrival, *Carnation, Heliotrope, La Malouine* and *Bluebell* sailed to rendezvous with convoy SL81 from Sierra Leone, bound for "Home". Next day we met up, seventeen ships escorted by armed merchant cruiser

Moreton Bay, destroyers *Campbeltown, St Albans, Wanderer* and *Wrestler*, and corvettes *Clematis* and *Cyclamen*. Most of these left for Gibraltar, *Wanderer* becoming our senior officer. It was common for HM ships to join or leave from time to time as ordered by Admiralty according to the perceived threat by U-boats. *Hydrangea, Wallflower* and *Zinnia* joined as the convoy progressed northward at 7½ knots.

U-boats were known to be patrolling the area, and the convoy had already changed course once to avoid them. This must have been effective for day by day passed in peace. Nevertheless, we assumed that the sailing of escorts from Gibraltar would have been observed and reported by enemy agents in Spain, and expected soon to see four-engined German Focke-Wulf reconnaissance aircraft making slow circles around us, beyond gun range, while transmitting homing signals to U-boats. But, for the present, shipboard routine was uninterrupted, and the weather was warm and sunny.

By now I was overcoming my homesickness. In the process, I had come upon a copy of "The Bulletin" on board. Goodness knows how it got there, but I devoured it; first the most interesting articles, then the others, and finally the advertisements; in fact, every word, from cover to cover. What cheered me up most were the short comments from country readers of animal behaviour that they had observed on their farms. Reading about home was a palliative. I was also taking more interest in the world around me, and feeling less sorry for myself. Initially I hated everything, including *Bluebell*, while, without my realising it, she was wooing me and would eventually win my undying love.

In order that I should gain maximum experience, I was standing three watches per day, totalling nine hours, while the other officers, excepting the Captain, were standing two watches, and had eight hours off between each. This resulted in my keeping watch with all of them in turn, which was interesting and educational. The Captain was always available and slept for short periods at a time. He would always come onto the bridge when I was on watch and make some remark to indicate that he was watching my progress. I was the first Australian he had sailed with, and our accents were quite different. One night, when I had been giving the quartermaster helm orders to follow a quick zig-zag pattern, the Captain came onto the bridge and said "Shean, I have been in the wheelhouse for the last hour and have not understood one word you have said. I don't know how the helmsman knows what to do." I took note of this and tried to be more clear and deliberate. When excited, I do speak too fast, and am still, to this day, trying to calm down.

When I was on watch with the First Lieutenant, we talked about most things and got used to each other. He had stroked for Cambridge, was a qualified engineer and had worked on turbine design. He was a keen navigator and always took dawn star sights. These he calculated in the covered enclosure at the rear part of the bridge while I kept watch. I learned from Wilf that he had always done this, even when there was no other officer on watch, and on one occasion, while his head was under the cover, *Bluebell* collided with something. That explained the rusty bow plate which I had pointed out to him and his non reply. But for all that, he was a competent and diligent officer.

On 2nd August, a signal was received from Admiralty advising that we were being shadowed by a U-boat, and the next day *Wallflower* saw two enemy aircraft, so it was probable that a "pack" was forming. Their strategy was to assemble ahead of the convoy, and when four or five had gathered, to attack on the surface at night, merchant ships and escorts both being suitable targets.

According to developing policy, SL81 included a CAM, or Catapult Armed Merchantman, a comparatively large ship with a rocket propelled catapult and a Sea Hurricane fighter, all mounted on the forecastle. Soon after *Wallflower's* sighting, there was a tongue of flame and a roar as the Hurricane took off, and pursued one of the now retreating German planes and shot it down. The Hurricane patrolled around the convoy until it ran short on fuel, then pancaked onto the sea ahead of its mother ship which lowered a boat and retrieved its pilot.

Later that day, *Wanderer* saw a U-boat on the surface. It dived as she approached to make depth charge attacks in conjunction with *St Albans*, six attacks in all. Bubbles of air bursting on the surface gave some indication of success, and they resumed their stations in the screen. By day this was well away from the convoy, at the limit of visibility.

On receipt of *Wanderer's* sighting report, *Bluebell's* officer of the watch had sounded submarine action stations by continuous ringing of alarm bells throughout the ship. At my action station back aft with my depth charges, throwers and crew, I had no knowledge of what was going on. Until *Bluebell* was to make an attack, there was little for us to do but wait. If we gained an asdic contact, orders would be given of depth settings and the number of charges to be used.

A depth charge was a steel drum of about four hundred pounds capacity, filled with high explosive. In a three inch diameter central steel tube, a depth sensitive pistol and detonator was fixed at one end and a priming charge inserted at the other, at the outer extremity if set to "safe" and fully inserted when armed, ready for use. The anti submarine control officer (A/SCO) at the asdic operating position on the bridge would advise the depth setting to be applied prior to each attack. In the event of *Bluebell* starting to sink, all charges should be rendered safe to avoid blowing up her own survivors, and for this reason, charges were normally set to safe and only armed prior to an attack. On release into the ocean, either from the rails over the stern, or from throwers which propelled them to port and starboard, they would sink until the set depth was reached and then explode, hopefully at a safe distance from *Bluebell* and close to a U-boat. Half were "heavy" charges, weighted to make them sink faster so that a three dimensional pattern resulted, ideally with the U-boat within that space.

It was the duty of the A/SCO to con the ship onto such a course and to order "Fire one... fire two... fire three" at such times as to cause the charges to reach the submarine's future position at the same time as she did. As can be imagined, this required much skill and no bad luck. There was never enough opportunity to practise, my only go having been on the simulator at *Rushcutter*, and anyway, I had not yet been given this duty aboard *Bluebell*.

As night fell, each escort ship closed in to maintain visual contact with their convoy, and to keep a vigilant lookout in the hope of spotting any U-boat approaching. At 2219, *Hydrangea* saw one, fired two rounds from her four inch gun, then made two depth charge attacks. They were rewarded by the appearance at the site of their last attack of a sheepskin jacket, a German sailor's collar, and a leather coat marked "SCHMIDT". (This was *U 401*.)

Notwithstanding the possible destruction of two U-boats, Admiralty signalled pm 4th, "Several U-Boats and enemy aircraft are in the vicinity of SL81." This intelligence was derived from listening for and determining the direction of U-boat and aircraft radio transmissions, at strategically placed receiving stations. The information always proved reliable, and the message was confirmed later in the day, indicating that enemy activity was intense, and the threat of attack increasing.

The middle watch, midnight to 0400, on 5th August, was my watch below. One developed a philosophy to combat the obvious risk of sleeping below decks when torpedo attack was imminent. This was that there was a duty watch on deck, and the safety of the ship was their responsibility. We were off-duty, and the thing to do was to sleep. Not logical perhaps, but it did enable an essential to efficiency; sleep. I was awakened from mine by the sound of an explosion, not close, but quite audible as sound travels fast and powerfully through the water, and the sea was a quarter of an inch from the side of my bunk. I was already getting on my feet, into my seaboots and reaching for my coat, when the action station bells rang, and in a minute was groping my way aft over a pitching, pitch dark deck. One by one my DC crew "closed up", which I reported to the bridge. The OOW said that *Wanderer* had signalled that two ships, *Belgravian* and *Swiftpool* had been torpedoed, and that *Bluebell* was to pick up survivors.

We set about rigging the rope scrambling net over the starboard side as *Bluebell*, moving faster than usual, rolled her scuppers into the sea which gushed in and along the deck. The "Ding" of the engine room telegraph came clearly to our ears, and the vibration of shaft and propeller ceased. Looking ahead, we could see a group of tiny red lights bobbing on the sea surface. A short run of the propeller astern and we were stopped close to the swimming seamen. Bob Sherwood could certainly handle his ship.

With heaving line and boathook, we helped the ablest men close alongside and up the net. Some voices called from the blackness. We could only call back, being forbidden to leave the ship. If their swimming mates could bring them close, we could climb down the net and lift them aboard. Time was passing.

"How are you going, Shean?" asked the Captain down the voice pipe, "We can't remain stopped long or we will be the next target."

"Aye, aye, Sir. Please give me a few minutes. Most of them are aboard."

When all those within reach, and the able swimmers, were on deck, I called the bridge.

"We have all we can save, Sir. The other lights must be on dead men. They're all covered in oil."

"Right, we must move."

The telegraph rang and the steam engine turned the screw, faster as the swirl stretched out astern into the dark, towards a few points of red light. Those men nearly survived.

Some of the rescued men had been burned or had swallowed oil fuel, which covered them all. The fittest were taken below and made as comfortable as possible in the magazine, entered down through a steel hatch set in the deck of the wardroom flat, immediately outside my cabin doorway. The injured men were laid out on temporary beds on deck in the forecastle. All were put into dry clothing, and first aid administered. We had a sick berth attendant, but no sick bay.

SS Belgravian was still afloat and on fire. The other, *SS Swiftpool*, had sunk. Meanwhile, *Zinnia* had seen a U-boat and, with *Campion*, attacked with depth charges, resulting in a floating patch of oil. This U-boat had already been hit by a shell from a merchant ship and was thought to have sunk.

Soon after 0500, there were more explosions as torpedoes struck steam ships *Cape Rodney*, *Harlingen* and *Kumasian*. As day dawned on 5th August, *Belgravian* was burning, *Cape Rodney* sinking, and *Harlingen* floating, disabled. *Bluebell* secured from action stations, with more than twenty survivors aboard. *Hydrangea* had over eighty. Admiralty signalled that *Tug Zwart Zee* had left Greenock to take *Harlingen* in tow, but she sank before noon. Next, Admiralty advised that three Focke-Wulf's were in our vicinity, and within the hour an escorting aircraft had seen and attacked a U-boat with bombs and torpedo.

Heavy weather was developing, wind reaching gale force from the north-west. *Cape Rodney*, with *Hydrangea* standing by, was still afloat, but *Wanderer* doubted she could be salvaged. She was 150 miles west of Ireland, many days' tow from Britain.

During the morning, two of our rescued men had died. They were sewn in canvas and weighted. A timber platform was rigged on the starboard bulwarks, the bodies laid on it side by side, feet outboard, and covered with a union flag. The Captain came aft with a Prayer Book, read the short service, and ordered "Stop engine." I relayed this to the bridge through the depth charge crew voice pipe. The wheelhouse rang the order through to the engine room and the peal of the telegraph bell came clearly to those gathered nearby. Normally, this, to me, was a pleasant sound, but that was an occasion of sadness, almost of desperation. Those notes sounded the beginning of months of mourning for mothers, widows, and children.

As soon as the engine stopped, and the telegraph had rung to the wheelhouse "Main engine stopped", the inboard end of the platform was raised and the two merchant seamen slid from the ship which had tried to protect and save them, into the sea. "Half ahead" from the Captain, relay to the wheelhouse, ringing of the telegraph, and we were underway. Nobody spoke.

Admiralty signalled that more air cover would be provided that night, and the planes would drop flares. At 2400 I was coming down from the bridge having finished my watch, when I saw a man sitting on deck with his back against the funnel.

"Hello, it's you, Steward Gawn. Not in your bed?"

"No Sir. Not worth the risk. If the ship's going to sink, I want to be ready to get off." Obviously he was extremely anxious.

"Tonight, Gawn, we have a good chance of getting through." I told him. "We have had Coastal Command aircraft sweeping the ocean for U-boats today, and will have more tonight.

MS Bluebell in 1942, after refit in which her forecastle was extended, mast moved aft of the bridge and asdic operators to the re part. The camouflage paint on her topsides was light grey over dark grey, designed for Mid Atlantic service.

MS Carnation off Gilbraltar, seen from Bluebell's main deck beneath the Carley raft support, during fleet manoeuvres. Both re making full speed as shown by the unusually large waves with spray blowing back from the crests; great spectacle! epth charges in their throwers and their reloading davits are on the left.

At Gibraltar, the Author paints her pennant number "K80" on the stern. The starboard open door is the outlet from depth charges mounted on rails. There was a second set of rails and door to port, one for normal, the other for heavy charges.

Bluebell, port side looking forward, Lieut Geoffrey Walker stands next to the ten inch signal projector and faces the RDF "lighthouse" antenna which is partly obscured by the white ensign. During refit the mast was moved abaft the bridge and the galley moved forward, as seen by its "Charlie Noble" flue with double outlet, right of the

I am not worried."

"No thank you Sir, I'll stay here."

So I left him keeping his lonely vigil in his life-jacket, and with his "Abandon Ship" bag by his side. I felt sorry for him, enduring, as he was, continual anxiety. It had not occurred to me that, while serving our meals with courteous efficiency, he was very uneasy every second. I thought that we had all accepted the reality of risk that the Atlantic might one day roll over us; that death is not as bad as the contemplation of it; so we thought about other things. And this was the man who kept me going with hot soup on our outward-bound convoy. I was only seasick; he was sick of the sea.

On 7th August, *Zwart Zee* took *Cape Rodney* in tow. *Zinnia* had put a volunteer crew aboard to raise steam. Next day, water was still rising in her hold, so this crew was taken off a few hours before she foundered. So six ships had been sunk by a pack of U-boats, now known to have numbered thirteen.

On 8th August, without further incident, the convoy rounded the north of Ireland and entered the Irish Sea. Ships here split off into groups bound for the Clyde, Bristol and Liverpool, and our crew were becoming excited at the prospect of home leave. Liverpool was a popular port, having many amenities for sailors, and being not too far from other parts of Britain. It was not popular with me, but that gradually changed.

In the ship's mail to be posted on arrival was my first letter to my friend and former neighbour Jim Goss. This has survived as one of the few records of my thoughts at that time. While there is nothing of military significance, there is a distinct change from the lighthearted, even frivolous style of the first pages, written outward bound, to the thoughtful closing paragraphs which followed my first experience of action in the battle of the Atlantic.

CHAPTER FIVE

SEA ROUTINE and 0G71

One of the good things about being at sea is the ordered routine of shipboard life. If a day starts at midnight, the best place to start it is in your bunk. When officers were organised into three watches, which soon included me, every third night I was off duty from 2000 till 0400 if all were going well. The middle watch 2400 until 0400 is the least interesting and therefore seems the longest. It is followed by the morning watch, one of the best. At the start, all is black and dull. Presumably you have had nearly eight hours in the bunk, and are well rested, alert and in good spirits. One naval maxim is "All time not spent in sleep is wasted" and this applies mainly to watchkeepers.

The oncoming officer of the watch receives his briefing from his offgoing colleague, expresses his satisfaction that he "Has it all" and instantly finds himself alone, assuming that the lookouts, having less to hand over, have already left the bridge and their reliefs are now searching the sea's face for anything at all. Check all round to see that lookouts, signalman and asdic operator are at their posts, take a sweep around the horizon using binoculars, then, if all is clear and the nearest ships in convoy are where they should be, duck under the hood to read the log and latest signals. Some may be marked for attention and signing by the OOW. Next, visit each lookout and operator in turn, have a brief chat, alert them to anything important, look at the compass to check course, then search the sea again. Thus the dark, silent hours drag by, unless some incident arises to speed the clock. A ship astern of station, perhaps. While everyone is on watch looking for a U-boat, it is most unlikely that any one man will ever see one. But they are there, somewhere, looking for us. The first to make a sighting has first strike. But the odds are against us, being a much larger visual target. All the same, a sharp lookout must be kept.

Eventually, there is an almost imperceptible lightening of the eastern sky. Call down to the wheelhouse and ask the relief helmsman to make some kye (thick, strong, navy cocoa). Presently this comes up and all receive a recharge and look out more intently. Something may become visible in this first light. All this time, there are the regular helm orders to maintain a zig-zag, away from the convoy until it is lost in the dark, then back again until it reappears. If we have advanced ahead of our station, zig a little wider out and back until we are in the correct position to preserve even spacing of escorts around their charges.

As day breaks, the ship comes to life. All along, of course, the engine has maintained correct revolutions, boilers have rushed their steam to the engine and received it back as water from the feed pump, all sotto-voce so as not to betray our presence or to wake the sleeping men on "watch below". But now the curtain across the entrance to the forecastle divides, and a seabooted sailor scurries aft along the low main deck to the galley for a jug of something. Then more people appear, ready to perform their part of ship duties, scrubbing decks or whatever else, in the charge of a leading hand. The first lieutenant makes his way from point to point. His is the ship to maintain and it keeps him, and he keeps everyone else busy. Then it is "Cooks to the Galley" and a representative from each "Mess" goes aft to the galley and carries back along the open deck a precious tray of food. After breakfast there is more activity as hands perform the many maintenance and training activities.

By 0800, the ship's clock, if it could, would have struck eight bells, and the forenoon watchkeepers appear in succession to relieve the morning watchkeepers for their breakfast and part-of-ship work. So the watches change, to the afternoon at noon, the first dog at 1600 and the last dog at 1800, till the so-called first watch at 2000 completes the daily round. I suppose that must mean the first watch of the night.

My part-of-ship duty at sea, apart from the asdic, was mainly involved with confidential books. Signal Recoding Tables were important, to maintain confidentiality of signals broadcast by radio. They changed regularly, and sometimes irregularly, when one book, somewhere in the world, was suspected to have fallen into enemy hands. By reading all incoming signals, I was mostly able to supply the leading telegraphist with the next set of recoding tables in good time, but occasionally he would, very apologetically, awaken me from my bunk with the observation that "There must have been a change, Sir. We have a signal addressed to us which makes not one word of sense." Of course, that was as it should be if we did not have the correct tables, as we hoped the enemy had not. I would labour out of my bunk, unlock the safe, and hand him the next book, stay with him to see the result, and if the signal now decoded into English, return to my bunk.

Confidential books are regarded seriously by the Admiralty. They are in the charge of an officer who must sign for the receipt of each one and for its disposal. Loss of a CB is regarded as a serious matter. All this is in the interest of secrecy of important information and is a necessity in wartime, and for many aspects in peacetime. On joining *Bluebell* I took over from Wilf, a careful and reliable officer, who mustered all books, identified them against the register in my presence, and obtained my signature. I had to read all signals to keep up to date on which signal publications were in use. Other information came aboard with the ship's mail as soon as we berthed after a convoy. There was a good deal of work involved at this stage, new books to be signed for and entered into the register, superseded books to be returned or destroyed, and a declaration made as to their disposal, and some to be corrected.

There was one trap into which I fell. Some recoding tables had a loose supplement tucked in at the back. It had the same identification number with a suffix, and normally came into use and was superseded and destroyed along with the parent volume. On one occasion, a signal was received to destroy SP (Signal Publication) No. XXX, which I did. Months later, on submitting my report on CBs in my charge, I was asked why I did not have the supplement to SP No. XXX. I reported that it had been destroyed with the SP. The fact was that I had failed to remove the supplement and retain it. Nothing more was said. If it had been peacetime, I would probably have been reprimanded, although destruction of a volume could cause only inconvenience, whereas loss of one could be a serious breach of security. Our lives depended on security, so I felt worried about this oversight. At the same time, the supplement was never used, and I believe the mistake was partly on the part of the Navy in omitting to include the supplement in the instruction to destroy.

Another anomaly, though not serious, concerned an Aircraft Recognition Manual, which was not in our CB Library. It was only classified as "Restricted". Other classifications were "Confidential", "Secret" and "Most Secret" - to which popular comment was added "Burn before reading". Corrections started to arrive for this book which we did not have. As you might expect, new and modified aircraft were coming into operation frequently. Every time we came into port, in the big bag of books would be a bundle of replacement or added pages to the Aircraft Recognition Manual. By the time I handed over to my successor, I am sure we had a complete set of silhouettes, and were wanting only the cover.

It was my duty as CB Officer, in the case of abandoning ship, to destroy all secret publications, but fortunately this did not happen. The books were in a cast-iron safe in the captain's cabin. It would certainly sink beyond recovery if we were in deep water at the time, but it would take a strong working party to move it to the ship's side. Supposing this were successfully carried out, and I managed to survive and get back to Britain, no doubt the same CB authority in the Admiralty would want a signed declaration listing every publication thus disposed of.

Accountability in the duty of wine caterer was far less demanding, largely due to the accommodating policy of our suppliers, Saccone and Speed Ltd. They had warehouses in Liverpool and all other major ports, including Gibraltar. They retained ownership of stocks on board, and we paid as we consumed. This had two important advantages. Should the ship be sunk, the Company would not make demands on surviving officers for lost stocks. Also, at Gib, for example, beer was in short supply while wines were plentiful, from Spain and Portugal, at favourable prices. I would therefore take aboard full stocks of beer and spirits in Liverpool, and transfer the surplus to HM Ships at Gib, and take on a storeroom full of wines, to be distributed in Liverpool, to the benefit of other ships.

The only burden was in handling the stocks. I would request of the First Lieut two hands to load or unload supplies, usually to be told that there was none available. They were all busy on essential ship work. Always some compromise was reached, and we always shifted the cargo, not that it was a huge amount, possibly no more than a ton. At Gib one time, his hands were busy painting ship. I offered to take up a paint brush in exchange for two strong seamen, which he finally agreed to. The seamen did not mind because they were given a sample to test to make sure of the quality. On this occasion, one of them took a photo of me on a pontoon at *Bluebell's* stern, repainting her Number *"K80"*. Later, I photographed the painting party, suspended on planks around the superstructure. These pictures are in two albums of *Bluebell* photographs. Some of the men I remember by name, others not. I often look at these faces and wonder which survived the war, and which are still alive. I am 72 so they would average the same.

Having been in Liverpool for four days, we sailed again on 13th August 1941, in Escort Group 37, for OG71. *HMS Leith*, a sloop, was SO, with Norwegian destroyer *Bath*, and corvettes *Campanula, Campion, Wallflower* and *Zinnia*. There were five merchant ships from Liverpool, joined next day by ten from Milford Haven, and on the third day by the Clyde section, making twenty eight in all. The Clyde section included a tug, *Empire Oak*. The Commodore of the convoy was in *SS Aguila*, who also carried twenty one WRNS and a naval nurse. The Wrens were a select group of proficient cipher personnel, required to augment the staff of FOC Northern Atlantic in Gibraltar. From their position at the head of the centre column, they would have a brief view of the escorting ships each evening as darkness was falling and they took up their close screening positions for the night and, if they were early risers, again at dawn as the screen opened out to the limit of visibility. No doubt the sight of seven, and later more, warships, gave them some confidence; even a feeling of safety.

On 17th, a Focke-Wulf was sighted astern of the convoy

and a Coastal Command Catalina kept us company for a time. These two aircraft kept clear of each other. A "Cat" was not equipped nor fast enough to hunt a F.W., and the latter's job was to find convoys and to direct U-boats to them. Admiralty twice signalled *Leith* that two enemy aircraft were in our vicinity, and to expect attack.

Next day, two Junker bombers appeared and made unsuccessful attacks. Admiralty advised at 0204 that one U-boat might be shadowing, at 1114, three or four, and later, four or five, and that destroyer *Wanderer* had been sent to join. At 2110 Admiralty advised that we were still being shadowed. The U-boats were apparently busy sending position and sighting reports and action was imminent. We could only keep a good lookout and listening watch on asdic. To transmit might give away our precise position but might, on the other hand, detect a U-boat. It was our strategy not to transmit unless the close presence of a U-boat was suspected, or if our position was known to the enemy, after a sighting or attack, for example.

At an hour and a quarter after midnight, SS *Alva* was torpedoed, and *Zinnia* picked up survivors as she sank. *Bluebell* went to action stations, as no doubt did every escort vessel, but no enemy was located. The U-boats were probably within the convoy on the surface, for at 0220 Norwegian destroyer *Bath* was torpedoed and sank, survivors being rescued by *Hydrangea*. Then at 0309 *Aguila* and *Ciscar* were hit. Both ships sank. In *Aguila* the only survivors were men already on deck who swam off as she quickly heeled over and went down. All of the Wrens and the nurse would have been in their cabins, with insufficient time to reach the upper deck. Tug *Empire Oak* stood by rescuing the few survivors, but there was not one woman among them.

At 1029, C in C WA ordered destroyers *Gurkha* and *Lance* to join OG71. During the afternoon and evening, Admiralty confirmed that we were still being shadowed. The probability was that U-boats dived immediately after firing torpedoes, proceeded submerged to one side, and when beyond visibility, surfaced and ran at high speed ahead to maintain a safe distance until the next attack.

There were no attacks on 20th, and *Hydrangea* left for Gibraltar with her crowd of survivors.   Next day *HMS Boreas* joined, and in the afternoon Focke-Wulfs were twice seen astern of us.   At 2000 *Bluebell* was sent off in the darkness to a position some forty miles north west to create a diversion.   At midnight starshells were fired and depth charges dropped, illuminating the ocean from depth to surface with an instant flash of white light.   We made a false enemy sighting report by radio and returned to our station on the starboard side of the convoy at dawn.   This ruse may have succeeded as there had been no further attacks.

Later that day, 22nd August, four U-boats were reported to be in our area.   A Catalina was seen, and *HMS Wivern* joined. Admiralty advised that up to nine U-boats were shadowing, the convoy having been reported on five occasions.   *Boreas, Lance* and *Wivern* were sent to hunt around the convoy but without result.

At 2228, Tug *Empire Oak* and *SS Clonlara* were torpedoed, *Campanula* and *Campion* standing by to pick up survivors. Stationed one thousand yards to starboard of the convoy, we heard two explosions at 2240.   We received instruction from *Leith* to stand by *Zinnia* to port of the rear ship.   We arrived to find *Campanula* and *Campion* already there.   *Zinnia* had been torpedoed, sank in less than a minute, and few survivors had been found.

An hour and a quarter into the next day, 23rd August, we heard two more explosions.   *SS Aldergrove* had been sunk, and *SS Stork* set on fire.   *Bluebell* had returned to the starboard side, and what was left of the convoy pressed on, *Wallflower* and *Campanula* proceeding to Gibraltar with survivors.   There was no further action.   We had lost seven ships and two of our escort, but not one U-boat sighting or asdic contact had been made.   What was wrong? It seemed that we were ineffective, though nobody could tell what losses there would have been had we not been there.   The lack of any opportunity to strike back was demoralising.   Nevertheless, we had to persevere in spite of discouragement.

For Britain to maintain her war effort against Nazi Germany, it was essential for ships and cargoes to get through, in both directions.   Against this large merchant fleet, it was Hitler's strategy to give priority to U-boat building and so to establish an effective blockade; to starve Britain of food and materials. It was our task to beat this attempt, and in the face of U-boat proliferation, to maintain a defensive screen.

It is inevitable, after a period of difficulty has passed, that circumstances subsequently improve. From the low point in any experience, if one survives, things get better. Therefore, when one is in an adverse situation, he should take heart, continue to do his best, and to anticipate improvement. Of course, he is not to know at any stage that things are still not deteriorating, or that he will survive to triumph. I had observed in my studies of mathematics at University, in periods of incomprehensibility, that these were always followed by enlightenment, if I persevered. Many famous people have told us this, from Kipling ("If") to Churchill, whose darkest became our finest hour. I know now that this **was** our darkest hour. The only fine thing about it was that our determination was undiminished.

It is worth noting that one of the officers in *Campanula* was Nicholas Monsarrat, who wrote about corvettes, his best known book being "The Cruel Sea". In this book which although fictional, is based to some extent on fact, the reader will recognise incidents of convoy OG71, particularly the sad loss of the Nurse and Wrens, for which we all felt some responsibility.

CHAPTER SIX

FLEET MANOEUVRES and HG72

At Gibraltar there was an opportunity for the Escort Group to act together in training manoeuvres which could not be carried out while escorting, or in our home port of Liverpool, where ships would be dispersed among several docks, preoccupied with maintenance, and have half their crews on leave. One of the first was a summons to watchkeeping officers to be aboard *HMS Leith*, our "flagship", at 0900 one day for signal training. Actually, *Leith* was senior officer of the escort group; at least her commanding officer was. I can see that I need to be more clear in the use of words. Naval jargon means much to me, both referentially and emotionally as my Professor of English, Walter Murdoch used to say, but little to many others.

"Captain" can mean the rank of an officer with four gold rings on his sleeve. He is senior to a commander and junior to a commodore. His rank is that of captain, though he may not be captain of a ship. The captain of a ship is officially her commanding officer, and may have any rank from captain down to sub lieutenant. *Bluebell's* captain, or commanding officer, was a lieutenant commander.

"Flagship" is generally understood to mean the senior ship of a group. Strictly, it means that the officer commanding the Group or Fleet, is in that ship. In a big fleet of major war vessels, this officer could be an admiral, rear admiral, or commodore. There is a distinctive flag to signify the command of each of these, and it is flown by the ship where he is, hence the term "Flagship".

The senior officer of our escort group was a commander in rank, so he did not have a flag to hoist in his ship, but there was no question that he was the boss. So, when he sent a signal requiring the attendance of all us sub lieuts at a place and time, that's where we were.

We packed into *Leith's* wardroom for his lecture, and though there was a grumble or two that this was a waste of time when we could be getting on with our own ship's duties prior to a run ashore, I was impressed and not a little excited at the sense of occasion. Here were the men who, for the past ten days, had kept watch during periods of calm and storm, endeavouring to guard the convoy from U-boat attack, and now, for the first time, were together, able to learn about each other; men "in the presence of history" as Churchill had said, back in school.

The commander entered, and the chatter subsided. He held up a weighted copy of the Signal Manual. "You all need to know what is in this book, and how to act on receipt of a signal," he said, with an emphasis which immediately dispelled any delusions of grandeur that lingered from my recent reflections.

"You probably know that the signal code is composed of three letter groups. You should know the meaning of the groups most frequently used. Now, there is one group 'XXX'," (I can't remember exactly what the three letters were. It does not matter now, but it did then.) "These letters mean 'You are astern of station'. When you lot are on watch, I need to have these flags hoisted all the time. You must be frightened of collision. Do you realise that if you should be five hundred yards astern of the next ship, and you are eight hundred yards behind, which you usually are, if you increase speed by one knot, it will take you six minutes to regain station, and a further fifteen minutes to reach the ship ahead. So don't be frightened to increase speed to catch up if you are astern."

He went on in this vein for a while, beating us down into the deck, but soon moderated to a man-to-man presentation of what we really did need to learn about our jobs as watchkeepers in charge of one of His Majesty's Ships at war. "You will notice that all possible combinations of three letter groups have been allocated a meaning in this Manual. The RN Signal School needed more, so what did they do? They started over again with the suffix 'Z'. Now only the Signal School could think of so clumsy a system."

I have thought often about this first Back to School in convoy escort group. The Commander had given us a well deserved dressing down, some valuable advice, and finally let us know that we were part of his Group, as compared to "those others" like His Majesty's Signal School. Thus the efficiency of, and pride in the Group was forged, little by little as opportunity arose.

Another day, the Group sailed into the Straits of Gibraltar for "fleet manoeuvres". I doubt whether this was worth the fuel it expended, but we all learned something. This may have been a little delusion of grandeur on the part of the Commander. Perhaps he was admiral for the day. There were signals for fleet manoeuvres, brief, concise and clear to all familiar with them. I had learned them at Flinders, and thought that I knew them, though I am not too sure if, now, I remembered them accurately. One was "Blue 9" which meant, when the flags were hoisted, "Ships will prepare to alter course together, ninety degrees to starboard." When all ships had acknowledged the senior officer's signal by hoisting the same individually, or "repeating", the senior officer executed the order by smartly lowering his signal, whereupon all ships did likewise, and the officer of the watch ordered to the helmsman "Starboard fifteen" and the steering wheel was spun to turn the rudder fifteen degrees. Corvettes, particularly at the twelve knots which we were making, spun quickly with this amount of rudder. As the compass showed ship's head approaching the new course, the OOW commanded "Wheel amidships. Steer XXX" (the new course). All orders were repeated by the helmsman. Meanwhile, all six ships turned as one. It looked great.

Usually on fleet manoeuvres, the commanding officer of each ship would be on the bridge and con the ship, meaning that he gave wheel and engine orders. On this occasion, we were steaming in line abreast at twelve knots, when *Leith* made a signal "Officers of the watch take charge". This meant me, and I was just a bit anxious. The "Blue 9" signal was made and repeated. I was watching *Leith* intently as was the Leading Signalman.

"Hoist down Sir," he called.

"Port fifteen," I called to the wheelhouse.

"Starboard, Sir," immediately said the leading signalman.

"Belay that; starboard fifteen," I called to the wheelhouse.

"Starboard fifteen; fifteen of starboard on, Sir," reported the quartermaster, and *Bluebell* swung to starboard into line ahead with the others. Saved from a muddle by an alert signalman, I was; perhaps, from disaster. At worst, we could have collided with the ship which previously had been on our port beam. More probably, I would have realised my mistake as soon as the other ship was seen to swing toward us. Then the wheel order would have been corrected, but we would have been out of station, and have received an immediate reprimand from the senior officer. This was and still is another lesson for me on the need to think clearly in times of stress. Recollection of this experience does not cause nightmares, but is ever present, like my gratitude to the leading signalman, who was typical of his ilk; intelligent, alert, watchful.

All officers of the watch had a turn of duty during these exercises. When relieved, I went to my cabin for my camera. Photography was my hobby and my camera an Ensign Double Eight, a 21st birthday present from Mum and Dad. It produced a negative about the size of a 35 millimetre film, and folded to fit easily into my pocket. Most of the pictures herein were taken with this camera. By the time I reached the main deck, we were on a full speed run. This was the first time I had seen *Bluebell* at top speed by day. She was making sixteen knots, slow by destroyer standards, but quite impressive for a "jumped up trawler". She pulled large waves along with her, as you will see if you look at the picture I took, with the Rock in the background, and corvette *Carnation* on our port beam. This was most exciting. The ship trembled and plunged through the long low swell with characteristic vertical oscillation, like quick reversals in an elevator. Every so often she would get out of step with the swell and rise faster than usual, causing stomachs to sink, and knees to bend. In destroyers, this phenomena is known as "milestones", and I felt proud that little old *Bluebell* had at least one thing in common with the glamour ships of the Battle of the Atlantic. It made little difference to my pride that, upon reaching the tenth milestone, I was seasick for the first time in months - when I thought I had it beaten. But this is not uncommon among sailors serving in "greyhounds of the deep" during rare bursts of speed.

No1 had put me in charge of one of the ship's boats. I kept it scrubbed, and was in charge whenever it was called away. He knew that I loved this because it was a taste of home and my sailing dinghy on *Medana*. Nothing looks smarter than a ship's boat with clean, light grey paint, and scrubbed timber gunwale, thwarts, floorboards and oars. At sea, both boats were kept swung out on the davits, ready to lower quickly. In this relative southern latitude and fine warm weather, I would spend some of my off-watch time in the afternoons sitting in my boat, writing home. Convoy details were, of course, secret, but I told my parents and sisters and the Gang, about *Bluebell*. My mother sent Steward Gawn a present for his kindness.

On the morning of 5th September, 1941, *Bluebell* left Gibraltar in company with destroyer *Croome*, corvettes *Campion*, *Campanula* and *Mallow* as escort for HG72 (homeward bound from Gibraltar, number 72). We were routed westward for seven hundred miles to keep a good distance from enemy held bases. It was now considered that HG71 should have been similarly routed, instead of taking a shorter course. We were to join up with SL85 and its escort, and turn north. In anticipation of this, and in the absence of enemy sightings or signals, *Croome* was despatched on the 8th to join escort of OG73. Shortly after, she made asdic contact with a target considered to be a submarine, attacked with depth charges, and saw evidence of a kill. (U-boat not identified)

On the following day, *Campion*, on the port of the screen, made an asdic contact, and, together with *Campanula*, carried out depth charge attacks. There was no convincing evidence of a U-boat and later, whales were seen. These could easily be mistaken for submarines so far as the asdic was concerned, and no doubt many were mercilessly destroyed. Many more must have suffered pain and discomfort to their sensitive hearing organs, due to distant explosions and constant propeller noise.

When we did join up with SL85, *HMS Walker* became SO of the group which now included destroyer *Boreas*, sloops *Rochester*, *Leith* and *Sandwich*, corvettes *Wallflower*, *Hydrangea*, *Carnation*, and *La Malouine*, the French *Commandante Domine*,

Armed Yacht *Philante*, and CAM *Maplin*. We were routed northward, well west of the Bay of Biscay, then north east to the south of Ireland and through St George's Channel.

On the morning of 14th, a fishing boat was sighted and boarded. She proved to be French, with a catch of tunny, and without radio, so was unlikely to threaten our security. Later that morning, *Leith* and *Vanoc* sighted a Focke-Wulf. *Maplin* launched her Hurricane which gave chase, but the FW disappeared into cloud, and was not seen again. Our pilot came down by parachute and was retrieved by *Rochester's* boat. He reported that the German had jettisoned his bombs before making altitude into cloud, so he would give us no further trouble.

That same evening, *Walker* and *Vanoc* left for Milford Haven to refuel. Forty-five minutes later, *Vanoc* was attacked by a Heinkel seaplane whose bombs failed to explode. Next day *Daru* was bombed by two seaplanes and sunk. It seemed incredible that after the shocking losses of HG71, the next should get through unharmed by U-boats. Prompt action by *Croome*, *Maplin* and her Hurricane, and perhaps *Campion* and *Campanula*, together with a safer route, no doubt contributed. It has also occurred to me over the years that, in attacks on OG71, the U-boats must have had chance on their side, besides having exercised a high degree of skill.

Considering the small size of flower class corvettes, as compared with sloops and destroyers, their much lower cost, and reduced time of building, one must appreciate the wisdom of selecting this design. Escort ships had to be built quickly to meet the emergency in 1939. *Bluebell* was in the first batch of 26 ordered in July 1939, and completed a year later. By September 1941 over 100 were operating. While specifically designed for anti-submarine service, they actually did not excel in any role, except availability. Destroyers were faster and more powerfully armed. Nevertheless, corvettes did their job, and while there were not always destroyers on our screen, corvettes were always there.

CHAPTER SEVEN

OG 75

On return to Liverpool from HG72, half the ship's company went on leave, while the other half stood by, carrying out routine duties as well as those related to being in harbour. The Captain, after debriefing at C in C WA's headquarters, went home, and the First Lieutenant took charge, as he did anyway on most matters. There were stores to be taken aboard and stowed, "self refit" items of maintenance to be carried out by members of the ship's company, confidential books to be received, returned, corrected or destroyed, ship's correspondence to be processed, including seaman's service papers and many other official forms, all of which had been accumulating while we had been escorting ships through the Battle of the Atlantic. Now came that other battle; the Paper War. Fortunately for me, Wilf dealt with most of this and could not go on leave until he had done so.

Living aboard in harbour was most inconvenient if boiler cleaning was on the work list. Our electricity and water heating came from steam. When boilers were cold, so was the rest of the ship. But it was late summer, so the discomfort was not great and when, on completion of work, one boiler was returned to service, and the ship lit up and warmed up, it was all the more appreciated. There was a diesel driven generator on the wharf to supply lighting power by day, but this was shut down at night so our activities had to finish not too late.

Those remaining with the ship did get to go ashore occasionally, but I never found an "up homers" in Liverpool. That is to say, I did not make friends where I could visit and put my feet under the table. No doubt there was plenty that was of interest in the city, but I was content to get on with ship's routine and look forward to getting to sea and on with the war again, so that I could get back to Australia. I was allocated a few days leave and used the second of my four-per-year free travel vouchers to travel by train to Sussex, to stay with Elsie's aunt, Mrs Sally Woodall, who ran a cycle shop in the main street of Burwash. It was enjoyable walking the quiet, beautiful countryside and meeting Sussex people. "Sussex by the Sea" had long been a favourite march tune, but I was disappointed to learn that there was no major port on the coast.

One day I borrowed a bike from the cycle shop and rode to Battle, and Hastings on the south coast. Upon arrival, I asked a policeman where the famous Battle had been.

"Why?" he asked, "Are you looking for a fight?". He said it was difficult to describe or some other evasive answer, so I left without finding it. It is just possible that he did not know. It would hardly be still classified information. One of the seasonal occupations in Burwash was hop-picking. I had a go at this and liked it. Mrs Woodall's daughter, Evelyn, had been engaged for the season and I helped her fill baskets. It was most enjoyable to be back in natural surroundings again. I loved shipboard life, but not all the time. Everybody needs a break.

On the way back, I stayed a day or two at the Overseas League in London, and called at Australia House to meet some others from home. This was a great place for Australians to gather, and the Boomerang Club offered canteen facilities as well as the efficient billeting service for those on leave with nowhere to go. Some of the names from the busy Visitors Book would be listed in Australian newspapers from time to time, bringing great joy to their parents at home, and wives too, though most of us were single. My leave passed quickly, and I was on the train for Lime Street Station and Clarence Dock, where *Bluebell* was nearly ready for the sea once more.

Singly and in groups, the crew returned, and finally the Captain for his briefing, and on Saturday 27th September, 1941, we were off to Gibraltar again. I was now standing watch on my own, the Captain having decided that my apprenticeship, if not completed, was sufficiently advanced. He was conservative, as small ship captains go, but there was nothing wrong with that. It tended to emphasis the importance of thoroughness in all aspects of being in charge of the ship. He would come up to the bridge at some time during every watch and chat with me for a while. On leaving to return to his bunk, he always said "Keep her moving about, Shean." This meant making frequent course alterations, or zig-zagging in order to make it difficult for any U-boat to score a torpedo hit.

Keeping watch on my own freed other officers for their other duties, and gave me a feeling of responsibility. I reflected on my father's stand not to let me drive the family car; therefore I had no licence, yet here I was, in charge of an HM ship. There is no doubt that young people, no matter how good their home, need to get away from it for a long period in the process of growing up. I received my Watchkeeping Certificate for Corvettes at age 23, for Major War Vessels at 26, and motor vehicle drivers licence at 27. My friends who served in the RAAF were similarly placed, having been captains of four-engined bombers before they could legally drive a motor car.

Doubling up on watch resulted in getting to know the other person very well. Wilf and I got along best of all the officers. He was a lover of fine music, and had done some composing. He showed me a short manuscript, a song called "The Soldier". The notes on paper did not mean much to me because I was not so far advanced with my reading of music that it was a second language, as it needs to be. Wilf said that his musical friends were not keen about it because at one point there was a discord. I can't remember much more about the song, but suspect that it was his expression of the tragedy of war. My father had played base drum in several brass bands, principally Perth City Band, but that did not impress Wilf. Brass bands were not his first choice.

On watch at one time would be the officer, a lookout on the stern and port and starboard wings of the bridge, a signalman and an asdic operator. On the deck below were the helmsman and two relief helmsmen who were also messengers, being sent around the ship to make kye (cocoa), call the next watch, and anything else. These last three took twenty minute "tricks" on the wheel, talking and smoking all the while. You can imagine the fug which prevailed all night in the wheelhouse, with doors and windows shut to keep the ship blacked out.

Behind the wheelhouse was the radio room, manned by the duty telegraphist. It was most important for continuous watch to be maintained for radio messages (signals). Ships maintained radio silence, but were always able to receive and traffic was frequent. Thus we were kept informed on the disposition of shadowing U-boats who made signals to Germany and to each other, signals which were "DF'd" by Admiralty; that is to say, the direction of these transmissions was found by monitoring radio receivers at strategic locations, giving the U-boat positions. Even if the signals could not be decoded, though generally they were, the number of them was some indication of the number of U-boats in our area, and the degree of activity. Admiralty signals were brought up to the officer of the watch at night so that he could take any necessary action.

Signals within the escort group were always made by signal lamp, the powerful ten-inch signal projector by day, and the smaller, sometimes blue-shaded aldis lamp, by night, but only if essential. Even an aldis lamp beam could be seen from many miles away at night, and could give the convoy's position away to a scouting U-boat. The ten-inch SP made its flashes by the opening and closing of venetian blind type shutters outside the front glass. The aldis, on the other hand, flashed by deflecting its beam down toward the recipient and up away from him. This it did by tilting the mirror mounted behind the bulb, or globe. The mirror focussed the light into a parallel beam, quite narrow, requiring the lamp to be aimed at the recipient using sights, like a gun. At night, a non addressee to one side could sometimes read another ship's signal by watching the beam rise and fall, a short fall being a dot, and a long one a dash.

We all became somewhat proficient at reading morse if the speed were moderate, but when two yeomen of signals were signalling each other, I had not a hope of keeping up. The procedure was first to call the addressee by a series of "A"s, dot dash, dot dash, dot dash, till the second ship answered "T", dash. Then the message flew. Each word, when understood, was acknowledged with a "T". Mostly, with long words, the recipient would guess the word after a few letters, acknowledge with a "T", and the sender would instantly start the next word. With good understanding between expert signalmen, small words were omitted, and long ones abbreviated so that sometimes no words were sent in full. When, for any reason, two escorts were steaming close abeam of each other, the two yeomen could be seen with their arms over the bridge rail, talking to each other by semaphore, using their fingers as flags. Nobody could eavesdrop at their speed.

This convoy was OG75 with the newly formed 37th Escort Group comprising *Rochester* (SO), *Bluebell, Campion, Carnation, Heliotrope, La Malouine* and *Mallow*. Destroyer *Lamerton* joined us for the start. CAM ship *Empire Gale* was present as well as another gale which plagued us for eight days. With a nominal speed of but seven knots, strong head winds and seas reduced effective speed to three or four at times. We hoped that these conditions would also prove difficult for the U-boats.

In small ships, "rounds" were carried out usually only once each day at sea. Ours were in the first watch at 2100, before all the "watch below" turned in. This was the duty officer's inspection of the ship to see that all was in order. In heavy weather, conditions in the forecastle where the ordinary, able and leading seamen lived, were awful. Water breaking over the bow leaked down the navel pipes which housed anchor cables from deck level to the chain locker. At messdeck level were clamps to stop the chain rattling in the steel pipes, and water leaked through the clamping holes onto the messdeck. Sailors getting in and out of their bunks and hammocks did so from a deck which was constantly awash with sea water. It is still on my conscience that I could have done something to make good this leak. I had still to learn that my superiors did not have all the initiative. Everybody had some contribution to make, and the sailors looked to their officers to act accordingly.

Two days out, Admiralty changed the route in order to keep clear of an area where FW's. were found to be operating, and all was quiet for the next two days. On 2nd October, one did sight the convoy, and again the following day. At 1100 Admiralty advised that we had been reported, and that two U-boats were astern. At midday, *Lamerton* saw an enemy aircraft. To try to prevent the U-boats from making contact, the convoy altered course twice in he afternoon, and again after dark. At 1800, Admiralty signalled "Expect air escort at night. U-Boats in your vicinity."

That night one of the escorts reported that she was investigating a possible submarine contact. Our officer of the watch informed the Captain, who ordered "Submarine action stations". I was asleep in my bunk and was awakened by the action stations bell. I tumbled out, pulled on my seaboots, grabbed my oilskin, mounted the companionway two steps at a time, pushed through the blackout curtain out onto the main deck, and picked my way aft between the many deck obstructions to where the depth charge crew were assembling. We set about arming the charges and setting them for counter attack. Presently, the voice pipe number (man) called to me.

"The Captain wants you, Sir." I went to the voice pipe.

"Shean here, Sir."

"What the bloody hell are you doing back there Shean?"

"I am at my action station, Sir," I replied, confident that I had him this time, but no!

"Your action station is on the bridge. Get up here at once."

"Aye aye, Sir," and forward I went, past the obstacles and up the series of steel ladders, wondering what had happened. Once on the bridge, I reported to the Captain.

"Your action station is on the asdic. Get there right away."

"Aye aye, Sir," said I, thinking but not saying - 1) that is where I should have been posted from the start, and 2) when, for whatever reason, the "Old Man" changed his mind, he might have told somebody! Never mind, here I was, on the job I was trained to do, though I felt uneasy about leaving my depth charge crew on their low, sea-washed deck, where so many rescues had been made.

I entered the asdic house, stood behind the recorder on the left of Petty Officer Aldridge who was operating, keeping a listening watch, and put on my earphones. There was nothing to be heard except the usual background sea noise. The escort reported that no submarine had been identified, and resumed her station on the screen. Sherwood ordered "Fall out action stations". The asdic operator on watch returned to the asdic from his action station; Aldridge and I returned to our bunks. On the day following night-action, everybody was tired and likely to be less efficient than they should be. Hence the Navy saying - "All time not spent in sleep is wasted".

It was Sunday 5th October, and the gale still opposed us. One day at sea is much like another, except that on Sunday a "Make and Mend" is piped in the afternoon. In olden times, seamen would make and mend clothes, but letter writing and clothes washing, or "dhobying" were now common activities. I was keeping the last dog watch, when up the companionway sprang Signalman Scott, a pleasant, witty Scotsman. He nipped quickly into the asdic hut before some sea spray caught him. I followed him in, observing that he had had a shower, donned a clean white polo neck sweater and freshly folded trousers - one fold for each of the world's seven oceans.

"You have had a scrub up, Scott," I said.

"Yes Sir," he replied, and pausing for emphasis, added, "Nothing, if not smart." Many times I have reflected upon this example of elevating one's spirits above the trials and discomfort of one's situation. I have tried to emulate Scott, because it does wonders for the rest of the crew and one's own morale, to take that first difficult step up, when it would be easier to drift down.

I mentioned washing. In most ships, certain enterprising sailors make a little money by taking in laundry for others. "Dhobying Firms" they are called, the subject of a little song that goes:

"I'm the dhobying firm
The money I earn,
I spend among all my messmates.
Liar!"

Talking of bathrooms reminds me of another occasion during that same gale when I was shaving with my cut-throat razor when the captain entered.

"Careful, Shean, you don't cut your throat. It will take a long time to grow again." He need not have worried. Though *Bluebell* was rolling and pitching heavily, I could manage to shave without injuring myself, having succeeded in all previous rough conditions except aboard the Perth to Kalgoorlie railway in the old days of three-foot six-inch gauge track. Then the motion was so violent I had to await the arrival of the train at a loop when it would stop long enough to allow a train to pass in the opposite direction, and for me to shave in safety.

Late that Sunday, Admiralty radioed a further warning of U-boats in the vicinity, and the weather was moderating. Next day, another course alteration was made. On Tuesday 7th, FOC North Atlantic despatched five destroyers to join the escort before dark on the 9th. There was a feeling of excitement and apprehension as the convoy sailed steadily southward, making better speed now that the seas had subsided.

For all the expectation, shipboard routine carried on, and I came down from the bridge that night having completed the last dog watch at 2000. Now, the Captain of every ship is apt to feel lonely because he spends less time with the ship's officers than we do with each other. Ours did eat in the wardroom, and that was where I found him as I entered to partake of late supper which Gawn had kept hot for me. The captain enjoyed a game of cribbage, and spoke to me while I ate.

"Well, Shean, how about a round of the board?" I obliged, of course, thinking of my cosy bunk and the morning watch. But he was a pleasant character whom nobody wished to offend, and that made for a happy ship. Although now standing watch on my own, I was still gaining experience. Getting along with my shipmates, from captain to ordinary seaman, was important.

On Wednesday 8th, Admiralty advised that aircraft had shadowed us, and to expect U-boat attack, and re-affirmed this twice as the afternoon wore on. One of the convoyed ships, *Soraston*, broke down, and was taken in tow by *Lamerton*, while *Heliotrope* stood by. The convoy had eight hundred and fifty miles to go which, at the present speed of six knots, would take six days. Notwithstanding the threats and warnings, nothing happened that night.

Next day, Thursday 9th, Admiralty advised that three FW's were looking for us. That, by comparison with their previous advice, was reassuring. We made two course alterations in case we had been spotted. Thus the game of hide-and-seek continued. Friday brought more news of U-boats in the vicinity, and aircraft sightings. It was probable that a concentration of U-boats would be encountered west of Gibraltar, and *Legion, Ariguani, Lively, Foresight, Fury* and *Forester* had arrived to augment our screen, which was now quite formidable.

The U-boats were certainly about because, on 14th October, as our charges steamed safely into Gibraltar, Corvette *Fleur de Lys* was torpedoed to the west. In fact six U-boats had been shadowing the convoy but none had succeeded in penetrating the escort screen. *Soraston*, to our deep satisfaction, arrived safely in Lisbon. To cap it all, we received a signal from FOCNA addressed to Commodore and escorts of OG75; "It reflects great credit that your convoy OG75 has arrived unscathed." 1056A/14 October 1941.

CHAPTER EIGHT

HG 75

The high concentration of U-boats, which had unsuccessfully hunted OG75, were still patrolling west of Gibraltar when the next homeward bound convoy was due to sail. So the convoy was delayed and two sweeps made in the hope of locating and destroying them. On Friday 17th October 1941, destroyers *Lamerton, Duncan* and *Vidette* swept out toward Cape St Vincent, while the 37th Escort Group combed the waters closer to the strait. *Rochester* (SO) led *Bluebell, Carnation, Heliotrope, La Malouine* and *Mallow* with quick results, as at 0330 Saturday, *Carnation* saw and attacked a U-boat.

Next day, *Rochester, Carnation* and *Mallow* made a combined attack on an asdic contact and were encouraged to see a spreading patch of oil, and further when *Bluebell*, on her way back to Gibraltar, recovered an air vessel from a German torpedo. Notwithstanding this evidence, however, we could not be sure that the U-boat pack was any smaller. (In fact, *U 204* had been sunk.)

Convoy HG75 sailed on Wednesday 22nd October, with destroyers *Cossack* (SO), *Lamerton, Legion, Vidette, Commandante Duboc* and the 37EG. At 2250 *Vidette* saw and attacked a U-boat, but due to the pressing of the wrong alarm, only six of the intended pattern of fourteen depth charges were dropped and no evidence of a kill was found. Nevertheless, there were no attacks that night, and our prime responsibility was to protect the merchant ships.

We were joined on this convoy by the newest development in the war against the U-boat, the escort carrier *Audacity*. She was the first of many converted large merchant ships and could land aircraft as well as launch them. She started service as *Empire Audacity* but was soon commissioned as an HM ship. It was reassuring to see her in convoy because we knew the value of air cover in at least forcing U-boats shadowing a convoy to submerge, and in keeping them down, until the ships had moved out of sight. A diesel-electric submarine did not, until very late in the war, have the speed and endurance when dived, to overtake a convoy. This she could only do when on the surface under diesel power and susceptible to sighting and sinking by these same carrier-borne aircraft. To launch her aircraft, *Audacity* would pull out of the convoy and steam at full speed into the wind. Thus she would have the necessary thirty knots air speed over her deck; similarly for landing, so she was vulnerable at these times.

For all our deterrent and evasive measures, a U-boat was seen and attacked by *Carnation* at 2300 on Thursday 23rd; five depth charges being dropped. *Bluebell* joined in the hunt, but contact was not regained. Half and hour later, *Cossack* was torpedoed. She did not sink and *HM Tug Thomas* left Gibraltar to help salvage her. The convoy of seventeen ships carried on, expecting further action. This was delayed but no less deliberate, for just before 0600 *Carsbreck, Alhama* and the Commodore's ship *Ariosto*, leading the centre column, were hit. Escorts fired starshell and snowflake rockets which illuminated the convoy, and were seen fifty miles away, but revealed no U-boats.

Possibly there were not many in the attack, as their technique was to penetrate between or under the escort ships, and to attack ships from the surface at point blank range, then to dive, and let the convoy pass over them. Asdic detection was not effective in the disturbed waters that would lie in the wake of so many ships, so we were not likely to find them after they had attacked. The U-boats would have to regain contact and get up ahead of the convoy on the surface during the day, which was probably what was going on at 1915 when two FW's were seen firing red signal flares. At least one U-boat was in position for another night attack, twelve miles to the north where a Catalina surprised him with a two depth charge attack in the late afternoon. At dusk, *Lamerton* made two attacks on an asdic contact. These counter measures were effective as there was no attack that night, and next day a Catalina sank a submarine from which survivors were rescued. She was the Italian

Ferraris.

By 0300 Sunday 26th October, the enemy was in position again and succeeded in hitting CAM ship *Ariguani* with a torpedo. Soon after 0500 *Heliotrope* made asdic contact and an attack, but the depth charges were not set in time so she had to do it again with nine charges, and a further one of seven. There should have been ten charges each time, but her starboard rails release-gear had jammed. These all too frequent failures of depth charges to be correctly dropped, propelled or detonated, were the result of insufficient practice, training and maintenance. I consider that we could all have tried harder, notwithstanding the lack of opportunity to experience realistic practice. Depth charges were expensive. We could not afford enough to let every crew member have a go at each step in the firing process.

HM Tug Thames left Gibraltar before noon to rendezvous with *Ariguani* and to tow her the five hundred miles, while *HM Tug Thomas* was already moving slowly that way with *HMS Cossack*. FW's were around again in the afternoon, so we could expect more that night. It was in this belief that I investigated an asdic contact at 0215. The range was six hundred yards, but at three hundred contact was lost. Eight charges were dropped just to be sure, though I was not confident that it was a submarine. It should have been ten, but the starboard firing buzzer failed to buzz, so the throwers did not fire.

Duncan saw a U-boat one thousand yards off the convoy's bow at 0500. It dived under the convoy but made no attack. Again at 0800 she saw a U-boat and attacked with six depth charges, her port thrower failing to fire. On her second attack fifteen minutes later, only three charges were ready. Further attacks were made with *Mallow*, but these were inconclusive.

We heard during the day that *Cossack* had foundered before reaching port. Two FW's circled us in the afternoon, and U-boat radio signals were intercepted, estimated to be twelve miles on our starboard beam, so a course alteration was made forty degrees to port after dark. Our remaining fourteen ships were in five columns, steering north west at seven and a half knots, and we were not yet half way home. Two of our screen were away escorting the ships under tow, leaving us with *Rochester, Duncan, Bluebell, La Malouine* and *Mallow.*

Ulea, rear ship of the port column, at 0408 saw a U-boat on her starboard bow, and four minutes later was struck by torpedo. *La Malouine* picked up survivors while we fired starshell and snowflake rockets and also rescued five men, returning to our station on the starboard beam. That was the only attack, unless other torpedoes had been fired and missed. It was suspected that a U-boat within the screen of escorts would fire a number in succession a few degrees apart. With fourteen ships in close formation, several hits would usually result. Thus the attack would be quick and she could dive, stay deep, and unless detected and attacked by depth charges, some of the crew could rest in preparation for the next night attack. There were in fact six U-boats in the pack, four of them having hunted OG75 without success.

That afternoon, destroyer *Duncan,* which had joined the screen, saw a U-boat five miles away from the convoy, and in association with *Lamerton,* which had just returned from refuelling at Ponta Delgardo, made asdic directed attacks. *Rochester* got radio bearings on a U-boat and searched without result. However, there were no attacks that night and it was *Duncan's* turn to visit the Azores for fuel. We corvettes, with our modest speed, did less dashing about and were thus able to cover the whole distance without replenishment.

This was the role in which we were cast; small, slow, lightly armed, and devoid of glamour. We were not exactly the pawns in this ocean-wide war game of chess, but neither were we knights. Our strength was in speed of building and consequently in numbers available. We were the common workmen of the sea. Most of our men were not professional sailors, but reservists, like myself, striving to become proficient in the all too short time available. Not that there was any less character or potential among our men than any other crew.

By day, the blackout shutters on the asdic hut windows were lowered. The asdic operator, seated on a high seat in the middle of the hut with the training (rotating) wheel in front of him, could see out over the bridge rail and splinter mattresses. As he could judge the amount by which he was rotating the oscillator by the feel of his wheel and his only other duty was to listen with headphones to the hydrophone for ship's and torpedo propeller noises and for echoes from his own transmissions, he was otherwise free to look about the general scene, all visible to him save fifty degrees each side of right astern. The operator I remember best is Able Seaman MacDonald. He was formerly a fisherman from Campbeltown on the Mull of Kintyre, Scotland. He had a strong voice, Scots of course, and was given to stuttering, especially when excited. He was also an observant fellow and frequently reported sighting before the lookouts and signal lamps flashing in our direction, before the "bunts" (buntings, or signalmen). He delighted in trapping the officer of the watch in conversation. When MacDonald was on duty, it was hazardous to go near the asdic hut. He had many amusing sayings too, but for the life of me, I cannot remember one; all the same, I can still feel his presence, turning the wheel, blurting out something to hold somebody's attention. He must have possessed that rare ability to comprehend more than one thing at a time, because with all the diversity of his attention, he was a reliable asdic operator and reported many contacts and sounds. I would not know how many he missed, but there would not be too many I'm sure. There was always something doing when Mac was on watch.

Another character in the memorable category, you have already met, Signalman Scott. He was also Scottish, of medium height, slightly thin, and always pleasant. When he and Mac were on together, there was plenty of chatter. It was not that Scott was distracted from his vigilance, because if there were any signals, MacDonald would see them first. I believe that these men were typical of those who are on top of their job. Their expertise was such that they took everything in their stride, did it well, and made it look easy.

A signalman had joined the ship, fresh from a short course, new to it all, and with most of the job still on top of him. One night when all was quiet except for the normal sounds of the ship, we were running alongside one of the ships in the starboard column, peering intently through binoculars at the darker than dark shape, weighing five thousand tons, a few yards on our port beam. *Bluebell*, too, was completely blacked out; no navigation lights, not a glimmer from any scuttle or door to betray her presence to the enemy. Suddenly, a brilliant wide beam of light flashed out toward the starboard horizon. I shot across the wing of the bridge to find our new signalman operating the ten inch signal projector.

"Put that out," I shouted. Blackness again, except for the dazzle-stars lingering in my eyes. There were no other lights visible, not even the subdued aldis lamp's flash which would have been used if a signal were being passed from another escort.

"What are you doing?" I asked the signalman.

"I was just testing the lamp," he said. They say one should never criticise a man for doing something. Maybe, but there is a time and place for everything. In a further discussion with him, he confided that he was unhappy in the Navy, and would rather be back home, where he used to keep pigs. He did get a draft, and I hope that he did find his niche in the Navy, as an officers' steward perhaps, because we were known as "pigs".

There is a procedure and scale for punishment available to officers of the watch, and indeed anybody with authority, and this case could have been reported and processed via the first lieutenant's defaulters hearing. I never did put anybody on a charge; I was probably fortunate in not having been involved in a serious case of misconduct. My signalman was a case of ignorance rather than deliberate misconduct. I have thought, from time to time, that I was not as effective an officer as I should have been, not having run anybody in. I discussed this with Ginger Coles, whom you will meet later, but he maintains that I had it right and that others were too prone to exercise their authority unwisely. He might have been speaking in self defence, being a man of independent thought and having been at the receiving end of many a charge and stoppage of leave, and indeed was the man, of all those who ever served under me, who came closest to opening my score.

When I said that we were reservists, that applied to all *Bluebell's* officers, and to most of the ratings. We were in the Navy for the period of hostilities only, abbreviated to "HO", otherwise "hostiles" or "indians".

HG75 was still steaming north, and enemy action seemed to have lessened, though we never knew whether it would continue that way. On the afternoon of Wednesday 29th, two FW's were seen to be flashing signals, presumably to a U-boat. Two of the escort searched along the bearing without seeing anything. No doubt the aircraft gave them warning and, in any case, a submarine crew, if alert, should always be able to avoid being sighted because of the comparatively large visual extent of a surface ship. These aircraft never flew over a convoy. Let me give you an explanation.

When describing *Bluebell's* anti-aircraft defence weapons, I left two for a later chapter because they are worthy of special mention. First of these was the Holman Projector. Holman, you may recognise, as the makers of compressed air equipment. This weapon could be powered by high pressure air or steam, the latter in our case because it was available. The projector comprised a small receiver or pressure vessel, with a six foot long pipe connected via a pedal operated valve. The pipe was sized to accommodate a hand grenade with its safety lever in position, and the assembly was mounted, like most weapons, on pivots which allowed rotation horizontally and vertically. In other words, it could point in any direction above the horizon, not moved by handwheels and gears like the four inch gun, but freely, by hand.

The method of use was, at the sounding of action stations for air attack - signalled by a series of short rings of the action stations alarm bells - for the operator to open the steam supply valve and heat the receiver till it had full steam pressure. On the approach of enemy aircraft, the operator would take a hand grenade from an adjacent locker, remove the pin and drop it, with lever in position, down the pipe. If the aircraft were approaching within range, which was rather short, like fifty yards, the operator would swing the projector to point to where the aircraft was going to be, and at the correct moment tread on the pedal. Steam would be released into the pipe below the grenade and propel it along the pipe, and hopefully toward the aircraft. At the standard time interval, the grenade would explode. All things being as required, the shrapnel would hit the aircraft and bring it down. I never saw this weapon used in anger, as they say, but frequently for amusement by the bored operator at his action station with nothing likely to come within range. It happened that the ship's potato locker was mounted on the upper deck nearby. Selected potatoes fitted the pipe quite nicely, and made effective, if harmless, projectiles for practice.

The second unusual defence against enemy aircraft was the PAC (parachute and cable) rocket. There were two, mounted port and starboard on top of the asdic hut. Each comprised a vertical tube about two feet long and containing a rocket to which was attached a long wire coiled within a bag, which normally hung at the base of the tube. The operator took the bag and hung it on his left arm, while in his right hand he held the firing toggle, a wooden handle connected to the rocket firing pin by a light line. No aiming was provided. If an enemy aircraft made to fly at low altitude over the ship, the toggle was to be pulled at the moment which would result in the rocket streaking up with its wire and suspending it, complete with a parachute at each end, in the path of the aircraft.

At my first participation in a practise A.A. action stations, my role was that of PAC Rocket Operator; actually to fire one. As I prepared to do so, I noticed all bridge personnel withdrawing to a safe distance. Standing alone, in ignorance of any risk, I pulled the toggle and away went the rocket, up, up, whipping the wire out from the bag on my left arm. It all went beautifully. There was a long strand of wire, gently falling, with a parachute at each end, until it all finished in the ocean. It was not until after this day that I learned that the wire had been known to tangle, causing injury to the operator's arm. It then occurred to me that the bag of wire might just as well be suspended from the hut so that the operator could extend the toggle line and, like the others, stand well clear.

On another day, with the other ships of the 37th Escort Group, we exercised A.A. action stations, and had a practice shoot. I was then in charge of the quadruple 0.5 inch gun abaft the funnel. This exercise included someone else firing a PAC rocket which would then become the target for my gun to aim at. Off went the rocket, my gun aimers slewed and elevated the gun and opened fire, following the upper parachute's gentle descent. As it hit the water, we ceased fire.

"Good shooting," I told them.   Presently, the ship next to starboard started flashing with his signal projector.

"Thanks for the bullet.   Would you like it back?"   In the excitement of the action, I had failed to notice that as my gun followed the descending target, this ship had come into the line of fire.   Not very good.

Nothing further happened to impede HG 75's progress.   On Thursday 30th, a Liberator bomber from Britain appeared to reconnoitre for us, and *HMS Londonderry* joined, becoming Senior Officer.   That may seem a little rude, *Rochester* having led us through the thick of the action, but the "Navy List", which is the Seniority Bible, takes precedence and defines the pecking order, but absolutely.

There being no further interference from our enemy, HG75 arrived in home waters on Monday 3rd November, and *Bluebell* was ordered to carry on to the River Tyne for refit.

Corvette and Submarine

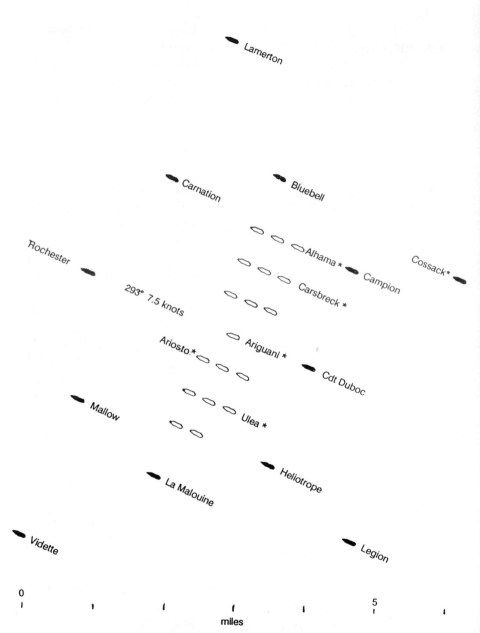

Lamerton

Carnation

Bluebell

Alhama *

Rochester

293° 7.5 knots

Campion

Cossack *

Carsbreck *

Ariosto.*

Ariguani *

Cdt Duboc

Mallow

Ulea *

Heliotrope

La Malouine

Vidette

Legion

0   5

miles

ships marked   *   were torpedoed

CONVOY HG75 AS AT 2130   23 OCTOBER 1941

CHAPTER NINE

REFIT

On Tuesday 4th November, 1941, we were taken into Tyne Dock in South Shields, and berthed alongside at Redhead's Yard. The principal work was the fitting of radar, or "RDF" as it was to be called in order to preserve its secrecy. Radio Direction Finding was a well established technique known to everybody and a common piece of equipment aboard ships, so we could refer to our new device by this name without giving away secrets. Ours was Set Type 271 and that was about the extent of my knowledge of it. Notwithstanding, I was made responsible for it because asdic was already my baby and RDF was more like asdic than anything else. Nobody could dispute the logic of this, but I knew nothing about it; however four able seamen, trained in the operation and maintenance of this set, joined the ship so I depended on them for technical expertise.

The equipment was large by present day standards. As I write this, equivalent radar for yachts comprises an antenna which could be carried in one hand, and an electronics and display unit which could be carried in the other. Type 271 occupied an additional steel hut placed at the rear of the bridge. There were racks of thermionic valves and all manner of components covering one wall of this hut, while the rotating antenna occupied a lighthouse type structure on top. The operator was shut inside the hut, turning the antenna, by means of a handwheel, to port 180°, then clockwise to ahead and 180° to starboard, then back to port and so on; archaic by today's standards, but a wonderful new facility at the time. The display was the now familiar cathode-ray tube, a simple forerunner of the television screen, which presented the operator with a spiky horizontal line. This had a high spike at the left representing the ship, and, if ships or land or anything else which could reflect electromagnetic waves were within range, other spikes further to the right. The distance on the display indicated the actual distance, or range, from the ship. Extreme range was about twenty miles. Aircraft may have been detected at this range, but ships could be contacted only up to ten miles, and periscopes, or surfaced submarines, at a much shorter range. On the other hand, RDF was effective at night as well as day, and promised much in our task of detecting U-boats approaching convoys. It also assisted the officer of the watch by providing accurate range and bearing on ships in convoy or points of land and islands. "Bearing" is the direction or compass bearing of such objects, and had to be checked visually because sometimes side echoes were indicated. This was not entirely new to us because the asdic behaved in a similar way, giving echoes off the sea bed, ship's wakes, whales, schools of fish, tidal streams as well as, sometimes, submarines.

Of the four additional personnel, Able Seaman Minns was the senior. He might have reached that able rate before the others, or perhaps their names started with O, P, Q or some later letter, I cannot remember. But I do remember Minns. He was tall, pleasant, and keen on his work. Also, he paid me the compliment of consulting me whenever Type 271 was misbehaving. I always responded with enthusiasm, if little else. Having studied three years of engineering, I had learned that there was much still to be known about everything. And here was this newly invented marvel, the product of the best brains in Britain, barely understood by an excellent able seaman with several weeks' electronic training, standing, inoperative, before a junior sub lieut with no electronic training, begging to be cured. The best I could do was to encourage Minns, supporting his every suggestion, handing him whichever tool he needed, like an operating theatre nurse, until at length the spiky line shivered across the screen again, and the Battle of the Atlantic could resume. But I have allowed my enthusiasm for this new RDF to carry me ahead of this period of refit, and you must hear more about other aspects.

Wilf was of literary mind, so he had accepted the duty of captain's secretary, attending to correspondence, pay and similar matters. This he did at the small folding desk in our cabin, until at this refit, he persuaded the dockyard overseer, by dint of fast talking and a bottle of Scotch, to provide minimal office furniture below the steep steel steps down to the wardroom flat. When he was in occupation, the space was completely filled; not that Wilf was fat, but he was tall and built in proportion. I drew a sign and fixed it to the side of the steps "Ship's Office. W.C. Swift."

My work I continued to carry out at my small folding "office" next to my high bunk, high in order to provide space for drawers below. There I pasted corrections into confidential books, wrote reports on asdic and RDF, pondered over instruction manuals, and generally attended to technicalities. There was a joke circulating at the time concerning an inmate of a mental institution who broke out, entered the laundry of a nearby village, forced his attentions upon some of the lady workers, and ran off. The next morning's newspaper carried a headline "NUT SCREWS WASHERS AND BOLTS". Wilf considered this an appropriate title for my place of technical endeavour, and labelled it accordingly.

Sub Lt "Bill" Adamson joined the ship at about this time. He was a big fellow, older than the rest of us, and had been around a lot. Down his cheek he had a long scar, collected, he claimed, in the Spanish Civil War. His voice was proportioned to his ample frame, and he was frequently emphasising his scathing opinion on various service imperfections. People who offended him he described as "He's a bloody corn". Such opinions were confined to other than present company, and as we were always at relatively close quarters, he was good and entertaining company. I suppose that he was junior to me, but I would never try to "pull rank" on Bill. His disdain for the frequent "pipes" or orders conveyed by the ship's public address system, he voiced by mimicking "Do you hear there? All those who do not wuppety wup today will wuppety wup tomorrow."

As at any port, as soon as *Bluebell* berthed, sacks of ship's mail were delivered alongside and whisked aboard by a working party under the First Lieutenant's direction. Personal mail for the ship's company would be sorted and delivered first. At the next

"Stand Easy" (tea break), sailors, petty officers and officers would be silent while they devoured news from home. It was not all good of course. There was frequently a sudden change in fortune for one of the crew. Fortunately for me no really bad news arrived from home during my time in the Navy, but often, after reading two months' accumulation of letters, my feelings would be so mixed, I would feel like laughing and crying at the same time. Many of the Gang wrote to me, besides my parents, sisters and other relations. Replying was left till later, when we were back at sea.

My older sister Beryl, or Bid as I call her, had a baby daughter just before I joined the Navy. Her name is Wendy, so I bought a nice edition of J.M. Barrie's "Peter Pan and Wendy". Wendy now has two boys of her own, Simon and Tim. Recently she lent me the book; it is inscribed "*HMS Bluebell*, at sea. To Dear Wendy, with wishes for a Merry Christmas, Lucky New Year, a Good Easter, or a Happy Birthday. I can't tell when you will receive this. Plenty of love, Max (uncle), 14th November, 1941".

Mail was slow, but usually reliable, which I thought remarkable in view of the number of ships we were losing in some convoys. My mother frequently sent food parcels, always with fruit cake, which was popular in the wardroom. I also received a parcel of knitted woollies from the University of WA girls group, who were doing their bit for students in the forces. Mine was from Heather Pearce and made me feel warm on the outside and the inside at once.

During refit the ship was partly uninhabitable due to modification going on in all places. Therefore, we found digs ashore. I had a very nice billet in South Shields, recommended by officers of a ship completing refit as we arrived. It was difficult for landladies to cater under food rationing, so we were issued with food ration and clothing coupons as well and could keep at least one outfit of civilian clothes. We preferred to wear civvies on leave, of course, but wore uniform travelling each way.

One of the features of the district was William Woodhave's lifeboat which was housed under a roof in a park within sight of the sea. There was also The Grotto Tavern at the foot of a cliff, reached by lift. On a Sunday afternoon I visited this romantic spot, which must have been a smugglers' lair like most such places.

However, it had become a smokers' lair and one could hardly see across the interior, so, after a quick drink, this one ascended again by the lift and enjoyed the comparative clarity of the open air, although never too pure in these industrial parts.

Every member of the ship's company, except for the "natives" - those who lived near the port - travelled off on leave at the first opportunity. We split the refit period, half on leave, the rest standing by the ship for the first half of the time, then changing over. I went to Sussex again, to Burwash, where Mrs Woodall was always kind and full of good cheer. I got to know her brother Dave quite well. He was a track maintenance man for Southern Railway and spent much of his time pulling the rails back into position. The trains, he told me, pulled the tracks along after them in the direction of travel, about four inches per year. He had a copy of The Anzac Book which he gave me, and which I still have.

Following refit, *Bluebell* was sent to Tobermory in the Island of Mull off the west coast of Scotland, for "working up". This comprised a series of exercises to train the crew in their various duties under the direction of a senior officer specialising in this activity. The Officer was the legendary Commodore Stevenson, an enthusiastic and fiery man who put everything into it, and ensured that everybody did likewise. There was little rest when a ship was under the control of *HMS Western Isles*. Headquarters were in the Western Isles Hotel which commands a view of Tobermory Bay. Apart from harbour exercises like "Away sea boat's crew", laying out an anchor, anti-aircraft action stations, fire drill and so on, we put to sea to exercise with a submarine. This was a unique opportunity, my first practice since the simulator at *Rushcutter*. I found that detection was not as sure at sea as with the simulator, and felt less confident afterwards.

There was always debate on the strategy of anti-submarine defence. One argument was that ships had a better chance of getting through on their own. This may have been so for fast ships, above twelve knots say, but for eight-knot ships that we were escorting, observations were that, at this severe stage of battle, fifteen percent of independently routed ships were lost compared with five percent of convoyed ships. To date we had lost seventeen of about one hundred and twenty ships in convoy, some fourteen percent. We must do better than this.

Another debate was whether an escort ship should leave her station to hunt and destroy a U-boat, or keep station and attack only while close to the convoy. The policy was to observe the latter practice. Our prime aim was to get the ships through, not to kill U-boats if that put the ships at greater risk. I supported this strategy, although I felt frustrated like everyone else that we were not hitting back as much as we would like. If there were only one U-boat threatening at any one time, escorts could safely leave the convoy and hunt it to destruction, but that was seldom the case. Escorts on station, evenly spaced around their charges, did provide the best deterrent to U-boats attacking at night, even though the screen so provided was not impenetrable.

It was always on my mind, when on watch and keeping almost constant lookout through binoculars with seven times magnification and fifty millimetre field lenses, that *Bluebell* was a far larger visual target to the U-boat than he was to us. Therefore, the sighting odds were in his favour. In fact, during my twelve convoys to and from Gibraltar, occupying one hundred and twenty days, and being shadowed or attacked on one third of them, I never saw a U-boat. Notwithstanding, I believe that we were doing the best thing. What we will never know is how many attacks we prevented by just being on station, close in at night, and at the limit of visibility by day.

In the ship's delivery of confidential books was a Monthly Intelligence Report. This was of great interest, containing as it did information on sinkings of merchantmen and U-boats and also of escorts. I recall Lt Walker observing that corvettes were improving because one had sunk in thirty seconds after being torpedoed, while the next took one minute.

The answer to the "hunt or protect" question came in the formation of support groups, separate from the escort groups. These evolved from our sister group, the Thirty Sixth Escort Group, led by Commander, later Captain, F J Walker. This energetic and enterprising man took the initiative to form a group of ships into an efficient and persevering hunt and destroy group. He needed additional escorts in convoy to be able to do this profitably. Looking back, I am tempted to think that I was unfortunate not to have been part of the 36th instead of the 37th Escort Group. But who can tell? They had the glamour of the offensive. We shepherded our ships through. Who had the greatest success in this respect? I guess that Walker succeeded in both. But I do believe that we could have done more intensive exercising and training, not that we were idle, but priority could have been increased toward activities which would have improved our performance.

After each convoy the Escort Group Commanding Officers would meet at the Gibraltar Headquarters of FOC North Atlantic, or in the Royal Exchange Building, where Admiral Sir Percy Noble, Commander in Chief, Western Approaches, was based, to conduct a de-briefing and to discuss strategies for the next convoy. I would have loved to have attended, so as to see the whole of the battle plan instead of what we could see from *Bluebell's* bridge. I doubt whether my contribution would have been significant, because I was still gaining experience, and would not have had the same views as I have now that it has all taken place.

When Lt Cdr Sherwood returned to the ship after these conferences, he always called the officers together in the wardroom and reported on what had come out of their discussions. While our wardroom meetings were conducted in the normal manner of *Bluebell's* administration, they were in fact high points in a great dramatic event. If only a recording could have been made of one, what a significant piece of historical evidence it would be today.

20° west

10° west

SCOTLAND

Oban

Clyde

Londonderry

Newcastle

Liverpool

Harlingen
+ Cape Rodney

+ Kumasian
Swiftpool
Belgravian

IRELAND

WALES

ENGLAND

Daru +

+ Bath

50° north

+ Ciscar
Alva
Aguila

Brest

NORTH ATLANTIC OCEAN

FRANCE

Empire Oak
Clanlara
+ Stork
Aldergrove
Zinnia

SPAIN

PORTUGAL

40° north

Lisbon

Carsbreck Ariosto
Alhama Ulea Cossack +

Gibraltar

+ shows position of ships sunk by U-boat

MOROCCO

PREFERRED OG CONVOY ROUTE

s in convoy; our reason for being. We were seldom as close as this in daylight and did not get to know many of them by
e. The corvette in the foreground may be La Malouine who flew her two ensigns, French and British, at her stern. Ours
from the funnel and became rather sooty.

-Lieut Wilfred Stiff keeping a sharp lookout through his Pattern 1900A binoculars. Seagulls habitually hovered over the
ge, gliding in the updraft, conserving their energy but putting bridge personnel at constant risk.

This landing party at Fingals Cave is described in the text. The skiff had to be secured fore and aft across the entrance channel, to keep her off the hard, sharp hexagonal basalt columns of which the cave is formed. Luckily it was a clam day but there was still considerable surge.

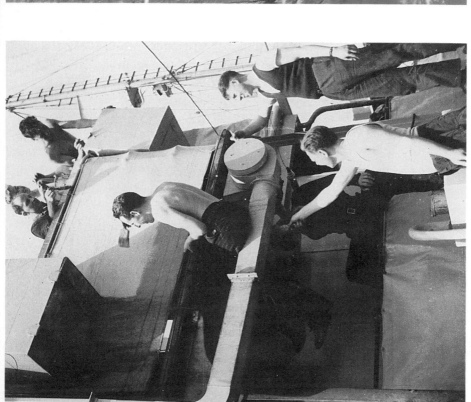

Gibraltar days were sunny, suitable for painting ship. This painting party were busy on the starboard side of the bridge. Able Seaman Minns, RDF Operator is shirtless, at the centre of the picture.

CHAPTER TEN

LONDONDERRY and OG 77

From refit and workup at Tobermory, *Bluebell* sailed for Londonderry to await her next Gibraltar convoy. On the way, all officers of the watch looked expectantly toward the RDF to answer all of our prayers. Breakdowns were frequent, demanding immediate attention by Minns and myself, pondering, probing and persevering, never giving up until it was working again. We badly needed this new magic eye and could not allow it to shut for longer than necessary. And when it was open, what it revealed took much skill in interpretation. A strong echo would register not only when the antenna was pointing at the object, but sometimes when looking to one side, requiring operator experience in classifying each contact so that the OOW could be informed correctly. A cooperation had to be developed between the three; RDF, Operator and OOW.

On arrival at Londonderry we secured alongside a timber wharf, so that the OOD had to watch mooring lines and fenders as the tide rose and fell twice a day. At Gibraltar there was little rise and fall, and in Clarence Dock water was shut in when the river level fell.

On the night of Thursday 27th November 1941, while we were still alongside, I was out on the main deck when there came on the still air the sound of revellers singing, not tunefully, but happily. One voice stood out from the rest as being of fine timbre and wild intonation. It could be only Peter William Taylor. Up onto the wharf I climbed, and intercepted four of the crew from *HM Trawler Vizalma*, arm in arm for mutual support, swaying down the boards. Peter and I were delighted to see each other, and lost no time in descending to the wardroom for another drink, which Peter did not need and took a long time to consume. With characteristic bonhomie, he entertained and was soon on the most friendly terms with all the wardroom personnel, especially Lt Cdr Sherwood, RNR.   Whereas we were always fairly formal in our relationship with our CO, Peter was sitting alongside him with his arm around his shoulders, calling him Bob.

Peter enthralled all with colourful accounts of *Vizalma* in heavy weather off Greenland and other trials of his sea life to date, while I listened in some apprehension as to how our Skipper would take it.   In fact, he took it with good humour and enjoyment.   Peter was a good ambassador.   It was hard to be indifferent toward him. In his presence, I was the quiet partner, the 'straight' man.   Next day we sailed, and I was not to cross Peter's bows again until it was all over, four years later.

Some sailors are superstitious about sailing on a Friday, but in wartime no day can be wasted, so we left Londonderry on that day, 28th November 1941 - thirteen months since my appointment in the RANVR.   The escort for OG77 was led by sloops *Black Swan* and *Fowey*, with *Bluebell, Campion, Carnation, Heliotrope, La Malouine, Mallow* and *Myosotis*.   I hope that you notice that the corvettes are in alphabetical order.   If it were otherwise, good manners would require that *Bluebell* should be placed last.   In fact, we were last in seniority when I joined, but were gradually moving to higher places, which meant that our position in the screen was no longer at the rear, but always on the starboard flank, so much so that I would not have felt at home anywhere else.

There were twenty six ships, including *CAM Empire Dell*. On the second day we altered course to avoid U-boats and a southerly gale developed on the fourth, reducing convoy speed from seven and a half knots to two and a half.   This made station keeping difficult for merchant ships if they were lightly loaded.   Severe pitching frequently brought the propeller out of the water, causing the engine to race.   This had to be controlled by hand throttling and the ship lost speed.   One of my engineering colleagues once experienced this difficulty and fell astern of the convoy.   A destroyer came close alongside and called through her loud hailer "I say, old boy, please try to keep up with the convoy."   Our Skipper, being from the Merchant Service, would express his concern in other words.   Chasing up stragglers was a common activity and important to the welfare of these ships, as U-boats frequently succeeded in sinking single ships without escorts.

Bluebell's incessant pitching and rolling must have found a weak spot in her RDF because late on the seventh day out, Able Seaman Minns called me from my cosy bunk to look at the set, which was failing intermittently.   I turned out and followed him up the series of steps to the bridge and into the hut.   There, another operator was doing his best with a trace which kept disappearing from the screen, until it finally refused to appear at all.   Minns said that he had carried out all the tests according to the book, without result, and that he regretted having to get me from my bunk.   By this time I was properly awake and told him 'not to worry, it was a nice night for a walk', or one of the usual reassurances.   The most popular one is, 'not to worry, I had to get up anyway to visit the heads (lavatory)'.

If Minns couldn't fix it, what chance did Shean have?   I did not say this of course; must not discourage the troops.   I asked the operator to continue to rotate the antenna to its limits, first to port, then starboard.   The trace appeared, briefly, occasionally.   It appeared sometimes when the antenna was at its starboard limit.

"Perhaps one of the cables to the antenna is faulty, Minns" I said.   "Train it forward while I go up to the antenna compartment and see what can be seen."

Up I went, through the small manhole above the operator, into the lighthouse where the half-moon shaped antenna was facing ahead.   There was a general fear that if one placed himself in front of an RDF antenna while it was transmitting, one would become sterile, or impotent, or both.   Whether there was any scientific backing for this hypothesis we did not know, but just to be sure, I took care that no part of my body was raised to that level except, at times, my head.   There were several electrical cables suspended from the antenna, circling the mounting and descending through deck glands to the electronics racks below.   One by one these were taken in hand, stretched and compressed, until an excited call from Minns, "That's the one, Sir.   The trace came on then."   Concentrating on that cable, a thick black one, I pushed and pulled each part in turn until it was established that there was a break within the cable where it coiled around the base, winding and unwinding with each rotation of the antenna. The 271 was shut down and the cable unplugged.

"Do we have a spare, Minns?" I asked.

"I don't think we have, Sir, but I'll have a look." He hurried out as the officer of the watch came to the door.

"Having any joy?"

"Yes. We've located the trouble in a cable, and are looking for a replacement. Give us an hour."

He was obviously anxious to have it back in service. *Bluebell* had operated without an RDF from commissioning up until a few weeks ago, but now it was indispensable.

Minns puffed into the hut, having mounted the three ladders two steps at a time.

"Sorry Sir. No spare for that cable."

"Well, Minns, it may be a silly suggestion, but there is a cable that looks like this one, in the asdic spares kit. I'll get it and we can try." The cable was of the co-axial type; that is to say, it had a single core of copper wires twisted together, surrounded by a milk-coloured insulation, then a braided copper wire screen and a black rubber protective covering. This type was used to carry the signal current to and from the antenna or, in the case of the asdic, the oscillator/hydrophone.

It was my turn to come back puffing, with a coil of black cable. Minns and his oppo (opposite number, or shipmate) got to work transferring the plugs from the old cable to the new, having remembered, as I would not have done, to thread it first through the gland in the deckhead (ceiling) of the hut. They plugged in at each end, switched on the set, and after the valves had warmed up .... miracle of miracles, it worked.

"Bridge, RDF" from the operator.

"Bridge." came the reply from the OOW.

"RDF operational."

"Thank you. Make a sweep and report what you can see."

The operator reported the convoy and otherwise nothing, and routine was re-established within the hour. When later I reported this event to the Command RDF Officer, and the fact that an asdic signal cable served quite well in RDF Type 271, he said

"Well, it shouldn't have." I expect that he had improvised plenty in his time, and was giving me a punchline for my story.

On Thursday 11th December, Admiralty signalled that at 1032 hours, a U-boat had radioed a sighting, probably of OG77. *Bluebell* had been detailed off to escort ships bound for Lisbon and was proceeding at best speed, consistent with economy, to rejoin. I was asleep when, just before midnight, action station bells sounded. I tumbled out, put on boots and coat, and hurried to the bridge, visiting the heads on the way. This was not entirely from fright but a precaution as advised by CPO Beer at *Rushcutter*.

"Always take that opportunity," he said, "because once you reach your action station, it may be a long time before you get another. The short delay incurred will make little difference to the outcome of the war."

On reaching the asdic operating position, I learned that we had been zig-zagging at twelve knots, five miles ahead of the convoy, when at 2342 hours an RDF contact was made, 5000 yards on the port beam, and had altered course to investigate. The captain was already on the bridge instructing the signalman to inform *Black Swan* by radio. According to normal routine, asdic was maintaining listening watch.

At 2345, range by RDF having come down to 3000 yards, bow and stern waves were seen ahead by bridge personnel searching with binoculars, and identified as "submarine" moving to port at high speed. We altered course forty degrees to port to intercept, and increased to full speed. It was a calm night with good visibility, though I could see nothing but the dimly lit interior of the asdic hut as I stood at the recorder, on Aldridge's left, wearing headphones and listening intently for U-boat propeller sounds. I instructed him to commence transmission, sweeping forty degrees each side of the bow, or "red four oh to green four oh."

All personnel were now closed up at action stations, confirmed by the flood of reports from around the ship, by voicepipe to the forebridge, the part at the forward end in front of the asdic hut, running across from wing to wing. There, the captain, first lieutenant and signalman were peering ahead through their binoculars, along with the two lookouts. There was an air of excitement, heightened by the very pulsing of the ship as the engine reached maximum revolutions. My own heart was thumping as if it knew that this was the moment for which all the training had been undertaken. The chase was on.

Shortly, in the headphones, Aldridge and I heard high speed propeller noises, which I reported to the bridge as torpedoes running, starboard side. They passed to starboard harmlessly. Between asdic transmissions, submarine propeller noise was now audible and becoming louder. Six minutes later , torpedoes were again heard on the starboard bow. I reported to the Captain who altered course in order to present a minimum target, and when they had passed, resumed the course for pursuit of our target. Lookouts lost sight of him, and Sherwood ordered "Asdic take over".

I replied "Asdic take over, Sir," and ordered a course alteration to port, to the bearing of the loudest hydrophone sounds. Echoes were now heard, but less distinctly than they might have been. Probably the chase had become a stern chase due to our quarry having turned away, and we were transmitting through his wake. Then I heard the captain ordering a change of course, and knew that the U-boat was in sight again.

Once more, this series of events took place. I could hear the RDF operator's regular reports to the forebridge and it seemed that the submarine was drawing slowly ahead. Indeed, we knew that most U-boats were faster than we were. At 2349 he could be seen, on the same course as ourselves, by lookouts, but not by the gun crew. A starshell was fired, followed by direct action (high explosive) shell, a second starshell and a third, but they all failed to illuminate. The bridge personnel were temporarily blinded by the flash from the propelling charges, and I was momentarily deafened, so the cease-fire order was given.

Although it was unlikely that a hit had been made, the U-boat dived, and asdic finally did take over, maintaining firm contact from 1100 yards, bearing north and moving rapidly left. RDF had held contact throughout, despite shocks as the gun fired. Doppler was marked opening, meaning that the echo was distinctly lower in pitch compared with that of our transmission, which occurred when the target was receding.

I set course for depth charge attack, having already ordered the crews to prepare a pattern of five light charges set to detonate at 100 feet depth. Steaming still at full speed, range closed rapidly and contact was lost, as expected, at 400 yards. The recorder showed a neat oblique line of dashes, each representing an echo, and each closer to the base line than the last. I set and lined up the firing indicator, and called "Stand by" to the crews, then "Fire one... fire two... fire three," pressing the buzzer button each time.

It was 2357 when the thud of the propellant confirmed the throwing of the first depth charge, and many seconds later when the powerful explosions were heard and felt. The captain reported that he had seen the submarine's phosphorescent wake as we passed ahead of it, and that our charges had fallen on track and well ahead of the diving swirl. I reduced speed to ten knots while Aldridge searched astern and regained firm contact at 900 yards, indicating that the submarine had gone deeper.

By now I was feeling quite composed, and ordered preparation for a ten charge pattern, comprising five set to 150 feet, and five heavy charges set to 300. At 1200 yards range we turned to port and steadied with asdic contact ahead. It was drawing slowly right with no doppler. That is to say, the pitch of the echo was the same as that of our transmission, indicating that the target was neither approaching nor receding, but slowly crossing our path at right angles, if not stopped. On our first approach, doppler had been opening because he was receding at a detectable rate. I made a course alteration to starboard.

It was four minutes past midnight when I gave the orders to fire. At the reduced ship's speed of ten knots, there had been ample time to adjust course and so to make the most accurate attack. Seconds passed as we awaited the shock of our own charges. There was no mistaking it. *Bluebell* shuddered violently, continuing on the same course as Aldridge swept across the stern to regain contact. A less than sharp echo was received and held until range reached 700 yards, and then faded. No propeller or other sounds were heard. Could it be that the echo was from the water, disrupted by explosions, and if so, had the submarine gone so deep as to be beyond detection?

An all-round asdic sweep was commenced as we reached one thousand yards from the site of our second attack and turned to recross it.   I noticed a red-hot electronic component within the recorder, opened the cover and pulled the component from its circuit board.   The asdic bearing indicator light went out and automatic transmission ceased. We continued to search using the hand key transmission and judging direction from the handwheel and drive wheel on the oscillator flexible cable, but never regained contact. Twenty minutes having elapsed without detecting anything, Sherwood sent a signal to *Black Swan*

"Have made two attacks. Asdic fault. Have lost contact." Although this was true, it gave our senior officer the impression that contact was lost because of the fault, whereas it was lost from some other cause -sinking of the U-boat possibly. The reply read:

"Return to convoy.   Your asdic failure has cost you a DSO."

We obeyed this order without question, of course, as one did not argue with the senior officer, who had understandably delivered us a "bottle" (reprimand). We felt that it was unjustified because the asdic fault was accidental, not a matter of neglect, and in any case, was not responsible for the loss of contact. But we took it on the chin and resumed our customary position on close screen, to starboard of the starboard column of merchant ships. By this time, I also learned that two of our throwers had failed to function.

Crestfallen though we were, there was satisfaction in the outcome - that every ship reached its destination safely, despite the presence of U-boats. We had succeeded in our prime objective.

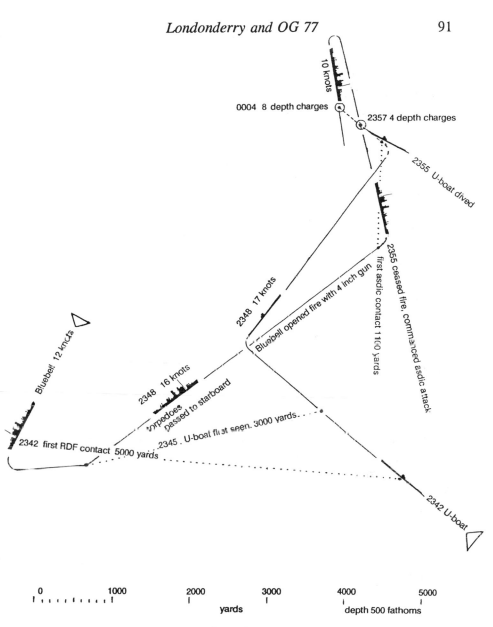

10 knots

0004 8 depth charges

2357 4 depth charges

2355 U-boat dived

2355 ceased fire, commenced asdic attack

first asdic contact 1100 yards

2348 17 knots

Bluebell opened fire with 4 inch gun

Bluebell 12 knots

2348 16 knots

torpedoes passed to starboard

2342 first RDF contact 5000 yards

2345 U-boat first seen. 3000 yards

2342 U-boat

| 0 | 1000 | 2000 | 3000 | 4000 | 5000 |

yards

depth 500 fathoms

Location: Atlantic Ocean, thirty miles south west of
Cape St Vincent. When U-boat was intercepted, Bluebell
was part of the escort of Gibraltar bound convoy OG77
which was on course 208 degrees at 8 knots, 5 miles
to the north, off this chart.
Times shown are one hour ahead of GMT eg 2345 [11.45 pm] = 2245GMT.

BLUEBELL'S ATTACK ON U-BOAT 11-12 DECEMBER 1941

CHAPTER ELEVEN

11th DECEMBER RESEARCHED

Because that day was one out of the ordinary, I have thought much about it, and since commencing to write this book, have sought further facts from different sources. Many times, I have reconsidered the conduct of the attack, asking myself "What could I have done to have produced a more definite result?"

It is now obvious that it would have been better to have ordered a fourteen charge pattern on the first attack. The five charge pattern which I did order was in accordance with both our training and standing instructions. I know now that U-boats promptly went deep, sometimes beyond 300 feet. Only by chance would an accurate attack result on a target moving at that depth. It would have been better tactics to have dropped the maximum number of charges in the first instance when he was still shallow and, as it happened, visible.

The proportion of misfires could have been reduced by more practical training of depth charge crews. U-boat crews spent weeks exercising in the comparatively safe waters of the Baltic where they became proficient in all aspects of handling their respective boats and weapons, before venturing forth on patrol. We escorts, on the other hand, were desperately needed at sea. In fact, at that time, *Bluebell* received a commendation from CinCWA for the efforts of her crew in keeping her seaworthy during months of near continuous service. It would only have been while on escort duty that further training could have been fitted in. With all crew members already working long hours, time for further training could only have been made if the Captain had given the matter high priority. Yet even one hour's exercise during each convoy would have done something toward ensuring that on the rare occasion of detecting a U-boat, we would have made the best of the opportunity.

When I first came across Roskill's "The War at Sea" I turned straight to the index to seek *Bluebell's* name and was excited to read "*Bluebell* sinks *U208*". The text in that edition revealed that on 11 December 1941 off Cape St Vincent this successful action had taken place. I wrote to Robert Sherwood to inform him and to Admiralty to seek further details, only to be told that subsequent research had identified our target as *U67* which was slightly damaged.

In the course of further research I twice visited the UK and consulted records at the Public Record Office at Kew, the RN Submarine Museum Archives at Gosport and MoD (Navy) Historical Section in London. Data obtained included convoy details, *Bluebell's* attack report, three publications by German authors crediting *Bluebell* with the sinking of U208 and an English translation of the War Diary of the BdU (Befehshaber der Unterseeboots, or U-boat Command).

The latter document listed the boats patrolling west of Portugal at the time as *U43, 67, 208, 332, 374, 434, 568, 574* and *575*. Those closest to OG77 were *U43, 67, 208* and *434*, so I obtained photocopies of their War Diaries in German together with the German Naval Grid Chart of the Atlantic which was necessary in plotting all positions referred to by grid number.

Many hours spent translating and plotting have yielded much interesting information, not only of this action but on the deterrent value of escorts, even corvettes. This I found encouraging, notwithstanding the passage of time. The events of the day were of particular interest and are set out below in chronological order. Times have been brought to convoy time, which was one hour fast on Greenwich Mean Time (GMT). U-boats' clocks were two hours fast on GMT. (Chart at end of chapter)

Thursday 11 December 1941.

Convoy OG77 was off the coast of Portugal proceeding at seven and a half knots toward Gibraltar. *U43* and *U67* were patrolling south west of Cape St Vincent. *U208*, to the best of BdU knowledge was west of Gibraltar and *U434* was patrolling west of Lisbon. *U43* commanded by Lüth and *U67* by Müller were Type IX, 1030 tons,18 knots with four bow and two stern torpedo tubes. *U208*, Schlieper and *U434*, Heyda were Type VIIc, 770 tons, 17 knots with four bow and one stern tube.

0858   *U434* reported to BdU "Convoy in Quadrant CG5588 (30 miles west of Lisbon) course 160 degrees, 6 knots." BdU signalled *U43* and *U67* to intercept and *U434* to shadow convoy. (The convoy was OG77 which had been routed much closer to the Portuguese coast than had previously been found prudent)

1233   (and at 1420) *U434* signalled an update on the convoy's position, stating that the 25 vessels had a strong escort.

1610   *U434* signalled that the convoy was in two groups. (Bluebell had been detached to escort the Lisbon-bound ships)

1713   *U434* updated her position by signal to BdU.

1900   *U67* logged that she was waiting in position ahead of the convoy, 20 miles south south west of Cape St Vincent, but sent no signal. *U43* meanwhile had dived several times to dodge Sunderland aircraft, work on diesel engines to eliminate smoke and to attend to batteries which were overheating and had lost 40 percent capacity (batteries had been damaged by sea water when *U43* accidentally sank in Lorient early 1941 When raised and overhauled, her batteries were not replaced). She was 25 miles north north west of Cape St Vincent, patrolling northward. (OG77 was just over the horizon to the west)

1930   *U43* saw a "destroyer" (actually *Bluebell*) bearing 100 degrees, course south, and turned onto a parallel course, preparing to attack.

2018   *U43* fired three torpedoes from bow tubes I,II and III, estimated target speed 10 knots, range 1500 metres, aimed at bow, midships and stern. Two broke surface and none hit. *U43* signalled BdU that he had made a "fault shot" on a destroyer and proceeded south eastward toward Cape St Vincent. (He thereby missed the convoy and took no further part in the action)

2112   *U434* signalled that she was in position behind the convoy. (Actually she was fifteen miles east of it. As a result of these signals having been DF'd (direction-found) by British radio stations, U-boat locations were now known and evasive routing of the convoy decided)

2149   *U67*, still 25 miles ahead of OG77 and 40 miles ahead of *Bluebell* as she steamed south to rejoin, saw two dark objects to the north and north east, the latter standing out clearly against the loom of Cape St Vincent light. These objects appeared to zig-zag about a southerly course leading *U67* to assume that they were advance units of a convoy escort. Later a third object, lower than the horizon was seen and classified as "fast motor boat". *U67* manoeuvred at full speed (18 knots) to get clear but without success, particularly with respect to the motor boat and thought that she might be receiving UK intelligence.

2314   *U67* prepared to fire bow tubes I,II and III at what he classified as a "*Dundee* class destroyer" but the motor boat kept too close.

2326   *U67* logged that the destroyer came close, travelling at 16 knots. During all this manoeuvring *U67* had moved only five miles to the south and recorded her position as 35 miles south-southwest of Cape St Vincent. The moon had not yet risen and the loom of the light was clearly visible on that clear, calm night, allowing U-boats and *Bluebell* accurate position fixing.

2343   *Bluebell*, now 10 miles north of *U67's* reported position, detected a suspicious object bearing 100 degrees, 2.5 miles on her port beam. She turned to port to bring it ahead and increased to full speed (16 knots).

2347   The object, seen to be making a wash, was identified as a U-boat on the surface moving fast to the left on a course approximating north west. When range had reduced to 1.5 miles course was altered 40 degrees to port to intercept.

2348   *Bluebell's* asdic detected torpedoes passing to starboard.

2349   U-boat had altered course away, to about north east and

	range started opening slowly.
2353	*Bluebell* fired starshell which did not function and gun action ceased. At this time *U67* fired torpedoes from both stern tubes, V and VI, at a "*Wishart* class destroyer". A "corvete" then came in sight and *U67* considered firing bow tubes at her.
2354	*Bluebell's* asdic detected more torpedoes running. Course was altered to evade then resumed for pursuit. Asdic contact was made on the U-boat and course altered to port at the commencement of the first asdic-directed attack. The U-boat could no longer be seen from the bridge and must have dived.
2356	*U67* dived.
2357	*Bluebell* dropped the first pattern of charges set to 100 feet. Of five ordered, four were dropped and seen to be on line with the phosphorescent wake of the U-boat and ahead of it. *U67* recorded hearing four depth charges but no damage.

Friday 12 December 1941.

0004	*Bluebell* dropped second pattern. Of ten ordered, possibly seven or eight detonated. *U67* recorded hearing three detonations. Several could have exploded simultaneously. *Bluebell* regained asdic contact but this faded at 700 yards range. (Bluebell's official report refers to a five charge pattern. I did order a ten charge pattern and know of only two misfires. This was confirmed by Wilf Stiff who was stationed aft and released extra charges from the rails for good measure.)
0018	As a result of the shock from her own charges, *Bluebell's* asdic developed a fault in the automatic transmission which was continued by hand.
0030	No further contact being gained, *Bluebell* reported by radio and was ordered by *Black Swan* to rejoin the convoy screen.
0050	*U67*, hearing no activity, surfaced to find nothing in sight.

Subsequent to this action, *U434* was ordered to patrol north east of Madeira where, on 18 December, she was detected and sunk by destroyers *Stanley* and *Blankney*, along with *U131*. *U67* was ordered to form part of a five boat patrol line south from Cape St Vincent. Of these, *U127* was sunk on 15 December and *U574* on 19th. *U67* survived until 16 July 1943 and *U43* until 30th of that month, but Lüth had left her by then.

Considering further the identity of *Bluebell's* target, Admiralty's contention that it was *U67* is understandable because she was in the area, saw *Bluebell's* gunfire and heard her depth charges. These 400 pound weapons seldom made a direct hit and unless they exploded within seven yards, were not likely to cause a sinking. Damage experienced by *U67* was less than that by *Bluebell* herself, who was retreating at ten knots and would be at least 100 yards away. *U67* must have been even more distant from each of the two patterns and yet the first of these was seen to fall on line and close ahead of a U-boat, as aimed. Therefore *U67* could not have been the target but was close enough to suffer slight damage.

The time of detonation of the first pattern was logged as 2357 by *Bluebell* and *U67* so other recorded times should be comparable. Bluebell logged torpedoes running at 2346 and again at 2354. The time of *U67's* salvo was 2353 and would be those logged by *Bluebell* one minute later. Who fired those heard at 2346? It must have been another U-boat.

Between 2149 and 2356, *U67* had been busy manoeuvring first to evade a destroyer and then to attack one. From information available these vessels have not been identified. After firing torpedoes at a destroyer and just prior to diving, *U67* sighted a "corvette", no doubt Bluebell as all others were with OG77 five miles to the north west and no other escort reported any sighting or action. *U67's* courses would have been many and varied and while they are not recorded in her war diary, her positions given at 2149 and 2314 are only 13 miles apart, despite her 18 knots and 25 miles covered during this period. She dived two minutes after the target U-boat.

The above indicates the presence of another U-boat and this could only have been *U208*, as stated by German publications. As she was lost on that patrol, her war diary is a reconstruction from such information as was available to BdU, comprising:

3 December   sailed from Brest with orders to make for an area 200 miles south-west of Cape St Vincent.

4 December   routine signal received that she was in the Bay of Biscay. (This was the last that was heard from her.)

6 December   BdU ordered *U208* to make best speed for her destination.

                (On 7 December destroyers *Hesperus* and *Harvester* saw and made three inconclusive attacks on a U-boat 100 miles south south east of Cape St Vincent. This was probably *U208*)]

12 December   BdU ordered *U208* to signal her position but received no reply and later assumed that she was lost as of this date.

While Admiralty considers that *U208* was lost in the action of 7 December, this is not proven and the following is submitted as an explanation of all known facts: *U208* suffered some damage in the 7 December action, including immobilisation of her radio transmitter; she continued to patrol west of the Straits of Gibraltar in the face of heavy British patrols and her own defects until she decided, as U-boats had done before, to return to base for repairs. As she neared Cape St Vincent she could have been seen and mistaken for a motor boat by *U67* and later was detected, correctly identified and successfully attacked by *Bluebell*, in the course of which *U208* made her own, unsuccessful, torpedo attack on *Bluebell*.

Other points of interest emerge from the analysis of available data. The "destroyer" at which *U43* fired three torpedoes on 11 December could only have been *Bluebell*. Positions and times coincide. In fading daylight a 1000 ton single funnelled corvette could well be taken for a 1100 ton two funnelled destroyer (Lüth was second only to Kretschmer in sinkings). Thus in the one day, *Bluebell* survived some seven torpedoes fired from three U-boats.

It is surprising that *U434*, who was in visual contact with OG77 for several hours, eventually lost contact by standing too far east. However we do not have her log and do not know to what extent she was obstructed by aircraft, as *U43* had been.

In summary, the combination of escort vigilance, air cover, radio direction finding, intelligence used to good effect by CinCWA leading to successful convoy re-routing, and *Bluebell's* action, prevented any attack from the four present U-boats and resulted in all ships of OG77 reaching harbour safely. Within the one week and the area west of Gibraltar, *U127, 134, 208, 434* and *574* were sunk. Had *Bluebell* been allowed to continue to search following her two atacks, she would probably have detected *U67* on RDF when she surfaced at 0050 hours on 12 December and have increased this score to six.

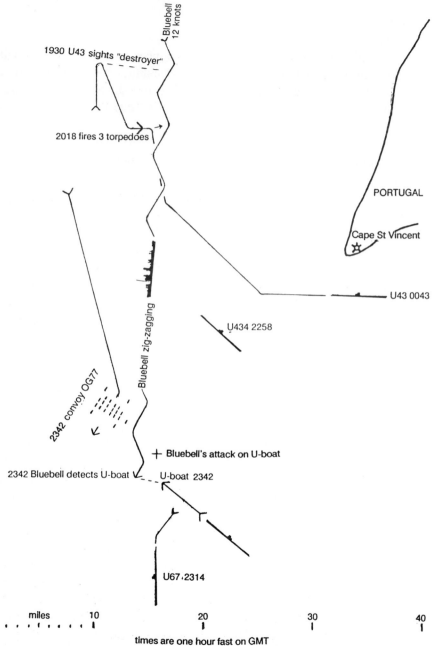

Bluebell 12 knots

1930 U43 sights "destroyer"

2018 fires 3 torpedoes

PORTUGAL

Cape St Vincent

U43 0043

U434 2258

Bluebell zig-zagging

2342 convoy OG77

+ Bluebell's attack on U-boat

2342 Bluebell detects U-boat   U-boat 2342

U67 .2314

0   miles   10   20   30   40

times are one hour fast on GMT

CONVOY OG 77 11 DECEMBER 1941

CHAPTER TWELVE

HG 77

It was Saturday, 13th December, when OG77 arrived in Gibraltar. One warship who had heard of our recent encounter had a broom lashed to her masthead, an historic symbol of sweeping the seas clear of enemy ships. That was comforting to see, though other news had not been so comforting. On 7th December, 1941, the Japanese had attacked the USA Fleet in Pearl Harbour, and three days later had sunk *HMS Prince of Wales* and *HMS Repulse*. Then, on 21st, *HMS Audacity*, who had joined OG77 for the last few days, and had become a symbol of success in the fight against the U-boat, was sunk.

We had a fortnight in harbour, so Wilf and I decided to apply for papers which would enable us to walk across the border to La Linea, the nearest Spanish town. We acquired a Spanish Identification Card, but had to wait till the next visit for a visa.

On one occasion, returning after a walk ashore, I was interested to see that there was a submarine in the dry dock at the south end of the harbour. Frequently submarines berthed near us at Gib, but this was the first time one had been exposed to full view as she sat high and dry on the blocks. I walked slowly around her, taking in details of her underwater features, propellers, hydroplanes, the horizontal rudders fore and aft, used for controlling depth, her torpedo tube caps and absence of upper deck obstructions except for conning tower and guns. While I was studying this interesting vessel, a petty officer on the casing, or deck, was watching me. As I reached her starboard side amidships, having completed a slow circle of observation, the PO walked down the gangplank, saying

"You seem to be interested. Would you like to see on board?"

"Yes," I said, "I've never been aboard a submarine," whereupon he led the way to the torpedo loading hatch set below the foredeck. Climbing down the steel ladder through the inclined circular hatchway, I found myself in the close quarters in which men and machinery compete for space. We traversed the boat from the torpedo tube compartment right forward, back past the sailors' and petty officers' messes, or living spaces, wardroom, control room where the periscopes appeared as massive silver steel columns descending from the deckhead above, into the circular wells below and aft, to the diesel engines and electric motors, passing small cubicles for radio and other equipment, all packed tightly against the circular hull.

It was really too much to comprehend at one viewing, despite the petty officer's expert commentary. This was a world like no other I had ever seen.

"Submarines," I thought, "must be an acquired taste. This PO seems enthusiastic, but I am overwhelmed and not a little scared by my experience." He escorted me to the gangplank and asked

"Are you interested in joining submarines, Sir?"

"No, not me!" I hastily retorted, "But I appreciate the time you have taken to show me over, and am most impressed. Goodbye." and hurried down to the dockside again, thankful that I was serving in *Bluebell* who, I now knew, had won me over. Later, much later, I came to realise two things; one, that my snappy retort to the petty officer was stupid and lacking in consideration for the feelings of a competent and loyal submarine crew member and, secondly, that if I thought submarines repulsive it was because I did not know the first thing about them or the men who serve in them.

On Christmas Eve, *Bluebell* received a signal to proceed at 0500 on 25th to carry out an asdic sweep at the western entry to the Strait, for twenty four hours. This was a frequent requirement in order to prevent U-boats from entering the Mediterranean. Important though the task was, we felt that it was rather unkind to send us to sea on Christmas Day. Notwithstanding this disappointment, the day was enjoyable. The weather was moderate and fine, no U-boats crossed our path and we had cakes for tea.

Now, this was a treat usually reserved for Sundays and looked forward to all week, even though there was a chemical taste to the cakes. This was traced, later in the New Year, to the main flour store, where chloride of lime, carried for the treatment of drinking water, was stored in a container leaning against the flour sacks. I suppose the strong chlorine smell meant little to the sailors who carried stores aboard, and at least our cakes would be free from bacterial contamination.

The sweep was over a rectangular course, the turning points all being within sight of land - Spain to the north and North Africa to the south. This was a good opportunity for us junior watchkeepers to practise coastal navigation in a real ship as compared with the classroom. Anticipating the time of arrival at each turning point was interesting, and any irregularities could be put down to technique intended to confuse the enemy. At the end of our stint, we handed over to our relieving corvette with good wishes for a happy Boxing Day, and returned to harbour, the better for having spent a sober day at sea.

HG77 was due to sail on Wednesday 31st December, so we would have a sober New Year's eve as well. Our now familiar escort prepared for the next bout with the U-boats; *Black Swan, Fowey, Bluebell, Campion, Carnation, Heliotrope, La Malouine, Myosotis, Stonecrop* and local destroyers *Bradford, Vidette* and *Wishart*. The last reminds me of Lord Louis Mountbatten, her one-time Commanding Officer, who made his introductory address to her ship's company with an adaptation of the Lord's Prayer, "Our Father, Wishart in Heaven...."

By virtue of my special training, supervision of the asdic, and its operators, was my prime duty. It became clear that the *Rushcutter* course was held in high regard by the RN people who had experience with its graduates. I had no difficulty in working in with *Bluebell's* asdic personnel, and our set was always functional. Other ships in the group would call for assistance if they had difficulties.

Early on 31st December, a corvette commanding officer asked Lt Cdr Sherwood if they could borrow me because the group was about to pick up convoy HG77 and head for home, and his asdic was out of action. I scurried along the wharf and down into the asdic compartment at the bottom of the ship, forward of centre. As sailing time approached, the ship's leading operator and I were still correcting faults. I asked the Captain to ask *Bluebell* if I could stay to finish the job and transfer at sea. This was approved, and work continued. By the time it was finished, and operating correctly, the convoy was well out to sea, and escorts on station.

I went onto the bridge and asked the officer of the watch to arrange my transfer. *Bluebell*, a speck on the horizon, was called up on the ten inch signal projector, the long range morse signalling lamp, and requested to close, in order to take an officer aboard. When the two ships were steaming side by side, the quartermaster piped "Away seaboat's crew". I climbed in as it hung on the davits, after the crew.

"Let go the gripes." These are the straps which pass from each davit head, diagonally around the boat, to stop it from swinging. "Turns for lowering." "Lower away." This is the exciting moment as the falls are eased, and the boat descends toward the heaving sea, both ends together hopefully. "Out pins." (From the Robinsons slipping gear, one forward and one aft.) As the boat lowered, the towing line, always rigged from the boat's bow forward to the forecastle, took up its slack and held the boat from swinging fore and aft. Two of the seamen crew held the boat off the ship's side with the looms of their oars. Three feet above the sea, "Vast lowering. Stand by to slip." "All ready in the boat?" The Coxswain aft called out, "Ready in the boat." "Slip." One of the boat's crew operated the slip lever as the well timed wave rose toward the boat, which fell with a splash and sheered away from the ship. The coxswain ordered "Let go forward. Oars." The forward hand let the towing rope go and returned to his thwart, placed his oar in position, horizontal, as the other three had already done. "Ready, give way together." And four oars propelled the boat forward.

As we moved across the heaving seas toward *Bluebell*, gently rolling as she glided slowly forward, I looked back and waved to the captain and officer of the watch who were still standing in the wing of the bridge. They waved their thanks. We came alongside *Bluebell* on her port quarter where the scramble net hung. I made a spring onto the net and clung like a spider for a moment, then climbed inboard, thanked the boat's crew and *Bluebell's* net handlers, and made my way to the bridge to report to the captain. A lamp signal was being received, not too fast for me to read

"Thanks for loan of your ping king. Where could we get one?" A moment's wait while our captain gave the text of a reply to our signalman. Nearing the bridge, I heard the signal lamp rattle out,

"You are welcome. They come up from Down Under."

U-boats were still about, and Admiralty's system of location was becoming more and more efficient. Ours was a small convoy of thirteen merchant ships with a large escort of twelve, initially, at least. Admiralty signalled course alterations to avoid U-boats on 3rd January and again on the following two days. From time to time, one of the escorts would report something suspicious, which was inevitable when so many ships were searching for something which they knew to exist. Whenever such a report was received, *Bluebell* went to action stations until the investigation was completed, often without confirming an enemy presence.

One night, after the ship's company had been at action stations for an hour without action, the Captain ordered "Fall out action stations." Signalman Scott called the quartermaster, repeating the order. He then went to the asdic voicepipe, which connected to the fore bridge as well as to the RDF hut on the after part of the bridge. "Hello," he called to the RDF Operator. The Captain heard a voice from the fore bridge voicepipe and answered "Yes." Said Signalman Scott, "Put away your brass rags, pack up your knitting, and shove off!" The Captain was so taken aback that he only had time to gulp before the RDF operator acknowledged the message, and the situation was saved. It may seem to you, in this age of ever developing communications, that a length of pipe to talk through would make only a good child's toy, but believe me, it had several advantages. Being simple it never failed, and as long as you found the correct one, even in the dark you could never get a wrong connection; well, hardly ever. To keep sea spray out of them they were fitted with a copper flap. Lifting and shutting this a few times sounded along the pipe and attracted the attention of the distant party.

There was, as you learned from Scott's experience, a possibility of confusion in the case of a three-way voicepipe, but there was only one other of these, that running down from the fore bridge to the captain's cabin, and on to the wardroom. The captain's branch was next to his bunk and was fitted with a flexible hose so that he could put it to his ear or mouth while lying down, instead of having to put his face to the pipe-end on the bulkhead. This was a refinement to which he was well entitled. However, one calm afternoon when we were off the southern Spanish coast, the officer of the watch became bored and decided to stir up his fellow Officers who, at the time, were having tea in the wardroom. They heard the familiar "Flap... flap". One of them went to the mouthpiece and was about to answer when he heard another voice doing the same. He waited, not wishing to interrupt the Captain who was the only other person on the connection, but all he heard was the sound of water trickling down, followed by a gasp - from you know who - awakening from a dog watch zizz rather more suddenly than usual. His flexible hose would have been at his ear as the flood arrived.

Admiralty's evasive routing proved effective, and no U-boat attacks occurred. But I did experience my only air attack. We had made our landfall on the south coast of Ireland, and were to approach Liverpool via St George's Channel, south of Ireland instead of north-about as previously. In this channel there was always a possibility of the convoy being sighted from the Irish coast by an enemy agent, and reported to Germany. This undoubtedly is what happened, because later in the day, from the east, came six German bombers, flying about two thousand feet up. All escorts opened fire, though my gun had insufficient range. All bombs were dropped from the same height and were clearly visible as they were falling, raising tall spouts of water which subsided to reveal every ship proceeding as before. That was another lucky convoy in that no ships were lost.

However, we were not yet home, and one minor incident

marred the homecoming.   The senior officer had made a signal to
his fleet by radio telegraphy in morse, and our telegraphist had
missed it.   This was discovered by our lack of response, and a mild
rebuke was administered; not a matter of great importance, we
thought, when the message was repeated to us.   As the convoy
steamed up the Irish Sea, the senior officer told off the individual
ships who were to escort certain merchantmen to the more distant
ports, like the Clyde, while the remainder made an early entry to
the Mersey, and leave.   *Bluebell* was detailed for the Oban section;
the SO added, for missing his earlier signal.   This meant an
additional day's sea-time, escorting the northbound ships up to
Scotland,   then   returning   to   Liverpool   ourselves.   The
disappointment around the ship at the extension of our sea-time by
one day was deep and lasting, with the duty telegraphist the least
popular man aboard, but once we had actually gone on leave, all
was forgotten.

CHAPTER THIRTEEN

WINTER

For the third time, I spent a week in Mrs Woodall's house in Burwash. I visited the former home of Rudyard Kipling, took long walks to enjoy the beauty of the countryside, had long chats with Dave and the many people whom I had come to know and, best of all, enjoyed my hostess's anecdotes of local folk and happenings. Everybody spoke with a pleasant accent, in contrast with mine. Their "r"s were round, as if they were all to commence the word "round". For example, she told me of a Burwash man who was standing at the altar with his bride, and had come to that part in the service where he was asked if he took this woman to be his lawful wedded wife, to which he replied "I come 'ere a'purrpose."

It was on my second last day of leave that the sky became grey and the temperature fell. Eventually, snowflakes started to fall, for the first time in my experience, and by evening the snow was starting to lie in places. My bedroom was upstairs, facing the street. In fact, the front wall of the house was on the edge of the footpath. When I awoke next morning, all was silent. Not a sound from the street, of vehicles or feet. The roads and roofs were thick with snow. I could not wait to get out in it and make a snowball. The village looked beautiful and the countryside more so. The children and I were probably the only ones enjoying it. For the adults it meant difficulty getting about, and mess around and within the front door.

There was no difficulty getting to the station for my return journey to London, and what a pretty journey it was, till we arrived in the city. There, I saw the other side of the picture; slush in every street and sidewalk, wet shoes, and cold feet. On arrival in

Liverpool late at night, I found the streets lined with hard frozen ridges of dirty snow where it had been scraped away by graders. Walking back to Clarence Dock was difficult and hazardous, carrying a case and trying to keep balance with the other arm.

Before arriving at the dock, I had already seen enough snow and felt tired and out of sorts. To top it off, I arrived aboard to find the ship dark and cold. Boiler cleaning was not yet finished, and the auxiliary generator was shut down for the night. I turned in with my romantic ideas of snow shattered. This was my first winter in these high latitudes; there were a few more to come.

Our next convoy was OG79, which left Liverpool on Monday 26th January 1942 with the same escort. We learned that the alternative convoy, HG78 had arrived, having been attacked by three U-boats, two of which were sunk. Our convoy had an uneventful run and while the threat must be regarded as undiminished, results showed that several factors were in our favour. Escort groups were larger and more experienced. RDF was proving its worth, so long as it could be kept operative. Now that the USA was at war with Germany, U-boats found easier targets on the western side of the Atlantic. Our air cover was always increasing and improving, with airborne RDF and spotlights. In order to cover greater distances from base to hunting areas, U-boats were forced to spend more time on the surface and engaged in gun battles with aircraft, with losses to both sides.

We arrived in Gibraltar with our twenty-five ships on 7th February, two inconclusive asdic attacks having been carried out; one by *Mallow* on the 1st, and the other by *Bluebell* on the 2nd. It was good to enjoy the Mediterranean climate again.

Wilf and I obtained visas and walked across the border to La Linea. This small Spanish town boasted a bullring. No fight was programmed during our stay, and would not attract me anyway. What humans do to one another is bad enough. What they do to animals is cruel. I was going to say 'beastly', but beasts would not do it. The town had an unprosperous appearance. In a bookshop window was a book on Prien's sinking of *HMS Royal Oak* at Scapa. Spain seemed to be a neutral country with sympathies toward our enemy, but that was merely an impression without much observation, and of a small town.

Gibraltar harbour was covered with fuel oil from ships which had survived a torpedo hit and were being repaired. During an "Away sea boat" exercise, I took my boat alongside a ship with bow damage and was able to float into the ship as far as her forward watertight bulkhead. We arranged a regatta with the other corvettes. They all had identical boats which made rowing races interesting. We also challenged them to a Carley raft paddle race. No 1, Wilf, Bill Adamson and I were *Bluebell's* crew. I do not recall the result except that we were all spotted with fuel oil by the finish. It was a useful experience, becoming familiar with our means of survival should *Bluebell* be sunk. Rafts were more likely to be launched safely than boats, because they simply slid down a frame into the sea, and would float either way up, even if punctured.

HG79 with the 37th Escort group left on Sunday 22nd February, there being twenty-seven ships, all of which arrived in Britain without serious incident. But it was late winter, and as our latitude increased the weather became reminiscent of the "mad March days" of Masefield, when his dirty British coasters with their salt caked smoke stacks were butting up the channel with manufactured cargoes. We were still in the Atlantic when a south west gale developed, pushing the ships along from behind. While heavy weather made it uncomfortable for all of us, ships and escorts alike, it must have been equally difficult for the enemy.

When on watch I marvelled at *Bluebell's* seaworthiness as developing swells, growing larger day by day, swept up on us from astern, threatening to engulf her. But she would gracefully rise and let the mountains of water roll under her from aft to forward, except for the occasional breaking crest which crashed down on the after deck and flowed forward, disappearing out of the scuppers. Photographs do not convey the scale of these sea mountains. You have to be there, see it for yourself, and feel your heart in your mouth.

HG79 arrived home on Friday 6th March. On our arrival in Liverpool after escorting the Clyde and Oban sections, in the ship's mail was a letter from Harvey, who was undergoing a course of training in Moreton-in-Marsh, inviting me to visit him there. I sent a telegram saying that I would arrive Monday 9th.

Harvey met me at the railway and, as we drove to his air station, pointed out the local churchyard where there were always fresh flowers marking the last landing place of those who were killed in training. Harvey said that the risks in training were equal to half of one tour of Ops over Germany. At the air station, I was recorded in as if on training myself, as S/L Shean.

"This," said Harvey, "makes you a squadron leader for the period of your stay." That was to be two days. On the second day I joined the trainee crew in an Avro Anson for a navigation exercise to York and back. This was the highlight, but all of the time in the RAAF was most enjoyable; a complete change, as, for the two days, I wore the uniform of an RAAF Sergeant.

I was obliged to report, regularly in writing, on the performance of the RDF as we were one of the first ships to be fitted. It gave me some satisfaction to report at this time, that our set had been in regular service except for occasional short periods, when ship's staff had always succeeded in rectifying defects. Another boost to my confidence came on 16th March 1942, when R E Sherwood, Lt Cdr RNR, signed my certificate of proficiency as watchkeeper for corvettes.

Next day, the 37th Escort Group sailed with 22 ships in OG81, a passage of 13 days without interference from the enemy. The only observation I can make is that on the 27th our former escort member *HMS Campbeltown* was deliberately steamed into the caisson of the large St Nazaire dry dock and then blown up, thus denying Germany the use of the dock to service their battleship *Tirpitz*.

Just one week in Gibraltar and we were escorting HG81, comprising 14 ships, back to Britain. The only incident was on 13th April when the convoy was reported by enemy aircraft, and all arrived in good order on Wednesday 15th. Although I did not know it at the time, this was the last of my Gibraltar convoys, and during my ten months aboard, we had endured some of the worst and finished in the best of the Battle of the Eastern Atlantic. *Bluebell* could be proud of the part she had played, along with her sister ships, not forgetting *Zinnia* and *Fleur de Lys*, corvette victims in the struggle.

Study of ship loss figures reminds me of an acknowledgment to be made. While sinkings by U-boat torpedo were heavy, those from mines were greater. Yet we had sailed in the company of escorts and merchantmen through channels and coastal waters which had frequently been mined, without a single loss from a mine, proof of the efficient work of minesweepers. If I have emphasised the hard work and little glamour of corvettes, surely minesweepers have done more with less. Some corvettes, I should add, were fitted for minesweeping.

There was an important factor in our success in convoying without loss so far in 1942, which added to those of increased efficiency and better equipment. Now that America was at war with Germany, allied ships plying the eastern seaboard of the USA soon became attractive targets for U-boats. It seemed to us that the American Navy were slow to learn from the British experience. There was free interchange of information, and this covered U-boat movements, on which Admiralty intelligence was of a high order, as I have already made clear. In spite of all this, America was slow to institute essential anti-submarine measures like ship and coastal blackout, strengthening of escorts, and air cover. As a result, U-boats moved across the Atlantic and went for the inadequately defended ships on the other side, relieving our convoys of some of the pressure of attack.

CHAPTER FOURTEEN

SECOND REFIT

Bluebell was again sent to South Shields for refit. This time, a considerable number of alterations and additions were planned.

The forecastle, the raised deck forward, was to be extended further aft to midships to provide more accommodation and space on deck for more weapons. The Lewis guns, which were never used effectively, were moved aft, 20mm Oerlikon anti-aircraft guns fitted each side of the bridge, one two pounder abaft the funnel, and a new anti-submarine weapon installed just abaft and to starboard of the four inch gun.

One of the difficulties in making an accurate attack with depth charges was that they had to be dropped from the stern of the ship, but ahead of the submarine, so that by the time they had reached detonation depth, the sub would have arrived at the same location. As they were dropped and thrown from the ship, she had to cross the submarine's path well ahead of it and lose asdic contact while doing so. This new weapon fired forward a circular pattern of 30 pound spigot mortar charges which exploded on contact. It was called "Hedgehog". The charges were carried in four groups of six, mounted on four beams, which rotated to maintain a steady forward direction as the ship rolled. All this was gyro controlled so we also gained a Sperry gyroscopic compass to supersede the magnetic compass, which was still carried for emergency. The 'brain' of this control system was delivered into my charge as I was duty officer at the time. I kept the cartage note as a souvenir. It was manufactured by the British United Shoe Machinery Company.

Modifications to the bridge included removal of the asdic hut to shore, where it served as ship's office for the refit period. A new asdic compartment was prefabricated and fixed low down at the forward end of the bridge, leaving clear visibility all round for the OOW standing near the centre. No more all-purpose watchkeeping for Able Seaman McDonald. To complete the tidying process, the mast was relocated abaft the bridge, advance in radio technology allowing use of shorter antennae.

At the start of this period, we received a signal from the Naval Officer Commanding Tyne Area to send all confidential books to his office for safe keeping and correction. This I gladly did because I was busy learning about our new weapons, keeping an eye on the progress of the work, and also wanted my share of leave.

As this was to be a longer refit than the first, both halves of the crew were to get leave. I was in the first batch. I had written to Australia House billeting service asking if it were possible for me to go somewhere in Scotland for my week commencing 11th June. I had a vague idea that our family had some Scottish connection way back, and I knew it to be a beautiful country. The reply came promptly, that I would be the guest of the British Legion in Aberfeldy, Perthshire. That sounded just the ticket, and so it was.

Acquiring my train ticket, I was told to change at Edinburgh, and at Ballinluig for Aberfeldy. I wondered how I would remember, let alone recognise, a place with a name like, what was it? Ballinluig, I was told again. Newcastle to Edinburgh was a fast run with many interesting sights like the approach to Berwick-on-Tweed and crossing the border soon after. At Edinburgh I took the train for Perth and Inverness. I was most impressed with the British rail system, being so much more comprehensive than our Western Australian Government Railways. One of the compartments I rode in was beautifully fitted out in a honey coloured timber, the name of which was engraved on a small plate above the door; "Queensland Maple".

It was interesting just to enter the other Perth, even for a few minutes. My recollection is of a tall brick chimney with PULLARS in large letters down its length, and a large DEWARS sign. Other travellers kindly undertook to let me know when we would approach Ballinluig, and assured me of an enjoyable stay in Aberfeldy. Everywhere in Britain, dominion servicemen were received with kindness, especially, it seemed to me already, in

Scotland. Perhaps I wanted it that way. At Ballinluig the small branch line locomotive with its one passenger coach and guard's van was waiting as the superior main-line locomotive came to a halt, waited briefly for a few passengers to alight, then, with a show of power, drew out its long train of coaches, bound for the pass of Killiecrankie and the north.

It took some time for the Ballinluig station master and my branch line engine driver to exchange vital information and gossip, but eventually we chuffed off, uphill alongside the swift flowing River Tay. I was still reflecting on having passed through Birnam, and on "Macbeth" which we had studied at school. It was a fascination for one who had grown up in the antipodes, to come face to face with previously familiar, if distant, names. After three stops, we came to the end of the line, Aberfeldy, where my host, Mr Bill Bennett, was waiting for me. He welcomed me and drove to "Inchadney", a neat two storey house facing the river, where I met Jess Anne, my hostess.

Bill was the newsagent and stationer. Next day, I walked the length of Aberfeldy and, coming upon "McLaren's" - the newsagency - entered to pay my respects to my hosts. There was a pretty girl, with typical highland complexion, behind the counter. Jess Anne introduced us.

"Max, this is Mary Golding. She has a boyfriend in the Navy. Mary, get John Sherrif's photo to show Max. Max has a girlfriend in Australia." So there we were, firmly in our places.

During the week, I had many trips around the lovely, grand countryside, one with the doctor, one the butcher, and another with the grocer. No doubt every local inhabitant already knew about this Australian in the Navy, from the other Perth. I loved this Scotland, if this were a true sample. Walking the narrow, tree lined roads between the mountains, provided the return to serenity which we all needed.

On the town noticeboard was a poster announcing the imminent arrival of a concert party, sponsored by the Council for the Encouragement of Music and the Arts, to perform in the Town Hall. It seemed that this was a very respectable occasion to which one could, with propriety, invite even a new acquaintance, so I revisited McLarens and asked Mary Golding if she would like to come with me to this concert. Politely, but firmly, she said

"No thank you." So I took her photo instead, later that day, as she was walking back to the shop with her friend Betty, and at the end of a wonderful week, returned to *Bluebell* and, not the warring seas, but the dockyard, which was much noisier.

The ship was in a real mess, this being a comprehensive refit. But, wonder of wonders, it was finished on time and a very different looking corvette put out into the Tyne to swing compasses. This was a matter of slowly swinging the ship several times to face every point of the compass, while the compass adjuster placed small magnets to compensate for the steel in the ship so that the magnetic compasses would point the right way. How he got his reference bearings with the ship being carried along sideways in the ebbing current, I don't know. Although we now had the superior gyroscopic compass, which did not depend upon the earth's magnetism, the old compasses were maintained for emergency use.

The first thing for my attention on return from leave was a signal from the WRNS officer in charge of confidential books at the Tyne Base, demanding an explanation as to why I had not been to her office to correct *Bluebell's* books. I called to see her and to explain that I had assumed that would have been done by her staff, as part of the service to us sea-weary mariners. Well, it wasn't, as she made clear. Not having much success with my ladies, was I? Perhaps I should have persevered, but that might have led to a fight, and my understanding was that the way to fight a lady was with your hat. You grabbed it, and ran. The books were delivered back to *Bluebell* for me to correct at sea, and we left the River Tyne for another work-up at Tobermory.

The Minches, the waterway between the Scottish coast and the Hebridean Islands, are spectacular. We had a wonderful opportunity to see the many fascinating islands like Skye, Rhum, Muck and Eigg.

By this time, Lt Cdr Sherwood had been appointed in command of a frigate, *HMS Tay* and Lt Walker became our commanding officer. A Lt Sinclair, RNR, took his place as First Lt, and S/Lt Dick Thurman, RANVR from Perth, joined as additional officer. One of the exercises was to put a landing party ashore on the Island of Staffa, better known as the site of Fingal's Cave. It was my good fortune to be put in charge of this landing. It was a calm day, and there was no difficulty in pulling our sixteen foot skiff right into the famous cave, and securing it with long ropes across the entrance to prevent the sea surge from washing it against the hard sharp basalt columns of which the island is composed. Carrying our tin hats and respirators, we scrambled onto and up the rock, each of the seamen also carrying a rifle. We met no opposition. The only inhabitants retreated as we walked up the steep slope to the centre of the island. We showed great care not to frighten them unduly because of the legend that sheep on a certain island had, for years, followed a feeding pattern of facing the sun and walking around the island clockwise each day. As a result, they all grew shorter in the right legs and longer in the left. One day, a careless landing party chased the sheep anti-clockwise around the island. Every sheep swung away to starboard (right) and disappeared into the ocean.

On our return to *Bluebell*, Lt Sinclair directed hoisting of the boat.

"You are a lucky man, Max," he said in his warm Scottish voice, "I would give my right arm to go ashore on that island."

While exercising one day, we came upon one of the old four funnelled ex-USA destroyers which Winston Churchill had acquired in return for the USA's leasing of certain British bases. These Great War ships had been maintained in the interim to some degree, but were far from perfect. This one was stopped. G H Walker made a signal, "Can we be of any assistance?"

"No thanks. This happens once every watch."

On completion of this workup, we were despatched to Londonderry to await assignment to a convoy to Murmansk, in North Russia. This prospect filled nobody with enthusiasm. Convoys routed north of Norway were far from home support by aircraft, and close to German airfields in Norway. For good measure, the German battle fleet was deployed in Norway for the purpose of commerce raiding, and therefore were a constant threat.

It included one of the world's most powerful ships, *Tirpitz*. Another discouragement was that the Russians would provide no support from their end, and took no responsibility for cargoes until unloaded at Murmansk. Hospitality was non-existent. On the other hand, it was in the interest of the Allies to supply equipment to boost the success of actions on the Russian-German front. It was also possible that, as winter approached, we could be iced in and obliged to stay there until spring.

Soon after we berthed alongside at Londonderry, Wilf and I went ashore to order some table waters for wardroom use. Our information was that the agent was in Cowie Street. Having no street directory, we asked a city man if he could direct us. He stroked his chin for a while, and said "No, I can't say that I know of a Cowie Street. Are you sure you don't mean Currie Street?"

"Perhaps we have got it wrong. Where is Currie Street, please?" More chin rubbing, then-

"Can't say I ever heard of it."

We did find Cowie Street eventually, but I had another purchase to make. If we were to be iced in at an inhospitable port for months, I needed a project to keep myself occupied, and had decided to buy a second-hand violin and to learn to play it. That should take a few months. I bought one for three pounds, and a tutor book for a few shillings. I still have the violin, and still can't play it, because there was a change in our sailing instructions. We were to return to the Tyne for further work, the fitting of additional weapons and de-icing equipment, or "arcticising" as it was termed.

CHAPTER FIFTEEN

RETRAINING

At the conclusion of each convoy I was obliged to submit a report to C in C W A on the performance of the Type 271 RDF, as mentioned earlier. By perseverance, and the ability of our team of operators, we had kept our set going since its installation. In May 1942, Able Seaman Minns and I each received a letter of commendation from Admiral Sir Percy Noble for the results we had achieved with this, the first RDF fitted to corvettes. On the strength of this, I made application to be permitted to undergo a course of training, at the Navy RDF Establishment, in June. This was courteously refused on the grounds that I was already an A/S specialist and was valuable serving in that capacity.

Lt Walker was Commanding Officer when we were sent for the third refit to the Tyne. One day I visited the Walker home on the upper reaches of the river and enjoyed the hospitality of a most pleasant and competent family. No doubt they were proud of their son and brother in his recent promotion to command the ship which he had long managed as 1st Lieut in this vital phase of the war at sea.

We received in the ship's mail all Admiralty signals in an "A" series, and all Admiralty Fleet Orders and Confidential AFOs, so there was plenty of reading to do in harbour. I recall one CAFO which referred to a control knob for a certain asdic set. It seems that it had been incorrectly engraved and the information was 'For "TOP" read "BOTTOM" to avoid confusion'.

CAFO 843/42 called for "Volunteers for special and hazardous service, who are: below age 24, unmarried, good swimmers and of strong and enduring physique." Everybody in *Bluebell* ignored this, automatically applying another Navy maxim;

"Keep your mouth shut, your bowels open, and never volunteer."
It must have met with universal disregard throughout the Royal
Navy because, soon after, an "A" series signal was received
drawing commanding officers' attention to it. Lt Walker brought
this signal, and CAFO, to each of us in turn for information.

"I am going to volunteer, Shean," he said.

"Very good Sir, please put me down too."

I asked Bill Adamson if he were going to be in it.

"No," he said, "I don't go looking for trouble."
Considering the long scar on his face, I thought that perhaps he had
good reason for revising his attitude to further adventure.

A week later, came a confidential signal from Admiralty,
requiring Lt Walker and S/Lt Shean to report to the Captain, 5th
Submarine Flotilla in *HMS Dolphin* at earliest convenience for
interview. If successful, they would be required for duty in *Dolphin*
14th September 1942. We journeyed to Portsmouth separately, I on
7th August. All I can recall about the interview was being told that
this "Special Service" was most terribly secret, so much so that I
could not be told what manner of vessel we would serve in except
that it was quite small, and navigated with the use of a periscope.
What did I tell that P O on the submarine at Gibraltar?

The outcome was that Walker was advised, with thanks, that
he would be more valuable serving in his present appointment,
whereas Shean was accepted. I stood by for the completion of the
refit, and on 14th September, packed early and went around the
crew to say goodbye. *Bluebell* was also off that day. Once down
the gangway, I stood and watched her cast off and draw out into the
stream on her way to Murmansk, gliding down river taking my
home with her, until she had vanished into the mist.

I walked sadly to the station, and boarded the London train,
then another to Portsmouth and the Navy boat across to *HMS
Dolphin*. By next morning our intake of twelve volunteers had
assembled and were briefed on what was to come. First there was
the Davis Submarine Escape Apparatus to be explained and tried on
the surface of the heated training tank. That accomplished, next
was an escape from a simulated submarine, to be repeated until we
became accustomed to it. As with any group of mutual strangers

assembled for the first time, a pecking order started to evolve, one or two vocal ones asserting their superiority. The DSEA familiarisation on the surface was fun. It comprised a rubber "lung" worn on the chest. It had a mouthpiece at the top, a steel cylinder of oxygen below, and a canister of "Protosorb" to remove carbon dioxide on exhalation, fixed in the middle. One also wore a nose clip to prevent oxygen escaping, and goggles. It took a little courage, once breathing from this bag of oxygen, to leap into the water and to breathe with head immersed, but it worked and soon everyone was doing it.

The next bit was not such a pushover. Getting into a steel chamber set into the bottom of the tank, with fifteen feet of water above it, was bad enough, but when three trainees and one instructor were inside, and the steel door banged shut and locked, confidence dwindled. Then it was that the noisy peckers went quiet, except for one who screamed "Let me out. Let me out. Let ...." This the instructor did, and that was the last we saw of that volunteer. For the remainder, we held onto our residual composure while water was admitted and the level rose.

One technique involved a twill, or canvas type trunk, which was unrolled down from the deckhead, or top of the chamber, around an escape hatch. As water rose, the internal pressure increased until it was equal to that of the water outside. When the instructor opened the hatch, the twill trunk kept most of the air from escaping, and one at a time, we breathed from the set, ducked down into the trunk, and floated up to the surface, holding out an apron of rubber sheet to control the rate of ascent. Rather frightening first time, but in warm water it became quite easy with practice. I suppose I had an advantage over some because of my earlier study of hydraulics from the lecturer who was partly responsible for my being in this predicament.

By the end of the week, three of the party had withdrawn. The remainder, feeling now something of an elite, were assembled before Lt Hezlet for further briefing, and this was to be the shock of my life. The purpose of our recruitment was to take part in a most important, and therefore top secret, mission. The vessel was a midget submarine designed to penetrate enemy harbour defences undetected. It had a "wet and dry" compartment similar to the one which we had mastered (?) during the past week. This was to enable a diver, namely one of us, to get out while submerged in an enemy harbour, to cut through anti-submarine nets, and to get back in again without upsetting the control of the submarine. The armament was a pair of explosive charges of two tons each, strapped to the sides of the boat, and the target was battleship *Tirpitz*.

Gasp!

Tirpitz was expected to be heavily defended, in a remote Norwegian Fjord. The crew of the submarine was three, a commanding officer, a first lieutenant, and an engine room artificer. All were required to be proficient as divers. We were now to proceed to a new base on the Island of Bute in the Firth of Clyde. The base was the former Kyles of Bute Hydropathic Hotel. Captain W E Banks, RN was to become Captain of this Twelfth Submarine Flotilla, and initially Commander D C Ingram, RN, was C O of *HMS Varbel*, as the shore establishment was called.

So! I was in the Submarine Service without even trying. Would I be able to cope? My knees were trembling. It took a long time to get used to the new situation. This sounded like a one-way excursion. All these thoughts made no difference of course. Having set my hand to the plough, I suppose the horse knew what was to be done, the horse being my other self, not the one doing the rationalising, the talking and doubting but that inner force that pushed forward seemingly regardless.

Walking through the dockyard on the way to Portsmouth Harbour Station, prominent on my right were the masts of Nelson's Flagship *HMS Victory*. I walked over to her, for reassurance perhaps. She was in her permanent dry dock. A bomb, not so long before, had hit the dockside and then the concrete plinth on which her keel rested. Climbing down under the ship's bottom I could see the splintered timber where the bomb had blown a hole through her planking. I took hold of a piece of oak, which had projected from the keel, and pulled. It came away in my hand so I slid it into the inside pocket of my uniform jacket. It is now mounted above my desk, heart of oak that had fought at Trafalgar, but at the time it shored up my knees so that they did not knock quite so much, and took my mind off the alarming prospect of my shaky future with the Royal Navy.

I rejoined my group at Euston Station and we took over a compartment in the night train for Glasgow. As usual, there were many service men and women. The adjacent compartment contained several WRNS who, we soon discovered, were also on draft for *HMS Varbel* in Bute. We all crowded into one compartment and happiness prevailed. One clear memory I have is of Bill Whittam, who was very tall, reclining at full length across the laps of six or seven Wrens. It was one way of accommodating so tall an officer in so crowded a space.

On arrival at Glasgow, we then took the train to Wemyss and the ferry to Rothesay Bay in the Island of Bute. There waited a truck, driven by yet another Wren, to take us the two miles to the hotel at Port Bannatyne. It was quite a grand building, stripped of carpets and most other comforts, but bustling with Wrens. Here we met members of the other intakes and found English, Irish, Welsh, Scots, Canadians, South Africans, New Zealanders and Australians, lieutenants, sub-lieutenants and midshipmen. Among the ratings there were fewer countries represented, but a good deal of experience, especially with the engine room artificers (ERA's). There were seamen, torpedomen and stokers, all to be trained in the operation and maintenance of the midget submarine. Some had submarine experience, but most were like me, about to taste something different.

Lectures started forthwith. The officers' mentor was Lt Hezlet, RN, a submarine commanding officer. We were to learn that S/M CO's had undergone a rigorous training and elimination course, and that those who graduated from their "Perisher", as the course was, and still is, known, were extraordinarily efficient. Our lectures were given in the north west corner of the dining room, a large room, as a hotel would need, with a view to the north over Port Bannatyne and into Loch Striven.

The need for top secrecy was well drummed into us. To have any chance of success, an attack on *Tirpitz* must be a surprise. We were not to tell anyone, however trustworthy, what they did not have to know. Two prototypes, *X3* and *X4* were already operating, in waters nearby. As one lecture was proceeding, Lt Hezlet stopped talking, motioning us to wait. WRNS stewards were arranging tables in the main area of the room. When at length they disappeared into the kitchen, he said in a low voice, "Look through the window now. You will see *X3* proceeding on the surface." We crowded to the window but he called us back. "You newts," he said, "Everyone will see you looking. Stay where you are and look carefully." We did our best to look without appearing to do so and, as a result, I saw nothing but water. But it did not matter, we were to see plenty of *X3* and *X4* in the future, and so were the people of Port Bannatyne, never mind the Wrens of *Varbel*. At lectures we learned the operating principles of submarines and details of X-craft design. I will explain the main features and include a section drawing at the end of this chapter.

First, there was the pressure hull, cylindrical with tapering sections at the ends. This was of quarter inch thick steel with strengthening frames welded at intervals inside. Now, if this were the correct weight, it could remain at any depth submerged, down to three hundred feet, the safety limit. At some greater depth the steel would buckle under increased pressure and the hull would collapse, suddenly; an implosion.

To provide buoyancy for surface operating, there were three "main ballast" tanks, No.1 outside the pressure hull forward, No.2 internal amidships, and No.3 internal, aft. Each had a vent valve at the top and a hole at the bottom. The midships and after tanks had a "kingston" valve in lieu of a hole. In the hull and the external hollow keel, were housed three steel high pressure air cylinders, the same as those used in industry. They were connected through a valve chest amidships to the top of each main ballast tank. When on the surface, these three tanks were full of air and the vent valves shut. So long as she remained the right way up, air could not escape through the holes at the bottom, and buoyancy, equal to three tons, was assured. To dive, the three vent valves were opened quickly, letting the air out and the water in at the bottom, and when the main ballast tanks were completely full, the hull could submerge. To surface, high pressure air was admitted to the main ballast tanks until all water had been displaced through the holes or kingston valves at the bottom, providing up to three tons of buoyancy.

In order to be sure of submerging completely and quickly, another internal, smaller tank, was provided amidships, called "Q" tank (for quick). This also had a kingston valve at the bottom, an inboard vent at the top, and a high pressure air connection. In diving trim, this tank was empty, but when on the surface, in enemy or contested waters, was kept full so that when main vents were opened, and the main ballast tanks nearly flooded, the hull would submerge due to the extra weight of the Q tank. As soon as the desired depth was reached, Q tank would be "blown" (air admitted) until it was empty. Its kingston valve would then be shut, and the air vented into the hull.

When a surface ship is laden with cargo, she sinks a little until, as Archimedes discovered, the weight of additional water so displaced equalled the weight of the cargo. Ships can travel light or laden, without much adjustment. Our submarine, by comparison, could not change her submerged displacement. Therefore, some control to enable adjustment of total weight was needed to compensate for changes like extra crew, food and drinking water. Another tank amidships, called the "compensating tank" was normally about half full of sea water and could be filled or emptied as required, using a compensating pump. Similarly, if the bow were too heavy, or the stern too light, the hull would settle down by the bow. To control fore and aft trim, a tank at each end, interconnected through a trim pump, had their contents pumped fore or aft until the hull remained level.

Propulsion was provided by a diesel engine, and when submerged by an electric motor, supplied by two large batteries. There were clutches between engine, motor and propeller, so that any combination could be used; motor driving propeller, engine driving propeller with motor idling, the same with motor charging batteries or engine driving motor, as a generator with propeller stopped. Driving everything was called a "running charge", putting some electricity back into the batteries and moving through the water as well, both at reduced power. A "standing charge" was with the propeller disengaged, making the full 42 horse-power available to the batteries. A set of hydroplanes on horizontal rudders, mounted aft, controlled the hull's inclination when underway.

There was an air compressor driven from the motor. One attack periscope, ten feet long, was mounted in a dome amidships. The periscope was to be raised only when necessary, and would be visible only at short range, the top being little thicker than a finger. Here, the watchkeeper could stand with six feet headroom. Elsewhere there was four and a half feet. A second, short periscope was also mounted in the dome, This could be used to watch the diver and for navigation only when at the surface, though not necessarily in full buoyancy. A Browne's gyro compass, one magnetic compass, and a Chernikeef log to measure speed and distance travelled, completed the navigation facilities.

Initially there was a hydrophone fitted on the short periscope. This did not function well, and was removed. External sounds, if they were loud, could be heard from within, without special equipment. Weak sounds could often be heard by holding a wooden hammer shaft with one end against the pressure hull, and one ear against the other. However reliable this method was, it gave no sense of direction. Nevertheless, it was very useful, and required a certain skill, as possessed by some ERAs.

There was enough flat space on the cover boards above the batteries forward for one, or at a pinch two men, to lie down and to sleep. In the control room was another space on the port side where a man could thread his legs between pipes and pumps to stretch out, with his head under the chart table. This was where the CO would take his rest as and when he could leave his post, not that he left it by much. It took but one step to reach the periscope once he had extricated himself. For all the inconvenience of this bunk, the few odd hours, or even minutes, which I was to spend in this position, were golden.

Cooking appliances consisted of a carpenter's double boiler glue pot, and an electric kettle. We did not really cook, but heated prepared food. For ventilation there was a Protosorb canister with circulating fan and two small cylinders of oxygen, but mostly we breathed the air we dived with, and it became stale with the passage of time.

Overall length was fifty-two feet, diameter five feet ten inches, and surfaced displacement thirty tons. Maximum speed on diesel was six knots, five or less when submerged, but not for long before the batteries would be exhausted; two knots was an economical speed. Range on diesel was one thousand miles. There were many other details, but we will come to them as we move into the training and operations which were on a tight timetable because the attack was planned for April 1943, only six months away.

These submarines were numbered, not named, with prefix "X". This may not have stood for anything in particular, experimental, unknown, or secret perhaps, and the numbers started at three, because there had already been vessels of other types numbered one and two.

As their role was to sink enemy ships in their own harbours, special provision was needed to overcome the known obstacles. Declared minefields there were, each with a safe channel for the enemy's own ships. It was reckoned that intelligence would provide this information. Detector loops, laid on the seabed in the approach, picked up any steel vessel's "signature" due to its magnetism. X-craft were degaussed, or demagnetised, and fitted with electro magnets energised from the batteries. The current in these could be adjusted according to the direction in which the craft was heading in order to counteract the magnetism induced by that of the Earth, so that, altogether, it would behave as if non-magnetic and give no indication on the loop, and not trigger magnetic mines. Hydrophones were another method of detecting any vessel underway. The propulsion machinery and auxiliaries like pumps and periscope hoist, were designed to be as quiet as possible, and trials were conducted as I will describe later. Sighting on the surface would be most unlikely because of the small profile, even in full buoyancy. In very calm conditions, X-craft could be "trimmed down" or reduced in buoyancy, so as to float with very little showing. By day they would be submerged. The periscope was to be raised only when necessary, and would be visible only at short range.

The most difficult defences to overcome were the anti-submarine and the anti-torpedo nets. The former could be cut using a hydraulic cutter supplied with high pressure water from the craft. A diver breathing oxygen could operate the cutter, and be safe, down to a depth of thirty feet. Getting him out and in was one of the special features of X-craft, which I will now describe.

You will recall that the centre main ballast tank was internal and had valves top and bottom. When submerged it was full of sea water. Above this tank, formed by bulkheads (walls) on the forward and after ends, was a compartment called the "W and D", standing for wet and dry. Each bulkhead had a circular doorway and door to give crew access through the hull. The main entry hatch was also right above this space, which accommodated a yacht's toilet. The W&D had valved connections from its top to the top of the ballast tank, and from its bottom, through a reversible pump, to the bottom of the ballast tank. Thus, by shutting the two sea valves and opening the other two, the pump could transfer the water from the ballast tank to the W&D, provided that the two internal doors were shut. Reversing the pump would return the water to the ballast tank. Thus, the diver could dress inside the craft, enter the compartment, shut the two doors, start breathing oxygen, open the internal valves, pump the water up until the compartment was full, and he, submerged. He would then shut the two internal valves, stop the pump, let a little water in from the sea by means of a small valve in the top hatch, till pressures inside and outside were equal, open the hatch, and get out, shutting the hatch again. He could then operate the cutter or do any other work and upon completion, return to the submarine by the reverse procedure. This did not always go as easily as it is described, and I will tell you more about it later. But this meant that A/S nets could be negotiated, without changing the trim or weight of the craft.

Anti-torpedo nets were another thing. These were of heavy and strong manufacture, as they would need to be to stop a torpedo travelling at thirty knots. Cutting was not practicable, but it should be possible to get an X-craft underneath. British nets were only a little deeper than the protected ship, so we thought *Tirpitz's* nets were probably similar. An alternative with either type of net was to negotiate the gate used by the German service boats. Altogether, provided that we were not expected, there was considered to be a good chance of penetrating all defences undetected, both entering and leaving.

X3 and *X4* were busily engaged meantime, in trials to verify the suitability of the design. Lt Meek, RN, and Lt Cameron, RNR, both experienced officers, were carrying out this programme, while we were given more basic instruction. Because there were only the two X-craft and more than forty crew members to be trained, alternative facilities were provided.

There were two twenty five foot motor launches with periscopes fitted in their forward cabins for navigation training. All we officers and ERAs spent mornings or afternoons finding our way by periscope around Rothesay Bay and Kames Bay. This was good practise because later we were to find that a submarine was much better to take bearings from than a launch, as it was more steady and did not vibrate as much; in fact, not at all when moving slowly submerged.

At the end of our first week we knew each other, and were settling in to this new endeavour. The other Australians were Lt Brian (Digger) McFarlane, RAN, a happy, short, fair man, from Victoria, S/Lt Ken Hudspeth, RANVR, formerly a school teacher in Hobart, S/Lt Jack Marsden, RANVR, a burly man of the world from South Australia, and S/Lt Henty Henty-Creer, RNVR, from the British film industry, tall and slim with sandy hair. Jack and I shared a "cabin" as the rooms were termed, though we were dissimilar in habit; he a hard player, and I rather reserved and quiet.

Two others whom I got to know well were our fellow train passenger S/Lt Lionel Barnett Colt Whittam, RNVR, a six foot four genial former commando, who called himself "Bill", and a six foot S/Lt Joe Brooks RN, a good looking, friendly, leisure-time artist with pencil, charcoal, and water colours. We three became close friends and spent our first free afternoon walking across the island to Etterick Bay. On the return walk we stopped at a farm called Cranslag Vourity to buy some milk to drink. We were on powdered milk in Varbel. There we were welcomed by Lizzie

Dickie, a tall, lovely lady, who ran the farm with her sister Jenny and brother John. They gladly served us with fresh milk, but refused to take payment, typical, we were to find, of Scottish country folk. They all knew, of course, of the new base and the strange small submarines. Country people do not miss a thing, but though we saw them frequently in the months to follow, they were understanding and careful enough never to mention our activities.

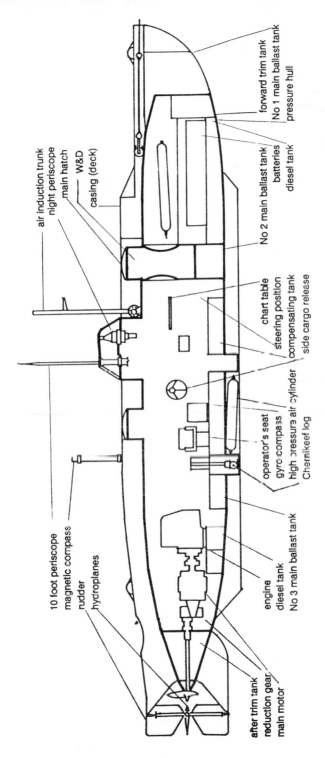

X CLASS MIDGET SUBMARINE

air induction trunk
night periscope
main hatch
W&D
casing (deck)

forward trim tank
No 1 main ballast tank
pressure hull

No 2 main ballast tank
batteries
diesel tank

chart table
steering position
compensating tank
side cargo release

operator's seat
gyro compass
high pressure air cylinder
Chernikeef log

10 foot periscope
magnetic compass
rudder
hydroplanes

after trim tank
reduction gear
main motor

engine
diesel tank
No 3 main ballast tank

CHAPTER SIXTEEN

LOCH STRIVEN

As the lectures progressed and the class became familiar, on paper at least, with this new weapon, practical training commenced. Diving was a large part of this because while the theoretical knowledge was soon imparted, practice and experience were most necessary in reaching the proficiency required to perform reliably under the rather demanding conditions.

Although all of our work was to be done using self contained oxygen breathing equipment, we were given a course in helmet diving. The heavy suits, large hand powered air pump, instructor and trainees were loaded into a motor cutter which proceeded to a sixty feet deep part of Kames Bay and anchored. The motor cutter was a timber open boat thirty two feet long, powered by a diesel engine and propeller fitted with Kitchener gear; a two section hoop which surrounded the propeller, serving as rudder, speed control and reverse gear.

Dressing in a Siebe Gorman diving suit was hard work. The fabric was heavy and stiff. One entered down through the neck. Brass backing plates were placed as a collar inside and outside the suit, with bolts projecting up through it and clamping them together. Onto these, the helmet was lowered and secured with a twist. Heavy boots were laced in place and finally, when a man had started turning the air pump handle, the glass facepiece was screwed into place. At this point the trainee, if he were at all susceptible to claustrophobia, would need all the self control he could muster in order to remain calm. Getting onto the ladder over the side of the boat was a mammoth task with those gigantic boots, but, once in the water, gravity ceased to exist, except for that of one's inner feelings. Likewise, descending the shot-rope, pausing from time to time to move the jaw in an effort to get air to flow somewhere within the head, and to equalise pressure on the ear drums, was quite pleasant as one realised, with agreeable surprise, that one was still breathing. Once on the seabed, the practice was to lie face down in order to register maximum pressure on the gauge up top, because the RN Diver's Allowance (not applicable to us) increased with depth.

Entertainment on the seabed was rather limited, but a set minimum period had to be endured, so we employed ourselves collecting scallops, while the unfortunates up top manning the air pump, were working like draught horses. It required as much effort to push air down sixty feet as it would to pump water up the same distance. Next after me came Fred Dennison-Jones, a whimsical Canadian, who was less than enthusiastic about this diving. Disregarding his many questions concerning the safety and inconvenience of helmet diving, the instructor and attendant bolted him into the suit, screwed home the helmet and window, and propelled him to the ladder. He had barely reached the bottom when he surfaced, laboured up the ladder, and mumbled something through his brass hat to the attendant ...

"He says his hands are cold," relayed the attendant to the instructor.

"Ask him if they are wet as well," came the unsympathetic reply, which was understood as an order to push him under again.

Once accomplished, the dive was a good experience, the worst part being the half-hour's hard labour on the pump, at which we all took turns. The group was next transfered by motor cutter to the head of Loch Striven, some ten miles north. This is a beautiful sea-loch with steep mountainous sides, one or two cottages on its banks part way up, and at the loch-head, a gently sloping alluvial area where the country retreat of a shipping company magnate had been established. These traditional Scottish stone buildings had been leased to the Navy to become *HMS Varbel II*, the diving training centre for the 12th Submarine Flotilla. Two Nissen huts, the ubiquitous half round wartime transportable buildings, had been erected near the shore to serve as store and workshop for diving gear. Anti-submarine and anti-torpedo nets, suspended on steel buoys, were placed out in deep water and a replica X craft section and barge were moored nearby.

The surroundings were lovely, steep hills covered with golden gorse, a swift flowing burn dividing a thick forest where we cut firewood for exercise and the wardroom fire, and a single narrow road up over the hills to Dunoon many miles away. Morning stillness in the loch, reflections of the steep banks, broken by the comparatively tiny, slow moving, craft, were a constant delight in fine weather.

The commanding officer was Commander TIS (Tizzy) Bell, RN, who, with Commander Varley, had designed and supervised the building of *X3* and *X4*, hence the name "Varbel". He was an energetic, single-minded man who urged us to train and strain until we were as fit as tigers. This was taken seriously by many of us who would rise early, take a run along the Dunoon Road, or up the hills, and return for breakfast of thin toast and ersatz scrambled egg, which meant that we were consuming more energy that we were getting, and hunger mounted day by day. There was another school of thought that argued that the way to train for life in a poorly ventilated submarine was to take all the rest available, and to spend off-duty time becoming accustomed to a self-generated tobacco fug before the log fire in the officers' mess, sipping gin. I must acknowledge that while I joined the tigers, the experienced fug generators were the more successful at crippling battleships.

More about the X-craft section. This was an exact replica of the W&D and a short section of the hull sealed with a blank bulkhead. The W&D had only one door internally, and a main hatch. There were all the valves and pumps necessary to enable the compartment to function as if it were part of an X-craft. This unit was suspended by wire ropes and a winch from a catamaran type barge, moored in water just deep enough for the unit to be lowered twenty feet. We were thus able to practise leaving and re-entering the "submarine" while *X3* and *X4* were free to carry out training in submarine handling.

Leaving via the W&D was one of life's experiences. The diving suits were of a light flexible material, convenient when negotiating small spaces and hatches. They were much easier to dress in than the helmet suit, but would not have been so protective and durable for regular divers' work. Ours were designed for the job in hand. There were several variations in detail until standardisation was reached on a suit which was entered, feet first, into the lower part through a pliable rubber trunk, at the stomach. The upper part was pulled over the head, which pushed up into the close fitting head-and-mouth piece. This always felt that it was lubricated with the previous wearer's saliva.

The lubricant was, in fact, the antiseptic in which suits were always cleansed after use. Nevertheless, it acquired the name "gob". Now, it may savour of class distinction, but this is how it was; that a sub lieutenant was prone to refer to this unpleasant feeling as having been caused by an ERA who used the suit previously and the term became "ERA gob". Eventually, some new trainee had to enquire as to "who was ERA Gob?"

Once dressed one soon became accustomed to the moisture within, so long as the suit constituted a complete barrier to the moisture without. The entry trunk was folded and sealed with a Jubilee clip, the DSEA type lung fastened on the chest, breathing pipe connected, and all was ready for a practice exit. We used the term "escape", but that was not appropriate. It was a normal, reversible process; exit, then re entry. The first time I went through, the sensations entered my memory for all time.

Once seated in the compartment, I switched onto oxygen, flushed two or three lungs full from the bag to the craft, then stayed on oxygen. All being well, I gave a thumbs up, shut the internal door, opened the water and return air valves, and started the pump. All these controls were duplicated in the "control room", so as soon as the instructor saw that the trainee was doing the correct thing, he would assist to save effort in his restricted space.

As water rose to visor level, there was a natural tendency to panic. This had to be resisted. This I did, but noted, for future, if any, reference, that surely this must be the most unnatural set of circumstances to which I had ever been subjected, but that it was ALL RIGHT, because the instructor said it was. It must have been, because I'm still breathing all this time later. But I did not know that then. When the water rose over my head and filled the compartment, it overflowed through the air return valve to the tank below, increasing the pressure as it did so. This was another shock to my feeling of well being, though I was expecting it. Now was the time to shut first the air valve, then the water inlet valve. That done, I equalised the water pressure by opening the small cock in the main hatch, released the hatch clip and pushed upward against it.   Nothing happened. There I was, immersed in water in a dark steel chamber, with a mere glimmer of light from the inspection window in the internal door, and the exit hatch was unyielding.   Then I noted that I was still breathing, just a little faster. "This won't do," I told myself, "Relax. Take your time. Everything will come right in the end."   I have always been unconvincing and would never have made a salesman. But in spite of all apprehensions and indications, the hatch did open as soon as water had flowed in through the widening gap at the seal to equalise the pressure difference which I was creating.   Suddenly, all was light. It was like Wagner's Sunrise that preceded Siegfried's Rhine Journey.   I floated up, shut the hatch by the same slow steady pressure, secured the clip, gave a thumbs up to the instructor through a small window, and swam to the surface.

There, watching for the first trainee, was the attendant. An exchange of thumbs up, and down I went again, moving my jaw to stop the pain at my ear drums, stopping, rising a little until it eased, then down onto the "submarine". Getting the hatch open from the outside was easy, but shutting it once inside was the most difficult act of all. A diver had no weight to apply to the hatch. The best he could do was to wedge himself somehow within the W&D, apply a steady pull, and wait. It took time for water once again to flow out around from one side of the hatch to the other through the narrowing gap as the seal closed.

After an age, the clip moved into place. It was then safe to open the lower water valve, then the air valve, and to pump down. Once the water level fell below my visor, I felt that it was as good as over. When the W&D was empty, I shut the two valves, stopped the pump and opened the inner door, removed my mouthpiece, shut off the oxygen, opened the visor, and mumbled "OK" to the instructor, who seemed quite pleased that it had gone painlessly.

Physically, yes, but mentally? I was not saying.   I was to go through this procedure many, many times, and was always relieved to get the hatch open on exit, and even more relieved to shut it successfully upon re-entry. This was a possible danger point. If the diver caused something like a strap on his gear to remain between the hatch and its seat, it would not seal, the clip would not move into place, his movement would be restricted, and he could not see what was wrong. If he continued with the procedure and opened any internal valve, water would rush in. An X-craft under these conditions would sink to the seabed unless the crew were quick enough to surface; allright in Loch Striven, but in an enemy harbour she would probably be destroyed.

Training was proceeding apace in *X3* and *X4*. With so many of us to be taken two or three at a time, it was a long programme. Time in the craft was at a premium. All day, crews would be diving, surfacing, making periscope sightings, carrying out all the evolutions of which we had to be capable, returning late afternoon to moor alongside the mother ship to re-charge batteries and high pressure air. We would make the best of our all too brief periods at the controls, forward in the control room with the steering wheel and main ballast vent and blow valves, and aft with engine, motor, trim pump and hydroplane controls.

At the height of this packed programme, *X3* suffered a serious setback. The diesel engine broke its crankshaft. *X3* motored alongside the mother ship *HM Drifter Present Help*, which was equipped with diesel generator and air compressor. Night after night a duty trainee would supervise the charge while ERA's, working in relays, dismantled the engine, replaced the crankshaft, and reassembled the engine. Completing this major refit within the very confined space was a tremendous and exhausting task, taking many weeks, while *X3* continued training by day, striving towards an April attack on *Tirpitz*.

Whenever an X-craft was exercising or training, two vessels were always available at immediate notice in case of the need for rescue and salvage. One was *HMS Alecto* or *HMS Tedworth*, ships with special diving equipment. The other was one of the boom ships, built to lift heavy loads by means of "horns" projecting over the bow. These were used mainly for laying moorings, A/S and A/T nets, and for salvage. If an X-craft should sink, *Alecto* or *Tedworth* was to arrive and send divers down to locate her, and to secure lifting wires from the boom vessel when she arrived.

One day in October 1942, *X3* was training members of our group and had trouble when she dived. The actions to be taken on the order "Dive. Dive. Dive." were divided between the helmsman forward and the hydroplanesman aft in the control room. The former immediately opened the three main ballast vents, shut the hull valve at the base of the induction trunk, which carried outside air down to the craft and the engine, and lowered this trunk, steering all the while. If Q tank had been flooded, he prepared to blow it empty when ordered to do so by the CO.

The man aft set the hydroplanes to dive, to give the craft a bow-down angle, stopped the diesel, shut two exhaust valves, disengaged the engine clutch, and started the main motor. He watched the craft angle, depth and levelled her at the required depth, pumping water in or out of the trim tanks as necessary to maintain depth and level.

On this occasion the helmsman forward was unable to shut the air inlet valve. Water gushed in so fast that she was on the seabed before the flow could be stopped and buoyancy restored. With no way of regaining control, most of the motors being underwater and inoperable, the crew abandoned ship using the method in which we had all been trained initially. All reached the surface easily, Commanding Officer John Lorimer assisting Taffy Lates and Len Gay to exit from the main hatch. Within seven hours, the rescue ships *Tedworth* and *Barfield* had *X3* afloat again, but it was many months before her equipment was restored.
I was at the Brown's Gyro Compass Works when *X3*'s compass arrived for overhaul. The company personnel could not hide their disgust at the way in which the Royal Navy had treated their delicate precision equipment.

By the time we had all been through this preliminary training, the first six operational X-craft were approaching completion at Vicker's yard in Barrow in Furness. Selection of the crews was imminent. It was well known that the senior lieutenants would receive commands, these being Meek, Martin, McFarlane, Place and Cameron. There was a post-examination feeling among the rest of us. It was a tribute to the Australian representation that the sixth command went to Ken Hudspeth. Henty-Creer was appointed first lieutenant to Willie Meek in *X5*, John Lorimer to *X6* with Don Cameron, Bill Whittam to *X7* with Godfrey Place, Jack Marsden with Digger in *X8*, an Australian combination, Joe Brooks with Terry Martin in *X9*, and Bruce Enzer with Ken Hudspeth in *X10*. Others were assigned as passage commanding officers because it would be necessary to tow the craft to the target area if it were as distant as north Norway, one thousand miles. To preserve the efficiency of the operational crews, a "passage crew" would man the craft on the arduous ocean passage. I seemed to have missed out on the guernseys, but was selected as reserve for any position; CO, first lieut, or passage CO. This I accepted with satisfaction. In fact, it was quite a favoured position in the order of seniority of those available.

This announcement triggered a wardroom party. So far as I remember, all accepted the appointments as wise and fair, and joined in the celebration with genuine goodwill. From this moment, there was a segregation among us, not complete, but subtle. The COs in particular were privy to the more secret information, while the rest of us worked away at various tasks as allocated.

An incident comes to mind that I must relate. "Bill" Whittam, I told you, was a tall, likeable man, courageous yet gentle. It was quite appropriate that he should fall for another tall person, a beautiful WRNS third officer, Ruth Barham. In their courting they were observed by Cdr Bell, who later became displeased with S/Lt Whittam over something which I do not recall. But, as a result, he submitted a report to Capt S12 (12th submarine flotilla), W E Banks. Bill told me about being called to the captain's office and being read a portion of it.... "... On my first encounter with this officer, he failed to salute as he had his arm around a Wren...." It seems that the main offence, whatever it was, was not too serious because Willie Banks concluded the interview by saying, "It's a sad heart that never rejoices." and tore up the report.   In reflecting now on subsequent events, I regard Willie Banks' action as inspired.

Prior to *X9*'s delivery from Barrow in Furness late January 1943, I travelled with Terry Martin, Joe Brooks and ERA Ingle-Claridge to the shipyard for the last days of construction, and accompanied her on her rail journey to Faslane in Gairloch for her launching. *X5, 6, 7* and *8* had already been launched. I was *X9*'s passage CO in those days, but that job did not last long, just long enough to take part in a couple of sets of trials.

One morning we set out on turning circle trials. The method chosen by our CO, but not normally employed to my knowledge, was to proceed past a buoy and, when it was abeam, to put on the desired degree of helm, hold it until she had turned one hundred and eighty degrees, and then steer the reciprocal course. I held a ball of string, the end of which was already made fast to the buoy, and had to keep it taut, and mark the string as the buoy came abeam each time. Then we were to measure the distance between the marks and that would be the turning circle diameter for that speed and degree of helm.

We charged for the buoy on the first run, which was to be at full speed and thirty degrees of rudder. I had the string taut and marked it as we passed close to the buoy. *X9* swung steadily to starboard at six knots as I paid out the string, soon realising that there would not be enough. I immediately told Terry, who called "Stop. Full astern." Joe was at the after control position, and carried out these orders promptly as they were relayed by ERA Ingle-Claridge at the forward position, but I ran out of string and had to let it go, telling Terry that I thought it was not a good method. He decided to call off further trials until he had decided on another way, and ordered "In engine clutch. Half ahead." There followed some ominous hammering down below, and I noticed the propeller swirl passing forward along the hull. That, I think, was the first engine to be wrecked. Joe had omitted to change the motor direction from astern to ahead before starting the engine, which had sucked in sea water through the exhaust and tried to compress it. After other engines suffered in the same way, safety interlocks were fitted between the engine clutch and astern switch.

I was appointed to *X6* that afternoon, thereby leaving Joe at the start of an unhappy commission. He was inclined to become utterly disgusted with things and like me, needed occasional reassurance. I did not witness the next incident, but heard about it soon after it happened. Terry Martin had just berthed *X9* alongside *Submarine Depot Ship Titania* and ordered "Finished main motor and steering." Joe, at the controls, removed the cover from the gyro compass and was stopping it when Terry decided to open the after hatch, which was usually left shut when the craft was afloat because of the electrical equipment close below it. As he did so, a sailor in *Titania* emptied a bucket of gash (rubbish), right down the hatch onto the gyro.

It was on 14th February 1943 that I received a surprise in the mail, in the form of a Valentine card in an envelope with an Aberfeldy postmark. There were kisses on the card. What could I do but acknowledge and ask if she would like me to spend my next leave in Aberfeldy? So the correspondence started. What did I say about being a poor communicator? So, from that time there were fewer train journeys to London and Burwash and more to Glasgow and Perthshire.

My next assignment, I clearly recall, was the first towing exercise. This was by submarine *Tuna* from Kames Bay to Eddrachillis Bay near Cape Wrath, in the north west of Scotland. I had been selected as CO of the passage crew of Don Cameron's *X6*. The manilla tow rope was about two inches thick, six hundred feet long, and had a telephone wire which usually broke, laid up within each strand. We also had a radio transceiver, and if these forms of communication failed, Submarine Underwater Explosive signals (Suzies) would be used, one to attract attention, two to dive, and three to surface. Commander Ingram, who succeeded Cdr Bell in Varbel II, was in overall charge in the towing submarine. This was to be the first ocean tow.

The X-craft was to stay dived most of the time so that best speed could be made, and to surface and run the engine to ventilate the craft as necessary. This was expected to be for fifteen minutes every six hours, and for a longer period after dark to enable batteries and air cylinders to be re-charged. The passage crew also included a stoker and a seaman electrician. The tow was to be a new experience for all of us, and would take thirty hours approximately.

Towing on the surface at up to eight knots in the calm waters of the Firth of Clyde was fine. *X6* kept on course behind *Tuna*, with five degrees of rise on her hydroplanes to keep her bow up. Her efficient hull speed was six knots. At speeds much above this, she would set up large waves at bow and stern with a trough amidships. As this trough increased with speed, she could eventually lose buoyancy altogether, and submerge.

This did, in fact, happen much later with *X8*. Digger was on deck, which was called a casing, and Jack in the control room. On this occasion the telephone happened to be working. Cdr Ingram was in the towing submarine's control room. Speed was increased above eight knots. Fully buoyant though she was, *X8* submerged. Jack telephoned immediately:

"Reduce speed! We've dived, and Mac is on the casing."

"Well, he shouldn't be," from Cdr Ingram. But they did reduce speed and *X8* surfaced. Mac was seen to be lying back along the casing, his foot caught in the periscope standard guard. Jack scampered up through the hatch in time to see Mac stir, much to his relief. Mac's uniform jacket had been swept up over his head, trapping a small bubble of air which had kept water out of his lungs.

Back now aboard *X6*, towing down the Clyde, past Ailsa Craig toward the Mull of Kintyre. Instructions were passed to us to dive and to surface each hour if the telephone failed, and to report by radio. Down we went, and up went the speed. This was easy to tell by the attendant noises. There was always something to rattle outside the hull. The hydroplane operator was having difficulty keeping a uniform depth of fifty feet. Presently she broke surface, took a bow down angle, and plummeted down, twenty feet, thirty, forty, fifty. Hydroplanes were, by this time, set amidships. Sixty, seventy, eighty, ninety, one hundred feet. There she steadied for a second while her bow came up. Ninety feet, eighty, and so on while the planes were reset to dive to try to slow her rate of rise.

Regardless of this, she splashed through the surface again, and porpoised once more for the depths at a steep angle.

I had called the submarine to request reduction of speed, but the phone had failed already. I went aft to the planes, climbing up the sloping deck of the control room. We had reached one hundred and twenty feet by this time. I ordered the operator to let me have a try and put the planes to dive, holding her at that depth. Slowly I reduced the angle on the planes. Her bow started to rise, pulled up by the tow rope. Very gradually, by anticipating her movements, these were brought under control, but it was an uneasy state of equilibrium, just on the balance. At fifty feet, she needed bow down angle to keep down at that depth. Some water was pumped into the compensating tank, and some from aft to forward. Eventually, she sat level at fifty feet, with planes amidships. So far, so good, but if the tow should part, we would no longer be pulled upwards, and with extra trim weight, and some of that forward, she would go deep.

This was explained to the crew. "If the noise suddenly stops, immediately pump out, pump aft, put planes to rise, and run the motor half speed ahead. If that does not restore control, shut main vents, and blow." The tow rope, being six hundred feet long, and our designed depth three hundred feet, even if the tow did not break it would be possible to reach a dangerous depth. By the time all three of us had practised controlling with the hydroplanes, keeping depth at fifty feet, it was time to surface and ventilate. Reduction in the noise level indicated speed reduction so we pumped out the midships main ballast tank to save high pressure air, planed to the surface, raised the induction trunk, declutched the propeller, and started the engine. Because we were not in full buoyancy nobody went on deck. I watched *Tuna* through the short periscope, though we were towing at such a bow up angle, I could only see over the bow when a wave lifted our stern. After fifteen minutes, we stopped engine, flooded the ballast tank, returned to fifty feet and the racket outside resumed as *Tuna* increased speed, north into the Minches.

After dark, the procedure was repeated, but this time we came to full buoyancy as the sea was rough, and I went onto the casing. A signal torch was calling us. I went below and got mine, came up, and acknowledged.

"Surface and report by radio, each hour commencing midnight."

This I acknowledged by just a "T" and went below. We were all tired. The fewer unnecessary manoeuvres the better. When all was going well at fifty feet, one of us at a time, could sleep, but surfacing and diving necessitated all hands at diving stations. Doing this every hour would mean no sleep. Fatigue is the sailor's worst enemy. But then, I was a trainee sub lieutenant, being instructed by an experienced commander.

After one hour charging, batteries were well up, and the air 'groups' as the cylinders were called, were at full pressure. We had been economical. The sea was rising, and the motion becoming unpleasant. Stoker Bill Ball and I were seasick. Upon returning to fifty feet, after one or two porpoises, the duty planesman regained control, and the third man got his head down forward on the platform above the batteries. I don't suppose he slept. It does not come easily on the first night at sea when one is unused to the noise, motion, and anxiety of being pulled through the water at an uncomfortable speed. But at least there were no waves down here, and I was starting to recuperate, when the clock reached twelve.

Pumping No 2 main ballast again, we regained the surface as soon as the speed noises stopped, and called *Tuna* by radio. It was even more rough than before, and I had difficulty listening to the handset and retching in the bilge at the same time. We made contact, reported all well, and dived again. The planesmen changed over, the relieved man going forward to rest. We promised to try to avoid porpoising so that he would not be slid back aft again. It was comparatively comfortable back at depth. At 0100 hours, the man forward was asleep, and the planesman clearly exhausted. I thought of the seas fifty feet above us, and the non-news we had to transmit, and decided to emulate Nelson. I could see no signal requiring us to the surface. So I told the planesman to turn-in in my bunk in the control room close at hand, and took the planes. He was asleep in an instant. It was quite pleasant with everything going well, the gyro compass singing close by and snores coming from two places at once. All I had to do was to keep *X6* at depth, and myself "on the surface", because, when not feeling sick, I felt tired, and was looking forward to getting to our destination. This was the nearest to exhaustion I had ever been.

At 0200 I called the man who had been sleeping forward and gave him the planes control. The other awoke and sat by him. I lay on my bunk with my legs threaded between pipes and motors, and slept immediately. So we went on, past 0300 and 0400, changing around every hour. At 0430, I was awakened by the sound of three Suzies. We surfaced and switched on the radio. Cdr Ingram's voice came as if from a great distance, but clearly enough to read.

"Why did you not report at 0100, 0200, 0300 and 0400?"

"I wanted to conserve HP air." I replied. "The crew were exhausted, and so was I. I regret not having complied with your instructions. It was unpleasant on the surface, but comfortable at fifty feet. The crew got some rest."

"Stand by to transfer crews in ten minutes."

"Aye aye, Sir."

I told the crew to come to full buoyancy and to tidy up as quickly as they could, and prepared to go onto the casing. The engine was started to ventilate. I went up on deck. We were proceeding slowly into a loch, with beauty all round. The sea was calm again, and I was glad that seasickness was over for the time being. It was not to my credit that I had not followed the set schedule. What I should have done was to have surfaced at 0100, and requested the cancellation of the following schedules and to surface again at 0500. It was an exercise to give experience, and we all knew more about ocean towing now.

There was activity on the after casing of the submarine. The dinghy had been inflated, Cameron and Lorimer were getting in. I called down the voice pipe, i.e., the air induction pipe, to stop engine and to stand by with engine clutch out, tail clutch in with batteries grouped down. The batteries could be connected, grouped up (in series) for maximum power, or grouped down (in parallel) for best economy. I wanted to hand over the boat with batteries and HP air fully charged. We tended to drift ahead under the weight of the tow, but *Tuna* gave a kick ahead occasionally to keep a distance. As the rubber dinghy approached, I called for one of my crew to come up, ready to transfer. The dinghy came alongside, two climbed out, and one in. It was hauled back and presently returned with the other crew member.

Meantime, I had briefed Don on our findings and details of the boat's condition. It was generally all right, but very humid and wet, despite the ventilating. He was impatient to be away, so as soon as my second crew member arrived on deck, we got into the dinghy and were hauled up to the submarine. If that were typical of a two hundred and fifty mile tow, I thought, what an ordeal a thousand mile tow would be. One would become accustomed to the conditions to some extent, but in that humidity, defects would occur increasingly, and there would be much to be done to keep all systems working.

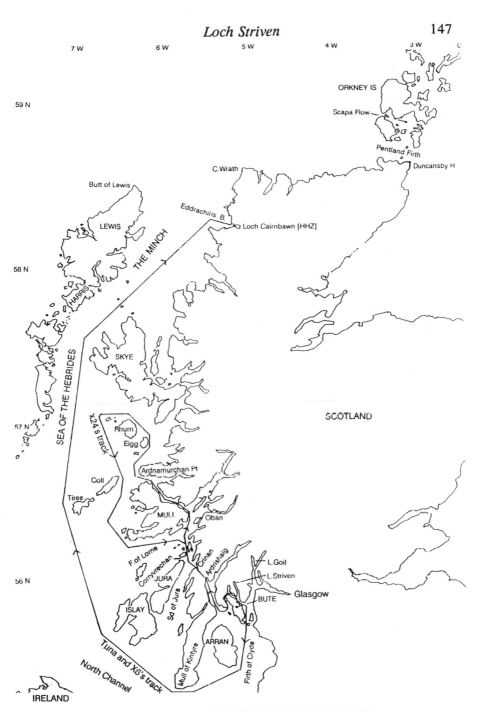

EXERCISES OFF THE WEST COAST OF SCOTLAND

CHAPTER SEVENTEEN

H H Z

X *6* slipped her towline, *Tuna* hauled it aboard, stowed it in the casing, and proceeded into Loch A'Chairn Bhain, known to us as Loch Cairnbawn, which leads off Eddrachillis Bay. Here was our mother ship *HMS Bonaventure*. She had been recently commissioned into the Royal Navy from the Clan Line, who had built her to handle heavy lifts. She could lift four X-craft onto her fore-deck, two onto her after-deck, and two into her after-hold. She had specialists in all trades, a well equipped workshop, and accommodation for crews of six X-craft. She was moored close to the shore on the south side of the loch. A small dam had been formed in a burn ashore, near her bow, and connected with fire hoses providing adequate highland water for all purposes. *Tuna* moored to the north of her, and I was taken aboard by motor cutter, with Cdr Ingram and my two crew. He was not pleased with me, and little was said during the short transfer. I felt that I should have done better, and if there were to be a next time, I would. But at least *X6* was delivered in good order, and I was to see later that that was not always the case. One of my shortcomings was that I did not give enough attention to communications. Another man would have convinced Cameron, Ingram, and everyone else, that he had achieved wonders in impossible circumstances. Never mind, the job was done; the first ocean tow had been successfully completed.

We were to spend months on all manner of exercises at HHZ, the code name for Loch Cairnbawn, or in Loch Striven. Loch Cairnbawn was several miles long, with a narrow, deep channel at its eastern end, opening onto two further long, deep waterways; Lochs Glen Dhu and Glen Coul, all steep-sided and sparsely populated.

I took passage back to the Clyde in *Tuna* and thoroughly enjoyed the voyage. Her Captain and crew thought that we had done well, and treated us accordingly. She negotiated several narrow waterways between islands of the Hebrides, past distilleries and small villages. It was a Cook's tour. I enjoyed the comparative comfort of a T boat, and noted the high standard of efficiency of all crew members. To be regarded as an equal was too good to be true, and my confidence rose hour by hour.

On 28th April 1943, I was promoted to lieutenant, having served two and a half years as a sub-lieutenant. Working from Varbel, all X-craft had completed their "first of class" trials to test their performance against design values. These had included measurements of speed on surface and dived, turning circle with different degrees of rudder, diving to maximum depth (300 feet), noise levels, magnetism levels, battery performance, fuel consumption, and so on, followed by crew training in navigation, attack, crash diving, depth keeping and net cutting. These mostly went well except for the latter and the programme had fallen behind schedule, so the attack on *Tirpitz* was postponed until September 1943.

In the early attempts to cut a submarine through a net, all divers had difficulty, and one was drowned. The exercise was stopped and I received a summons from Cdr Ingram, then Commanding Officer of Varbel II. He gave me a resume of recent events and said that progress was at a standstill, timing was becoming critical, morale was falling, and something must be done to overcome the difficulty, whatever it was, and to set a safe and efficient procedure for net penetration. Willie Meek had become discontented with the deferral of the operation and had returned to big submarines. Capt Banks had decided to appoint me in command of *X5*, Henty-Creer being 1st Lt, to concentrate on net penetration until the technique was established.

I thanked him for the opportunity, and set off by the next boat for Loch Striven where *X5* was at a mooring in readiness. It was a splendid appointment; interesting, challenging, exciting and sufficiently uncertain to inspire the boldest with a sense of care and awareness. What was more, I would be responsible for its success.

I contacted Henty and discussed our plan of action. First we spoke with those who witnessed the previous unsuccessful attempts. It came out that the divers got as far as exiting from the craft and starting to cut wires. After many cuts, the craft still had not penetrated the net. They tried to push it through between the wire ends, and at this stage, one diver had disappeared. He was later recovered from the seabed, too late for revival.

Henty himself had tried net cutting once, without success. It was when Willie Meek was *X5*'s CO and Henty her No 1. "Baldy" Hezlet was also on board, and their attitude was to show the flotilla how it was done. They were going to do it in style, first time. During the approach to the net, Henty was to get into the W&D, flood up, and wait. Baldy would knock on the door as a signal that the craft was in the net. They missed the net on the first run, so came round again, and missed it the second time. Thinking that Henty had been immersed long enough, Baldy hammered on the door to indicate that they had suspended the trial. Henty took this signal to mean that they were in the net, opened the top hatch and got out. He did notice a strong current, but, assuming that all was in order, pulled himself forward only to find that there was no net, only water. At this point, *X5* struck rocks at the edge of the loch, thus adding to the confusion. On their next attempt they did find the net, Henty got out, cut a large hole into which the craft settled down and moved no further. Henty got underneath, upside down, held the net with his hands, and pushed on the craft with his legs, until he passed out. He was rescued by an observing diver from the attendant boat.

It seemed to me that in Henty's characteristic determination to make a big impression, he was disregarding basic safe practices. Care was called for, like taking one step at a time, and not over exerting one's self when physically working under water. I had never been in an X-craft during such a trial. Henty and I sat in the mess at Varbel II on the evening of my arrival, with the logs burning and our fellow officers sipping warm, flat beer, from glass mugs. We had one too. We needed something to relieve the pessimism and to get the old enthusiasm going, not Dutch courage, but a snapping out of depression and a making of progress. I was mentally analysing the evidence.

It had struck me, listening to the accounts of recent failures, that there did not seem to be any pattern in the actual cutting. There had to be a best selection of wires to cut. What was it? I had also observed, from my own diving, that however clearly one might think on the surface, under water thought became muddled. It was therefore advisable to do the thinking first if possible, and to decide on a clear plan of working, a modus operandi if you prefer Latin. So, I fetched a sheet of paper and a pencil, and sketched a section of anti-submarine net approximately to scale, with the cross section of an X-craft with charges attached, end-on to the net. This was how an approach would be made, at right angles to the net, at thirty feet depth, the deepest a diver on oxygen could work in safety.(sketch at end of chapter)

I suggested to Henty that the bow would most probably nestle in one of the diamond shaped spaces, retained in this position by the four surrounding wires. The motor would be kept running at slow speed ahead to keep her there. Following the wires that lay across the top of the casing downwards, if the first cross-wire on each side were cut, the space between would increase from a three feet diamond to a six feet diamond. This would not be big enough. Cut the next cross-wire on each side and the diamond would become nine feet along the two top sides. The wires below the cuts would drop down and form a complete diamond shaped space of nine feet on each side. The sketch indicated that the craft would just fit through this space, provided that she could move down a little and not get out of position to one side or other.

Another thought struck me at this point. If the craft happened to be out of correct trim, let's say she were too heavy, the CO would not know. If she were moving through the water and not held by the net, she would slowly sink; her depth would be seen to be increasing. However, being held in the net, craft depth would be constant, and not therefore an indication that the trim needed adjustment. If this were the case, the craft would not move through the space, but would bear downward on the lower wires. It would be similar if she were too light, or off course to port or starboard. The CO could see if he were off course; in fact the helmsman would be controlling this as his normal duty, but only the diver could see if the trim needed adjustment.

We devised a simple system of hand signals to be made by the diver to the CO who would be watching through the short "night" periscope, as it was called. This instrument had a prism to enable scanning in the vertical plane. In other words, one could look up and down as well as around. The CO could acknowledge the diver's signals by moving this prism which was easily seen by the diver.

We then wrote a brief instruction for net penetration:

1. Pass the cutter through the same space as the craft is going to negotiate.
2. Examine the lie of the craft in the net. If she appears heavy or light, signal the CO accordingly; two hands up means pump out one hundred pounds; hands down means pump in. Repeat this signal as necessary until craft sits evenly, proving neutral buoyancy.
3. Diver penetrates net and remains on far side.
4. Cut the second cross-wire down each side.
5. Check lie of the craft. If trim is correct, cut first cross wire each side. Craft will move ahead.
6. Follow the net as it moves aft; clear any obstruction.
7. Stow the cutter and return to the W&D without delay. Craft may need to increase speed to control her depth.

That done, we turned in, proposing to try this technique next day. As a safety precaution, a boat was in attendance whenever a net penetration was in progress, and an observing diver to watch the craft's diver at work. Next day, Henty and I took *X5* away with her regular ERA and stoker. Henty wanted to make the first cut and dressed as I remained in command, diving to 30 feet on a course to intercept the net. Presently the craft stopped and swung off course a few degrees. Motor speed was reduced to slow ahead and the helmsman brought her back onto the former heading to keep her at right angles to the net, which I could just see through the

Sub-Lieuts Henty-Creer and Shean wait for diving instruction at Loch Striven. By today's standards our equipment appears archaic but despite awkwardness of dressing and undressing in an X-craft's limited space, breathing oxygen at dangerous depths and a high casualty rate, many, especially "charioteers" or "human-torpedomen, achieved great deeds with it.

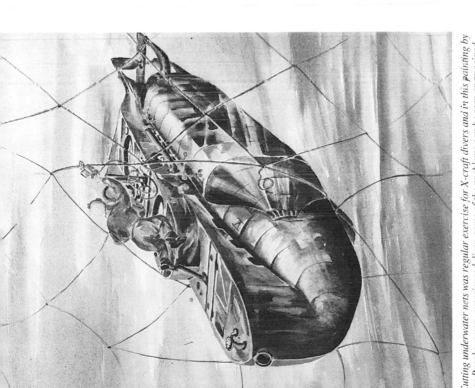

Cutting underwater nets was regular exercise for X-craft divers and in this painting by Joe Brooks, a very experienced diver, some of the problems can be seen or imagined. The feeling of loneliness, the cold, possibility of oxygen or equipment failure, the frequent poor visibility and the ever present enemy overhead made the diver's life a hazardous one.

While Tirpitz lies snug behind her protecting nets in Ka Fjord, North Notway, X5,6,7,8,9 and 10 have last minu maintenance and modifications in the Kames Bay float dock in preparation for Operation Source, the attack o German battle fleet.

X9" s crew, September 1943 Lt Terry Martin (CO), Lt Max Shean (Diver), Sub Lt Joe Brooks (First Lt), Sub Lt "Paddy" Kearon. (Passage CO) LTO "Darkie" Hart (passage crew) ERA "Ginger" Coles and Stoker "Ginger" Hollet (passage cre Deprived of the satisfaction and recognition of attacking the target, the passage crew endured the fatigue and discomfort of North Sea crossing in tow by a larger submarine, to perform a vital role in handing over the craft in seaworthy condition.

night periscope. I also saw the bottom of the attendant boat as she arrived and secured to a flotation buoy above us.

Henty was dressed by now, and entered the W&D. During his exit, and early period outside, he was having trouble breathing and returned to the craft. I pumped the W&D empty, opened the door, switched him back to breathing air and ordered "Stand by to surface. Shut main vents." This was repeated by the crew and vents were shut. An advantage of a small submarine is that the Skipper could see everything going on from his diving station at the periscopes.

"Stop motor." "Slow astern." I watched as she backed off and the net disappeared in the green water. "Stop." "Surface. Blow No 2 main ballast only." "Stop blowing." All these orders were repeated and executed promptly. I did not want to surface too quickly as the boat might be just above us.

Once on the surface I ordered full buoyancy The helmsman blew the three tanks. Henty opened the hatch and climbed onto the casing, and finished undressing. As we drifted in the calm loch, the boat came alongside, and we discussed the trial. It seemed that there was something wrong with the breathing set. It may have been one that was not prepared and taken from the diving store in the Nissen hut by mistake. There was a spare in the boat which the instructor verified as correct. We could try again with Henty conning the craft, and I as diver.

X5 got under way on motor as Henty and I went below. As he dived her, and manoeuvred toward the net, I dressed and entered the W&D. We were soon nosed into the net at thirty feet, as before. I felt a little anxious that no successful penetration had yet been achieved; we had had a bad start that morning, it was vital that we succeed and this was to be my first attempt. The diving part did not worry me because I had had a good run to date, with no serious setbacks.

The exit went allright. It was reassuring to see the attendant diver waiting for me, like a spider holding onto the net above the craft. We exchanged thumbs up as I went forward to examine the lie. She had her bow against one of the wires. I pushed the wire to one side, and she moved forward into a space and stopped again, all nice and gently. The water was clear and I could see the propeller spinning slowly between rudder and hydroplanes. The bow was bearing down on the net. I faced the night periscope and gave the hands moving up signal. The prism fluttered in acknowledgment. Next I heard the pump running and saw a cloudy stream of water discharging from her port side. The pump stopped. She seemed to be sitting evenly in the three foot diamond now.

I opened the door in the casing forward of the main hatch, took out the cutter, which looked like any other hydraulic hand tool, but with a strong hook at the business end, took out the twenty feet of hydraulic hose attached, shut and bolted the door. Moving to the bow, I passed the cutter and hose through the same space as the bow occupied and got through the adjacent space myself. In spite of our sketching of the previous evening, the wire pattern did not seem clear. I ran my hand down the wire from the port bow. First cross-wire, second cross-wire. This must be it. I hooked the cutter onto the wire and squeezed the trigger. With a steady hiss the blade moved slowly out from its guide toward the wire held in the hook. When they met, the blade continued as if there were no wire. Crunch, snap, and the wire fell apart. I released the trigger, and slowly the blade withdrew into its housing. I climbed up to the casing, felt for the wire on the starboard bow, slid down one cross-wire, two, hooked the cutter on and squeezed the trigger again.

Then, I looked once more at her position in the net. All four wires seemed to be equally loaded so the trim must be correct. I cut the first starboard cross-wire. The lower wires fell away, and *X5* moved forward until held by the remaining cross-wire under her bow. Checking that all was clear, and that the cutter hose was threaded through the same space as the craft, I cut the fourth wire according to our plan. All four lower wires dropped to form a large space into which *X5* moved, slowly at first, gathering way. I floated up over the casing, following the net back to the locker where I re-stowed the cutter and hose. By now the net had reached the rudder, dragging against the starboard side. The attendant diver was holding both thumbs up, sinking slowly to the end of his safety line as he did so. I waved two thumbs at him as he faded into the green distance. We were now free, through the net, and *X5* was sinking slowly. As I opened the hatch I saw the planes move to rise and heard the main motor increase speed. Before the wash over the deck increased, the hatch was shut, and the W&D was pumping down. As the water emptied, the pump was stopped, valves shut, and the internal door opened.

"That took twelve minutes," said Henty. I opened my visor, removed the mouthpiece and shut off the oxygen.

"The plan worked," I said to him, and, to the two crew, "Thanks for the ride. Very comfortable."

We surfaced downstream of the line of spherical steel buoys that suspended the net, and stopped. The boat was motoring around the end of the buoys, and came alongside. The diver had his head out of his suit. "A piece of cake," he said, descending to the use of Air Force slang. But he was not wrong. The problem was solved. We moored *X5*, took the boat ashore, and walked back to report, by phone, to Cdr Ingram, using ordinary words to preserve security. I said that the first trial had succeeded but that we would repeat the exercise a few times. He was pleased, and so were we. Our repeats went just as well, and, in fact, there were no further losses of life by divers on this evolution. *X5* was assigned to other work, but not before Henty and I had completed another trial.

There was concern that anti-torpedo nets around *Tirpitz* might extend right to the seabed unless the water was very deep. We had tried cutting a similar net but the steel grommets were so hard they broke the cutter blades. It was thought that it might be feasible to lift the bottom of the net using high pressure air in a steel cylinder, released into a strong air balloon attached to the bottom of the net. Our practice anti-torpedo net was sixty feet deep. At this depth, a diver on oxygen has limited endurance, about ten minutes.

As soon as a canvas balloon was ready, Henty and I went to the net in the attendant's boat, dressed in our suits. This time, we had safety "life" lines. There was a system of tug signals in common use. One tug from the instructor meant "Are you allright?" One tug in reply from the diver meant "I am allright." Four meant "Come up." or "I am coming up." This was usually not used by the diver except in an emergency, in which case the attendant would assist by heaving in on the line steadily. Coming up too quickly was not recommended.

Down went Henty, with the balloon. I followed with the cylinder on a rope. We did not often go down to sixty feet. It was rather dark down there, though the water was clear. At the bottom of the net Henty made the balloon fast. I secured the cylinder below with its outlet projecting up into the balloon, and opened the valve. Slowly the balloon rose and filled out. The lowest row of wire grommets lifted about a foot. It took some minutes for the air to transfer, during which time Henty had left the net and was swimming like a sea-horse, body vertical. His arms were stretched out in front of him. He was suspended at the end of his life line, turning slowly toward me. When he came round far enough, I looked at him through his visor. He had his eyes open, gazing fixedly ahead as though he were seeing nothing. I made some gesture, without any response, then shook him, still with no reaction. He was unconscious.

I took his lifeline and gave it a hard tug. An answering tug came down the line. I then gave it four good tugs. Back came four tugs, and up went Henty. I grabbed his foot as it passed me and went up with him. We arrived alongside the boat to an excited reception. I indicated that Henty needed attention and stayed in the water while he was pulled aboard. They quickly had him out of his suit. He was breathing and regaining consciousness. I said that we could leave the gear where it was and take Henty ashore. I climbed the ladder to see Henty sitting in the bow, looking far off, and shouting to one and all that he was unhappy with everybody and wanted to be ashore. From time to time he would stand in the bows and try to step over the side. After an hour or so, he was back to normal, with no harm done so far as I was aware.

I went back in the boat after Henty had been taken care of, descended to the depths with another diver to find the balloon fully inflated but very little more lifting of the net. That system was not suitable. We retrieved the balloon and cylinder, and returned to base. Henty's blackout was probably due to oxygen poisoning, as it was termed, caused by being too deep for too long. If I had stayed deep, eventually I could have succumbed, though there are warning signs of which we had been made aware, like twitching of the lips.

Another day I dived to the bottom of a net that went down one hundred and ten feet, to test a telephone headpiece. This had an earphone set into the headpiece over each ear. I went steadily down and up again, dwelling only a moment at the bottom to talk to the attendant above. There was no bother with consciousness and the phone worked, but when I undressed, I was bleeding from both ears, so did not try that one again. I never lost consciousness diving, whereas many others did. Success must have been at least partly due to an understanding of the chemistry and physiology of diving. For instance, I knew from studies that the Protosorb canister for carbon dioxide removal must have a capacity limit. Therefore, to work hard underwater could eventually overload the unit and cause heating and inadequate purification. Being of light build, I always tried to work efficiently. This applied also to the former net cutting difficulties. Why try to manhandle a submarine that is too heavy, to maintain her depth? Let the machinery do the hard work, and save yourself for the role of observer and director.

On 9th June 1943, Henty, who had received accelerated promotion to lieutenant after one year as sub lt, was appointed CO of *X5* and I, CO of *X3*, for continued training of new recruits. This reminds me to tell you a little more about Henty. He spoke frequently about after the war, when he wanted to be a film director or producer. He offered me a job as his technician. I, too, had ambitions, to return to university and to qualify as a professional engineer, but I do not think that he understood the difference. But he would have been an interesting character to work with. He had a flair for top billing, and would not be happy playing second fiddle to anyone, for long.

Henty had a winning personality, and used it to good effect. While I would pursue the job in hand with single minded enthusiasm, Henty spent sufficient of his time in conversation with senior officers who warmed to his engaging manner, leading to his accelerated promotion to lieutenant. All the while, he was writing his autobiography, which I have since read. This reveals his ability to present himself in the most favourable light, consistent with a statement which he once made to me, that "An impression is better than the solid fact." Better for impressing others, I agree, but not necessarily for operating and maintaining a submarine.

So it was that I had received my "second (lieutenant's) stripe", after two and a half years as sub lieutenant, during which time I had gained a watchkeeping certificate, and had been successful in directing an attack which had probably sunk a U-boat, while Henty achieved rapid promotion without such experience. It did not concern me at the time but, I believe, is a matter of some significance in view of subsequent happenings.

The mention of films stirs another recollection. We used to go to Dunoon, as necessary, to receive dental treatment aboard the S/M mother ship *HMS Forth* in the Holy Loch. I was to have a few fillings and arrived on board one day to find the quarterdeck busy with cameras, lamps, reflecting screens, producer, director, actors, and any number of others. I learned that the 'star' among us was Deborah Kerr in the production of "Perfect Strangers". She was playing opposite Robert Donat, who was not present, being disinclined to leave London. In any case, the scene being filmed did not include him. I have since seen the film, as you may have, but in case you have not, it tells of a London couple who lived their very ordinary lives, pre-war, happy with each other. When war broke out they both joined up, he in the Army I think, and she in the WRNS. She was, in fact, coxswain of *Forth's* motor boat in the film. Their service life so broadened their experience that each privately doubted whether he or she could settle down with the other after it was all over. In the scene under production at the time of my dental appointment, Deborah was coming aboard *Forth* after securing her motorboat to the boom, a wooden spar projecting from the ship's side. As she climbed beautifully over the guardrail, one of her Wren shipmates handed her a letter. She opened it, read it, and gazed wistfully over the waters of the loch. It transpired that the letter was from Robert saying he had leave and would be with her for a week or two. She wondered if she could take it with the old fuddy-duddy after a taste of life in the Navy. The camera had a view of a wide stretch of water behind Deborah as she climbed the rail and then leaned on it as she read her letter and gazed thoughtfully outboard. Something was needed to add interest to that water area, so one of *Forth's* boats spent the time circling. Deb climbed that ladder not once, but ten times, and it was still not to the director's satisfaction. The motor boat ran short on fuel, so the cameras had to stop whirring, and Shean missed his dental appointment while it refuelled and Deb got up and down that ladder another ten times. In the film the scene lasts thirty seconds.

There were plenty of setbacks during this busy time of preparation for the big attack. On one occasion, in *X10*, the crew had gone ashore on completion of battery charging, leaving her at a mooring in Kames Bay. The induction trunk was, as usual when moored, lowered level with the casing. Unfortunately, the crew had omitted to shut the air induction valve and the strong wind at the time caused waves to send slugs of water down through the trunk into the hull, until she lost buoyancy. Once the trunk was at water level, she quickly filled and sank. She was soon raised, overhauled, and returned to service. While items like gyro compass and batteries were damaged, the hull and most other equipment needed only to be washed with fresh water, dried, and re-lubricated, to be as good as new.

Most accidents were frightening but not tragic. A common one was, when opening up for diving, to omit to open the depth gauge hull valve. This gauge was really a pressure gauge, calibrated in feet. Upon diving, the planesman would see zero depth on the gauge and put more and more angle to dive on the planes, and pump in water while the craft would be plummeting down and finally dive into the mud on the seabed. Fortunately no harm would be done, except that the sudden stop would start the gyro compass wandering for the next few hours until the earth had rotated sufficiently for it to get its bearing.

It was customary to refer to such happenings as "cocks" or "stuff ups". Joe illustrated several of them in a sketch book which he entitled "Main Line Cocks", a main line being an important pipe line. "Cock" was also another name for valve. I will include two of these which feature "Digger" McFarlane in *X8*, the first involving the unintentional dive when on tow, already described. The second depicts *X8* making a practice attack on *Bonaventure*, with an Admiralty scientist, and a new instrument, aboard. Jack Marsden was having difficulty keeping correct depth during the approach to target. Mac could not see because his periscope was submerged. Joe depicts the result clearly and dramatically in his drawing.(see end of chapter)

An interesting feature of design was the fuel storage. Six of the tanks were located under the batteries forward, and more under the engine aft. In all tanks, the hull comprised the tank bottom. The flat tops served as decks, and end plates completed them. There were interconnections from the top of one fuel tank section to the bottom of the next. To compensate for loss of weight as fuel was consumed, sea water was admitted to the first section. This obviated the need for a fuel forwarding pump as the sea pressure was sufficient to push fuel to the engine injector pump. The tanks were always full of diesel or water. When refuelling, diesel was pumped into the engine supply line and flowed back through the tanks, displacing water into the sea. When diesel rose to the sea surface we knew that refuelling was complete. When the craft dived, the sea inlet to the fuel system was shut off to avoid excessive pressure.

Tanks in the control room had flat tops which formed a deck to walk on, but they also had raised sides for more capacity and to provide mounting space for pumps and other equipment. Space was at a premium. The crew occupied what remained after the equipment had been located. The engine room was most crowded, as you can imagine, with a bus engine alongside a three-stage air compressor within a five foot ten inch tube, the bottom of which was occupied by tanks. Yet ERA's and stokers did work in the remaining space, even with the engine running. The motor and clutches were at the back of this lot, and needed attention occasionally.

Another interesting assignment I had at Loch Striven Head was to liaise with a Norwegian fishing boat, skippered by Lief Larsen, who was, even in those early days, famous for his daring and effective sorties back to the German occupied coast of Norway. In the same manner as human torpedos, or "chariots", had been towed into Fjords by fishing boats which could pass as local, it was thought that X-craft might also be towed by them. This single cylinder engined boat came to Loch Striven Head and took an X-craft in tow, both surfaced and dived. I was aboard the fishing boat as liaison officer. While the cooperation could not have been better, the engine was just not powerful enough to make sufficient speed, and the proposal was dropped. Nevertheless, it was a great experience to meet Lief, and his fellow Norwegians, who were as dedicated to the cause of defeating the Germans and freeing Norway from this despised occupation, as men could be. Also enjoyed were the friendly chats in the snug cabin in the fore ends of the fishing boat, with its peat-fired stove, and coffee brewing from beans, in a kettle.

Corvette and Submarine

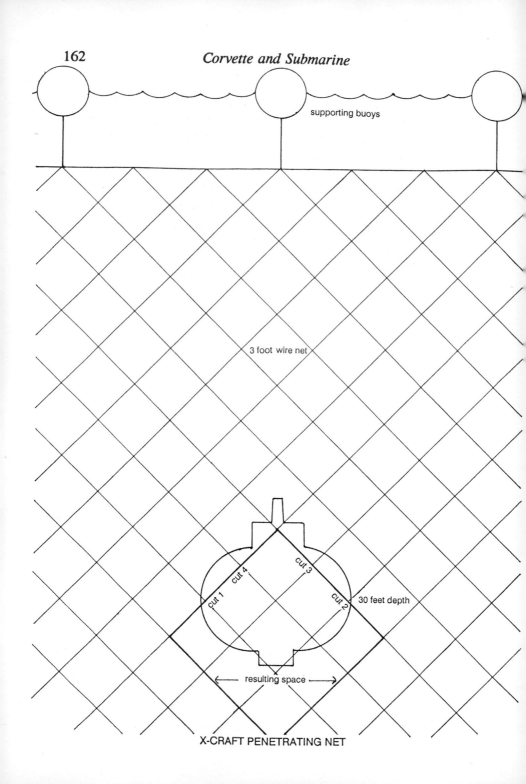

supporting buoys

3 foot wire net

cut 3

cut 4

cut 1

cut 2

30 feet depth

resulting space

X-CRAFT PENETRATING NET

Joe Brooks' cartoons were topical and pertinent. These two involve Brian McFarlane and Jack Marsden in X8. Above, under tow by S/M Tuna with Cdr Ingram aboard; heard on the telephone: "Slow down. We've dived and Mac is on the casing."
Reply from Cdr Ingram "Well he shouldn't be."

Approaching for a practice attack; "Get her up Jack! We must be somewhere near Bonaventure."

CHAPTER EIGHTEEN

FINAL PREPARATIONS

T he original plan had been to attack in April 1943, when there would be sufficient darkness for progress on the surface, yet not too much heavy weather. However, the craft and crews were just not ready. Some craft alterations were found necessary and it was becoming clear that all members of the crew could not be called on to perform net cutting. Divers needed to keep in training, whereas submarine crew personnel were preoccupied with essential submarine work.

All six craft were put up in the Kames Bay floating dock for alterations. I took a photo of them, and believe that it is one of only two existing pictures of all. One of the alterations was to the venting arrangements of No 1 main ballast tank, to enable it to vent more quickly and to reduce the time to dive. The automatic pilot, which never operated correctly, was removed to make room and buoyancy for echo detectors, which could measure the distance to the surface as well as to the seabed. The trimming pumps and some switches were fitted with sound absorbing mountings to reduce the level of underwater noise transmitted during their operation.

Gradually, flotilla activities moved from Clyde to HHZ. I was still spare man, keeping in touch as best I could, not being attached to any one boat. But all experiences were well discussed in the wardroom, so we all knew what was going on with every craft. There was some excitement one day when one of the craft, manoeuvring on motor, seemed to be out of control, going full astern, with controls set for slow ahead.

Main motors were compound wound, meaning that, in addition to a winding on the armature, the part that goes round and a field winding on the stator, the outside part that doesn't, there was also a "series" field winding connected in series with the armature. The current that flowed through the armature, also flowed through this series field winding. Correct operation, when preparing to put to sea, was first to switch on the main, or "shunt" field winding. Then, when ordered "Slow ahead", the planesman would close the ahead switches, which energised the series field and the armature, causing the motor to rotate in the ahead direction.

What had happened on this occasion, was that the operator had omitted to close the shunt field switch. There was only the series field energised, giving the motor a weaker magnetic field. Now, it may sound crazy, but a weak field makes a motor run fast, but why should it run astern? This was being discussed volubly at lunch that day and, as Fougasse had said, argument thrived because facts were scarce. After listening to the non-progress until coffee time, I said to the Electrical Lt Cdr who was next to me, "It sounds as if the series field winding is connected in reverse." He said nothing, but must have noted the remark, because he came to me during the afternoon, and said, "You were right. We examined it. It was incorrect, but it is right now, and the motor runs correctly. How did you know what was wrong?" Sailors, like non-sailors, all have trouble understanding electricity. It was my lucky day. I was just one ahead of him on that occasion.

Because of further troubles with net cutting, with divers having to bail out for no good reason except that they were out of practice, Capt S12 decided to bring in divers who had been trained for human torpedos, otherwise known as "chariots". This was a good idea from the point of view that they were expert divers, but they had no X-craft training, and were left to pick it up for themselves. There were further problems, and time was running out. The attack had been set for 22nd September. Two T class and four S class submarines had been scheduled to be at HHZ for towing trials immediately before leaving for Alten Fjord, which was where *Tirpitz* now spent most of her time.

Practice net penetrations went wrong and tension built up between X-craft and Chariot personnel. I was detailed off by Capt, S12, to resolve the matter. I did not welcome this brief because I did not quite know how to handle it. Nevertheless, I promptly met the Charioteers in the Staff Room on *Bonaventure*. Everybody was tense. I greeted them all.

"Let's all have a drink, and forget it for tonight. Tomorrow we may all be more relaxed." This was not accepted. Their attitude was as one.

"You tell us what you think is wrong." they said. So I went over my own early experience with the net cutting investigation, described the steps which evolved, and concluded by drawing a comparison. "You have been used to manhandling human torpedos weighing one ton. X-craft weigh thirty-five tons dived, with side charges. Don't try to push them. Use the submarine's own machinery."

They showed interest. Their attitude was cooperative. A great sense of relief came over me. I believed that these men would do the job because, proficient as they were, they were also prepared to learn that extra lesson. We worked together for the remaining period, I telling them about X-craft, and they putting it into practice.

If these accounts make it appear that all problems were solved by myself, let me say that there were many more difficulties solved by many others in the flotilla. Naturally, I know most about the ones in which I was involved. But, such engineering education as I had undergone at the University of WA was proving its worth.

In our leisure hours during that summer, we went ashore at every opportunity, walking the hills and mountains, and visiting nearby villages. Quinag was the dominant feature in the area. It overlooked the loch, a massive horseshoe shaped mountain, which we scaled frequently. There were deer roaming its slopes, but we saw them only at a distance. To the east was Kylesku, the site of a pre-war car ferry, and an existing pub. This had an austere interior, but the sailors frequented it, having nothing better within reach. Then, to the west was Nedd, a tiny hamlet, and further along the road, the village of Drumbeg, which had a school. The residents arranged many dances for the ship's company, and there was one marriage of a ship's officer to a Drumbeg lass. I recall one dance to which my party took a bottle of whisky, standard practice, no doubt. But it was a first for me, and I can still feel the exhilaration of the rising influence of a good dram followed by a vigorous reel.

In Drumbeg lived one Marion Stewart, who kept hens. She sold me some eggs on two occasions when I had leave due, so I had something to take to Mary, or was it to her mother? There were two motor cycles belonging to the ship: I used one of these when I went to collect the eggs, and, although the roads were steep and narrow, never was an egg broken. The purpose of the bikes was the courier run, every few days, to the nearest town with a Navy Office - Invergordon. Volunteers were called to do this run, and I did it twice. The road was lonely but beautiful, if you like the somewhat bleak and barren country of the far north, which I did. When light rain fell, stinging of the eyes forced a slow pace: we had no goggles. It was a change from the ship, and I had no submarine to care for at that time, being spare man.

In order to give skippers practice in avoiding being spotted by aircraft, all six craft were sailed from HHZ, southward, in the Minches, between the Inner and Outer Hebrides. They were 'hunted' by six Fleet Air Arm "Swordfish" biplanes from the Machrihanish Base. I was sent to Stornaway, on the Island of Harris, to liaise with the pilots, telling them what they were looking for, and where to look. They covered the exercise area two at a time, and I flew in the observer's seat on each sweep.

Swordfish had two open cockpits, the after one seating the observer, who could face aft. We flew at two thousand feet, and at eighty knots. If we were higher, the craft would appear too small to be seen, especially in the choppy waters, and, if too low, the field of cover would be reduced. After being in the air for half an hour, I saw a tiny white arrowhead, with another one immediately behind it, pointing south. I slapped the fuselage with my hand, as the pilot had done earlier, to attract attention. He looked at me and I pointed to the white arrows. He nodded, and next moment the Swordfish's tail went up, and all I could see was sky. At the bottom of his nearly vertical dive, the pilot pulled up again and there, almost within handshaking distance, was a skipper scrambling down the hatch of an X-craft. As we climbed back to our patrol altitude, I watched the craft as she slowly submerged. If she were our enemy, we should have made a kill.

X-craft took about sixty seconds to submerge from full buoyancy and, in such a sea, it would not be safe to proceed at reduced buoyancy. It took less than a minute for the Swordfish to dive from two thousand feet, so it was imperative for an X-craft to keep a good lookout for enemy aircraft at all times. The noise of his own diesel probably prevented the skipper from hearing us coming. We spotted one more craft before our endurance limit was reached, and we returned to Stornaway. I transferred to one of the next pair and flew off again.

I flew also with one of the third pair, and, altogether, four sightings were made. As the craft were to remain on the surface except for short periods when a Swordfish was sighted, they must have evaded more times than they were seen, and the exercise had proved well worthwhile. I loved it, especially at the end of the search time, when my pilot took me for a "hedge-hop" along the rocky coast of several islands, and made tight circles around one lighthouse. This was different from the usual sailor's view. It stood on a foam fringed rocky headland; a beautiful sight, which remains with me to this day.

As the date for departure drew near, many interesting things were happening. Officers came aboard to brief commanding officers for the attack. They had intelligence relating to many aspects of the operation. I was included in all of these, but not in subsequent discussions between skippers. Most interesting were the lectures on evasion of capture, in the event of having to abandon the craft, and to land in occupied Norway. It was possible to walk to Sweden, which was neutral and from where return to England was almost assured. Also, we were briefed on how to act if taken prisoner, and on escape techniques from PoW camps. All this sounded very exciting, so much so that a few were almost looking forward to the possibility. We were issued with survival kits and maps. There were also names of friendly contacts in Norway. These had to be memorised for fear of compromise and the sure retaliation against the Norwegian citizens by the Germans.

Finally, the six submarines arrived. Then, in the last practice of net cutting, the diver in *X9* lost confidence and pulled out, leaving a place into which I was appointed. A last minute draft is known, in the Navy, as a "pierhead jump", and this was one certainly. So, I rejoined Lt Terry Martin, S/Lt Joe Brooks, and joined ERA Vernon Coles who had also been recently appointed. S/Lt Paddy Kearon was passage crew CO with Leading Torpedo Operator A H Harte and Stoker G H Hollett. Our towing was to be by *Syrtis*, Lt Jupp, RN.

A few days before sailing, it was decided to photograph each crew, all crews together, and then all CO's together. It was like family grouping after a wedding. In the CO's picture, Digger McFarlane can be seen making a rude sign, with a smile, while Henty can't be seen at all. He had expressed displeasure at all this photographing, claiming that it showed lack of confidence in the operation on the part of the senior officers, and departed to his cabin.

A journalist and a press photographer came aboard in the last days, to prepare a press release should the attack succeed. Nothing had ever been published about X-craft, and it seemed odd to have these men present. All the same, they were made welcome, and took a picture of all the officers in their No 1 (best) uniforms prior to a mess dinner. After the dinner, some of the pent-up anxiety gave way to general revelry. A game started of collecting "medal ribbons", these being short pieces cut from braces which, in those days, were in general use to hold trousers up. Before long most of us had the shirts torn from our backs as well. I finished up in collar and cuffs. Well before this time, the two pressmen had retired to the safety of their cabin, but it was unanimously decided that another picture was needed, so they were brought, unwillingly, back to the mess for more pics.

The night before we sailed, the operational crew ERA's went ashore to the bar that they had rigged in a cow-shed, for a last drink together. Ralph Mortiboys, of *X5*, declined to go. He wanted to remain aboard *Bonaventure* to write to his widowed mother, because he had a premonition that he would not return from Alten Fjord.

CHAPTER NINETEEN

OPERATION SOURCE

On 11th September, 1943, six submarines were berthed alongside *HMS Alecto* and six X-craft were ready, with side charges fitted, alongside *HMS Bonaventure* in Loch Cairnbawn. Admiral Sir Claude Barry, Flag Officer Submarines, had come from "Northways", the S/M headquarters in London, to see the flotilla leave and to wish everyone well. He was a genial, thick-set man, with a fringe of hair above the neck, but none on top. He fulfilled my mental picture of Friar Tuck, and inspired all of us with his enthusiastic support. In the prevailing fine weather, the pairs of submarines and several ship's boats moving towards the sea created a scene reminiscent of a regatta.

As each pair of submarines approached the entrance to the loch, the Admiral's barge, with Captains Banks and Fell also on board, drew close alongside while words of encouragement were exchanged. I was on the conning tower of *Syrtis* when our turn came. The submarine captains each had some symbol of the chase. Lt Jupp had a forage cap and a bulb horn, as used long ago on automobiles. He was keen on using this when the Admiral came alongside, if he could do so without impertinence. The Admiral called out "Good luck, Jupp and Martin, and a safe return."

"Thank you, Sir. If we have any trouble, we'll take a taxi." Honk, honk, honk. This went down well with Sir Claude, and everyone else.

Soon we were on our own, *X9*, manned by S/Lt Paddy Kearon, Leading Torpedo Operator "Darkie" Harte, and Stoker "Ginger" Hollett, dived and speed was increased to ten knots for the thousand mile journey. Security precautions were extraordinary. According to the Prime Minister's definition, the hunt was for the most important target in the war at sea. It must not fail, and the enemy must not get the slightest hint that anything was afoot. The six pairs were routed separately on parallel tracks, ten miles apart. X-craft would be dived all day, except for a ten minute ventilating period at 0600, 1200 and 1800. After dark, they would surface to charge batteries and air for an hour or two. Within two hundred miles of Alten Fjord, the towing submarines also would dive by day. The most any aircraft would be likely to see would be a submarine apparently on patrol.

To guard against the possible compromising of radio signals, each submarine had a different re-coding book, and would not send signals except for matters of first importance and then only from a position far from the target area, north of the Arctic Circle, in the later stages. Targets had been allocated among the six X-craft. *X5*, *X6* and *X7* were to attack *Tirpitz*, and *X8*, *X9* and *X10* other capital ships which might include battle cruisers *Scharnhorst* and *Lützow*.

Aerial reconnaissance was made as frequently as possible, but was difficult because of the weather and the extreme range from Britain. Some flights were staged via Russia, but this required lengthy and delicate diplomatic negotiation. A good deal of information was radioed, at great risk to themselves and their families, by Norwegians. It was possible that changes would be made to the allocation of targets according to the disposition of German ships and the X-craft. This was the first time such an operation had been mounted, so flexibility was essential.

Towing routine had become standardised following trials like the one reported earlier, by *X6*. Telephones were not expected to last long, so a timetable for ventilating and charging was prearranged. SUE signals were available for emergencies. Passage crews undoubtedly had the more onerous task, as I well knew. My sympathies were with Paddy and his two crewmen.

We of the operational crew were comfortable during the passage. We did stand watch as lookouts to keep active and to provide another pair of eyes, but still had plenty of leisure time. The Daily Mirror produced a newspaper especially for submariners. Called "Good Morning", it was supplied in month bundles, not dated but sequentially numbered. This was important in order that the comic strips like 'Jane' and 'Zeke' would appear in logical sequence. There were features on submariners and their families, and pictures of the 'Windmill' girls, who were famous throughout Britain and, I should think, the world. The Windmill Theatre in London presented a variety show with emphasis on shapely girls: most Aussie servicemen attended at least one Windmill show during London leave at some time.

'Jane' was also a national institution. Like the Windmill girls, she frequently managed to lose her clothes, but acted with propriety none the less. 'Zeke' was an anthropologist, or something like that, and during this particular month's issues had one single ambition, to capture a prehistoric animal and so to be made a Fellow of the Zoological Society.

One morning, Joe was allowed to distribute that day's "Good Morning" throughout the messes in *Syrtis*. All seemed to be happy until members of each mess came to the wardroom with a complaint. "Something is wrong with this issue, Sir. Yesterday, Jane was about to do something or other, and today she is on about something entirely different." The fact was that Joe, in his eagerness to help, had issued the wrong number. I don't suppose many newspapermen have produced next week's news today.

Another time-passer was to play games on paper; a popular one being 'Hang the Man', in which one player thinks of a word which the other player must guess, letter by letter, losing a point for each incorrect guess. The points are scored by progressively drawing a gallows with rope and stick-man, ten pencil strokes in all. We spent so much time at this, it became nearly impossible to hang anybody, until Terry 'hung' his first lieut, Joe, with the word "ZekeFZS", considered to be of doubtful validity.

A further game arose out of the operational situation, as time passed. Our telegraphist intercepted a signal to Admiralty from one of our fleet. We were unable to decode it, but estimated from the strength of the signal, that it was transmitted from a position nearby. All we had was about twenty groups of five numbers. The telegraphist and submarine officers off-duty pondered at length. It had to be important, so it would not be just a weather

Commanding officers of the Operation Source X-craft muster aboard Bonaventure for a photograph before setting off. L to R: Harry Martin (X9), Ken Hudspeth (X10), Brian McFarlane (X8), Godfrey Place (X6) and Don Cameron (X6) Henty Henty-Creer (X5) is absent.

Bonaventure at HHZ with X5-10 on board and Titania with Thrasher, Truculent, Sceptre, Sea Nymph Stubborn and Syrtis alongside, ready for Operation Source, September 1943. Syrtis had several misfortunes. En route to Norway she lost X9 when tow parted, lost X22 in similar circumstances later in Pentland Firth and was lost herself off the Norwegian coast a few weeks later, all crew being lost each time.

X24's crew, March 1944: LTO "Lofty" Element, First Lt Joe Brooks, CO Max Shean, Passage CO "Willie" Britnell, Sub Lt Frank Ogden, and front, Passage ERA Syd Rudkin, Passage Crew Stoker Bill Gillard and ERA "Ginger" Coles, on Bonaventure's boat deck before the Bergen operation.

Basking in the Scottish sunshine before setting off for Bergen, Lt McIntosh, CO of Sceptre talks with Lt Max Shean, CO of X A superb and popular submariner, Ian McIntosh took part in Operation Source and both Bergen attacks. He had been awarded an MBE for captaining a 23 day open boat voyage after SS Britannia had been sunk by a German raider and later DSO, DSC and twice Mentioned in Despatches for submarine operations. "Bring 'em back alive" McIntosh.

report: at the same time, weather would be reported if radio silence were to be broken for any important reason. What were the possibilities? It could not be an enemy sighting report or this information would have been passed on to all by Admiralty. It could be difficulty with an X-craft. Had one been lost on tow?

After much thought and discussion, it was agreed that something was amiss with an X-craft, and so it was. *X8* had broken her tow and *Seanymph*, Lt J P H Oakley, RN, was searching for her, but we did not know that. In fact, we all knew nothing of the progress of the rest of the fleet until after the operation, by which time we had received several undecipherable signals, and were of the opinion that separate recoding tables were not a good idea. If six submarines had the one exclusive set, the risk of compromise before the attack was negligible, and the benefit to the participants considerable.

What was happening was that the four boats with manilla tow lines all had breakages. Nylon rope was a new material, developed for glider towing, and only two of these lines were available in time. These were used by *X5* and *X6*, and performed well. *X8* joined company with another submarine who directed her to her own. The Passage CO, Jack Smart, was exhausted after days of continuous watchkeeping, and was promptly relieved by McFarlane and his operational crew. Her side charges were starting to leak, and eventually had to be dumped. Although set not to detonate, they did so, and severely damaged *X-8*, which had to be scuttled.

X7, with Peter Philip in command, had several towline breakages, but succeeded in passing another towline each time, and got to the slipping position on time, a splendid effort of seamanship and endurance by a man who, in his youth, had been crippled by polio.

The worst setback was our own, on the morning of 16th September, two hundred and forty miles from the slipping position. At 0900, according to the now well established routine, *Syrtis* reduced speed for *X9* to surface for ventilation. There was no *X9*: only a slack towline streaming astern. *Syrtis* stopped, hands went aft along the casing to pull the line aboard. In the long swell, her

Corvette and Submarine

stern was rising and plunging, making it difficult to stand, let alone to pull in six hundred feet of heavy line. It was cold as well, for we were near the Arctic Circle. Part way in, the rope snagged under the submarine's stern and could not be freed. It had most likely fouled the port propeller. Lt Jupp ordered the X-craft diver to clear it. That was me. My diving suits were aboard *X9*. All that *Syrtis* had were the standard DSEA escape sets which provided breathing only; no protection from the cold water, neither had they any weights to compensate for their positive buoyancy.

I dressed in a pair of overalls and the DSEA set with some steel weights from the engine room, and went aft along the casing, where a rope had been rigged for support. Lt Jupp urged me to be quick. If we were surprised by enemy aircraft he would have to dive immediately. I climbed, with a lifeline attached, onto the after hydroplanes, switched to oxygen, and launched myself into the North Atlantic Ocean. It was cold. When my face went under, it took my breath away. I was floating. The weights were not only too light, but loose as well. They were long pieces of metal which swung about with my every movement. It was impossible to get down.

The water was absolutely clear. In the few moments that I could remain submerged, I noted the shafts of sunlight descending into the depths. It made me feel giddy. I tried to see the propellers, but, as *Syrtis* pitched in the heavy swell, the hydroplanes smacked the surface with an almighty splash, which forced me to the surface again. I was cold all over, and more frightened than I have ever been. This was not Loch Striven diving. It was beyond my ability to get down to the propellers. In a proper suit, correctly weighted, insulated from the cold, I could have swum down, but, floating as I was, and being pumped to the surface with every swell, it was more than I could do. But there was no giving up. The rope had to be cleared, otherwise we were limited to the use of the starboard propeller only.

I swam along the surface to get clear of the hydroplanes, and looked down. There were the infinite light beams converging toward the great deep, and there was the port propeller, with the rope around it, not tight, but in a big loop. That was fortunate so long as the propeller was not rotated. I looked up to the First Lieut on deck and removed my mouthpiece, "Do not turn the port propeller. Let out some slack on the tow, and carry it as far aft as you can." This they did. I saw, to my enormous relief, that the bight of rope was now lying aft of the propeller.

"Right. Heave in now."

The rope straightened above the propeller and slid across the top of the big shaft as the casing party heaved it aboard. Eventually the end came up, frayed from the break and having been towed for some time afterwards.

The casing party hauled me back to the hydroplanes and up on deck. The crew were complimentary as we hurried forward and up into the conning tower. *Syrtis* was already underway on diesels, and heading back along the way she had come.

"Well done Shean," from Jupp, and down I went to change.

The rush of engine air down the conning tower, as I stiffly clambered down the ladder, was hardly felt. I was numb.

That crisis over, we had time to consider the situation. *X9* must have broken her tow soon after diving at 0120 according to the engineer officer, who came up with hourly fuel consumption figures. If we retraced our track for the same time, at the same speed, we should meet up with her. This we did, without success. All that was seen was an oil slick running in the direction of the Norwegian coast. This may or may not have meant that *X9* headed that way. The logical course for Paddy to steer would be the one we were on, prior to the tow parting, which he would know. We turned, and covered the distance again, still without sighting anything. *X9* was lost, for the time being, or forever, we did not know. The situation must be radioed to Admiralty, and to do this, we had to travel north to the Arctic Circle. We turned north.

Of the operational crew members, I believe that Joe was most affected, although we all felt the absence of Paddy and his two shipmates, and also what looked like the end of our chance to attack the German fleet. So far as we knew, the other five were still OK, though in fact it was only four. I thought of Paddy. He was a cheerful Irishman, short, slightly on the heavy side of average, fair, with a broad countenance and a smile to go with it. He had a third officer WRNS acquaintance at *HMS Ambrose*, the submarine base for Allied boats, at Dundee, where my Mary was now a Wren herself.   On his last leave, Paddy had gone to Dundee to see "Touche" as he called her, and carried a letter from me to Mary. Paddy's friend was probably French; I think her name was La Touche. I had not got to know his other crew members very well because of my pierhead jump only a matter of days earlier.

Leading Torpedo Operator "Darkie" Harte, was a quiet, industrious Londoner.   Stoker "Ginger" Hollett was a ball of fire, always cheerful, always doing something in the boat of his own initiative; a very good submariner.

A signal to all submarines struck a note of resolution, if not desperation:

"All X-craft attack *Tirpitz.*"

We were out of it, except that any submarine could attack any major warship, but nothing less.   This proved frustrating for Jupp because, as we approached the slipping position submerged, he sighted a U-boat on the surface, and had to hold fire.   As if that were not enough, the U-boat altered course and came within range a second time.   We X-craft hands were not too popular for the rest of that day.

Our orders were to continue to patrol off the entrance to Alten Fjord for several days after the attack day, 22nd September, to torpedo any major ships flushed out, and to tow any X-craft needing one. There was an emergency rendezvous in a bay north of the entrance.   We entered this bay one still night while I was keeping lookout on the periscope standard.   There was no moon.   It was black and calm as we crept through the narrow waterway, and cold.   After an hour on lookout duty, fingers would be numb. Suddenly, the sky lit up with a vivid display of the aurora borealis. It was as if a giant were shaking an enormous fluorescent silk scarf above us. We could have read by its light, and a lookout ashore could have seen us clearly. *Syrtis* quietly headed for the open sea, counting the minutes and awaiting gunfire.   But the rendezvous had been well chosen, and there was nobody there to see us.   All the same, it was an anxious few minutes.   Eventually, we turned sadly from the recovery area empty handed, and headed for the Shetland Islands.

X10, with Ken Hudspeth, was being towed in the same direction, as it happened, having been defeated by defects in the last stage of approach to *Tirpitz*. He too, thought that five other craft were attacking. In fact, three were - *X6* and *X7* successfully, and *X5* nobody knows. All three sank in Kaa Fjord. *X6* attacked and then scuttled alongside *Tirpitz*, and all four crew were taken prisoner. *X7*, after attacking, was damaged by the resulting explosion, surfaced, and was sunk by gunfire, the skipper and diver escaping. They were taken to prison camp in Germany with *X6*'s crew. *X5* was sunk by gunfire seven hundred yards from Tirpitz: there were no survivors, so little more was ever known.

X10 was scuttled on her tow home, following several tow breakages and a deterioration in the weather. So, the tally was six X-craft and nine men lost in the process of crippling one battleship. Tirpitz did not sink, but she never fulfilled a battleship's role again.

Syrtis berthed at Shetland where we had our first hot bath in weeks at the servicemen's quarters ashore. Of course, I had had a dip in the North Atlantic, but that was salt, and cold. This was hot and fresh, and I wallowed in it. Then *Syrtis* returned us to *Bonaventure* at HHZ, where debriefing took place. Skippers Martin, McFarlane and Hudspeth, went to London for FOS's analysis of the operation. I was given a week's leave while our future was being decided. Six more X-craft were building, but their future deployment had to be considered in the light of the full results of "Source", on which intelligence reports were still awaited.

Bonaventure returned to Kames Bay, and off I went to Aberfeldy. This was, I believe, my third visit. Mary and her parents had invited me to stay with them on my next leave, and this I was glad to do. The disappointment of the last days was weighing heavily on all crew members. We knew only of our losses. Bill Whittam, in particular, I missed. To this day, whenever a period of silence is observed for departed comrades, he comes to mind. I think of his ravishing Ruth, their love, his remains recovered from the wreck of *X7* and buried in Norway and of her lonely sorrow.

There were the other eight whom, apart from Henty and

Paddy, I did not know as well, all missed by someone. And our entire flotilla wiped out. This was my immediate view of things. The overall fact was that it was a splendid achievement. Compare it with the sinking of the sister ship, *Bismarck*, which took a large fleet of the Royal Navy and the loss of the battle cruiser *Hood* with all but three of her crew.

It was a subdued Australian proceeding on post-operational leave, who alighted at the now familiar Aberfeldy station, to be met by Mary, who had left the WRNS to look after her ailing mother. I probably was poor company because I was in the depression period that follows all bouts of action. The Aberfeldy people were kind to me as they always were. One day I was loaned a .22 rifle, and walked off into the woods looking for a rabbit for supper. There were some, but I was such a poor shot, my bag remained empty. In desperation, I took aim at a knot on a tree and fired several shots around it.

Presently, a shout came from behind. A farmer was striding across a field.

"Good afternoon," I said, hopefully. Obviously I had been poaching.

"You are after my rabbits," he shouted.

"I was firing at a tree," I said, and took him over to show him. Luckily I had hit the tree. It was a large one.

"Who are you, anyway?" he asked. "I don't say I recognise you. You are not from these parts."

"No," I said, "I am from Australia, in the Navy. I'm staying with the Goldings during my leave."

"Oh," he was embarrassed, "You know, there are some folk around here that poach, and they're hard to catch," adding, after a pause, "but if you are from Australia, that's different. You can take a rabbit if you want one. There are some over in yon field," pointing to where I had been. I thanked him, and returned to 18 Kenmore Street for a more certain meal.

The following Saturday evening, Mary's father, George Golding, and I visited the Black Watch Inn for a quiet whisky together. This national drink was in short supply, and available only to local regulars, and then only one or two nips in one evening. The landlord had generously conferred "local status" upon me, a high honour indeed. The small bar was crowded. As we two stood together sipping slowly to make it last, who came toward us through the crowd, but my farmer. He took from his coat pocket a handful of .22 bullets and gave them to me.

"Take these, they are hard to come by."

Two days later, Mary and I had been to Inchadney to dine with my former hosts, Jess Anne and Bill Bennett. Walking home in the twilight, we took a turn down the Kenmore Road, past the Twin Trees. It was said that if a lass could squeeze through the narrow space between the two trunks, she would marry. Mary stayed on the footpath, but I got to thinking that I was fond of her, and could not imagine dropping her as a friend at any time. There seemed to be only one outcome.

"How would you like to come to Australia after the war? I know it is a big question for a girl to consider, so think it over in the next few weeks. There is no hurry."

"Yes," she said, "I'll come."

That was the 14th October, 1943. We were officially engaged on the 18th, by which time I had bought a ring.

At about this time, the *Tirpitz* story was released to the British press. There was quite a story, with a big photo of the ship herself, in the Glasgow Herald. A good many Aberfeldy folk put two and two together, but nobody said anything to me. No names were mentioned in the paper, for which I was thankful. I told Mary that that was where I had been, but nothing more. She had a right to know something about the bloke she was hitching up to.

It was a great pleasure to do the rounds and to meet all my future in-laws. None threw up his hands in horror. One was quite objective about it; Auntie Chris. She was a former teacher, widowed by the early death of her Merchant Navy Officer husband, and residing in the "smiddy" in Kinloch Rannoch, on the road to the Isles. When Mary and I called to inform her, she said "Sit down, and let me have a good look at you." We sat on opposite sides of a round table. She moved the vase of flowers to one side, and gave me an oral examination, about my prospects, family, and so on. Finally, she said, "Yes, you will do." and made a cup of tea, served with the incomparable Scottish cakes and shortbread. I knew where I stood with future Aunt Chrissie, and that was the way it turned out. A blacksmith's daughter, she lived in the smiddy cottage with her sons Duncan and John, and her brothers Tommie and Josie. I could write a book about that family, as indeed Duncan has done, and many a captivating tale it tells.

CHAPTER TWENTY

X 20 - 25

On return to *Varbel*, apart from celebrating my new involvement, we took up our new responsibilities. The second six craft were under construction, neither at Vickers nor any other shipyard, but at inland towns unused to the sight of naval officers on duty. These craft were designated X20, X21, X22, X23, X24 and X25. I was appointed to X22, in command. This was good news indeed, but more was to come. My crew were S/Lt Brooks and ERA Coles. I could not have asked for more. As the deliveries were not due for a while, I asked to be permitted to visit the manufacturers of some of the more important components. This was agreed to. I went to Manchester and spent a day at the Patricroft Works of the Gardner Engine Company. These were well laid out workshops, clean and tidy, with a high standard of quality control As an added enjoyment, I was taken to a delightful inn for lunch by the Gardner brothers themselves, in a car fitted with one of their own engines. Diesel powered cars were rare in those days.

While in that city, I also visited the Chloride Electrical Storage Company, who made the Exide batteries for all X craft. Here I learned more about care and maintenance of lead acid batteries, information which is still useful today. One of the most valuable pieces of information for a submariner who must frequently recharge his batteries as much as possible, in the time available without damaging them, was that, with the power of our engine, we could start charging at full power, watching battery voltage. When this reached two-point-four volts per cell, which, with fifty five cells, was one hundred and thirty two volts, charging rate must be reduced, progressively, to maintain and not exceed that voltage. This would achieve recharge in the minimum time without ill effect.

This was a very useful rule, which I still use. Throughout my submarine experience, I never had trouble with batteries, or engines, and considered these visits good value indeed.

Among the few papers still in my possession is a pink NAVAL MESSAGE form, S1320f. All forms used by ships had a number prefixed by "S". It reads -

"SECRET CYPHER

TO: F.O.S. (Flag Officer Submarines)   FROM: S.12
Following appointments are submitted, to take effect forthwith.

X.20   Commanding Officer Lieutenant K R HUDSPETH, R.A.N.V.R.
         First Lieutenant   Sub Lieut. B E ENZER, R.N.V.R.
         E.R.A. TILLEY

X.22   Commanding Officer Lieutenant M SHEAN, R.A.N.V.R.
         First Lieutenant   Sub Lieut. J BROOKS, R.N.
         E.R.A. V COLES.

Crews will report a.m. tomorrow 27th October to Commander RENDEL at Huddersfield.

        ---261500 A October   Date 26/10/43"

That was another of the more significant pieces of paper in my life. It gave me my first operational command, and brought Joe, Ginger and me together in one crew. We had, of course, been together in *X9*, but Ginger and I had joined immediately prior to departure for Alten Fjord aboard *Syrtis*, and I had spent very little time in her. This was exciting, going to the builders to take delivery of a submarine on behalf of Admiralty. The six of us took the train to Huddersfield next day, and reported to Cdr Rendel, who had a temporary office in the works of Thomas Broadbent and Company, who were building *X20*. He was a short, energetic man, lively and good fun.

One of the first things, upon receiving command of a new boat, was to choose a name. Officially, X-craft were referred to by their numbers, but crews preferred names which, according to custom, should begin with the class letter, like *Syrtis* for an "S" class boat. There are not many suitable words beginning with "X" so our custom was to choose names beginning with "EX". We had chosen "*Exploit*", and told Cdr Rendel, who considered it a good name. ERA Coles said "I think that the engine should have a name too, Sir. Would you choose one for us before we take delivery, please."

"Yes, certainly, Coles," he replied with characteristic enthusiasm. "I will start thinking this very day."

X22 was being built at Chesterfield, thirty miles to the south-east, by H V Markham and Son. Cdr Rendel was the Admiralty representative, overseeing the building of two X-craft at each works, the third being Marshall, at Gainsborough. We three *X22* crew, having been brought up to date by the commander, took the train to Chesterfield and walked to Markhams. Here we were shown into a large building with tarpaulin screens over all doors to keep any but the essential workmen from seeing what was going on and there, fresh in her black paint, was *X22*.

"Does that look right?" asked the works manager, "We have never built a submarine before." It looked right to us, in fact, the more we saw of it, the better we liked it. The company had done it well.

"Is there anything you want us to do?" asked the works manager.

"Yes," said ERA Coles, "I would like three wheel keys to operate valves, please."

"Right, you shall have them," replied the works manager. "What are they like. Draw me one." There was the problem. Trying to convey the design of a three dimensional, unfamiliar object like a wheel key, on a two dimensional sheet of paper, is not easy, unless you are a draftsman in a drawing office, but Ginger Coles persevered, and with much scribbling and waving of hands, the idea was grasped, and the keys duly completed.

Our experience on *X5 - X10* was that soon after launching, moving parts became stiff to operate as rust took hold. Therefore, we asked if all parts could be thoroughly greased. The job was well done. They greased not only the internals of all valves, but the handwheels as well. But never mind, she was well built. This company had carried out other important contracts for Admiralty, and maintained a high standard. The works manager showed us a set of torpedo tubes under construction. These, he said, were for a destroyer and his employees took great pride in their work, and an interest in the recipient ship. The midget submarine was also an important contract but, being classified "secret", could not be discussed and therefore did not stimulate the employees, except those working on it, and they could not discuss it with others. Their usual products were, I understand, for collieries. They were nothing if not versatile, as Signalman Scott would say.

On the Sunday of our stand-by period, we were kindly invited by Works Manager Fred Williams, to his home for dinner. It was a memorable occasion. We met his wife and two daughters. The two young ladies, in their Sunday best I would imagine, waited at table, bringing hot pots skirted in snow white cloth. Everything else about the meal was also beautifully done. We were being honoured. Whether or not we deserved it, we enjoyed it. There are not many meals that one remembers after forty odd years.

Mr Williams told an anecdote as the meal progressed. It concerned a resident of Chesterfield who bought a second-hand cuckoo clock which wouldn't go. He took it apart, cleaned it, rebushed the bearings that were worn, reassembled and oiled it. He had two gears left over, but it started keeping time all right, until it came to the hour, when the cuckoo came out, tail first, and called "OO CUCK, OO CUCK."

The other improbable story concerning Chesterfield referred to its church with a crooked spire. Legend had it that the young ladies of that city had been renowned more for their beauty than their chastity. One day, a bride arrived who was both beautiful and chaste. The weathercock was so keen not to miss so rare a sight that he leaned over to look down, and bent the spire. City folk are waiting for another such bride to come to the church. She will enter by the opposite door so that the cock can look over the other way and straighten his steeple.

On his first visit to Markham's during our stand-by period, Cdr Rendel came up to the three of us in the large shed where *X22* was standing, near completion.

"I think we have the name for you, Coles," he said, in his enthusiastic manner. "We all know how important the Island of Malta is to the conduct of the war in the Mediterranean. Now, not everybody knows that, close to Malta, is a small island called 'Gozo'. It struck me that this would be a suitable name for a submarine's diesel engine. It has the right sound about it; besides, if ever you have engine trouble, you can say 'Go, Gozo, go!' Now, what do you think of that?" Ginge had a pleasant chuckle to show when he was really amused, and this name struck home with him.

"Thank you, Sir. Gozo it will be." And Gozo it was. Markham's kindly engraved a suitable brass plate, and fixed it to the front of the engine, next to the decompression lever which was provided for hand starting; not that we ever had to start by hand, nor did we ever have a moment's trouble with Gozo. But, if we had, we were all sure that he would be as good as his name, and respond to our elbow grease before we ran out of it. It may not be peeping too much into the future to tell you that when, months later, Ginge and I commissioned another X-craft, the engine was adorned with a similar brass plate engraved "Gozo II", a plate which Ginger still has.

X22, like all her older sisters, was taken from the builder's yard by rail. A special train was arranged, comprising locomotive, tender, small spacing wagon, the main long low flat top bogie wagon to carry her, a second spacing wagon, because she overhung each end, a passenger coach for us three, and the guard van. To hide her from public view, tarpaulins were lashed all over her. The visible profile, like that of a sweater girl, could not have been of anything other than what she was.

Travelling in one's own private train was the closest to royalty that any of us was likely to get. Markhams had packed us a fine hamper for the journey to Faslane on the Gairloch, north of the Firth of Clyde. We spent some time in the cab, stoking the boiler and keeping a good lookout which, we were horrified to see, the locomotive crew did not. No doubt they knew when to look for signals, but for the rest of the time, they had their backs to the engine. I suppose that, as they were in it, they must have had their backs to the front of the engine, if that makes it any clearer. However you say it, they trusted the system of signals and points setting to protect them, and us, from collision, and puffed on through the night.

At Faslane, a large floating crane lifted *X22* and swung her gently up off the wagon, out over the water, and down alongside the crane barge. A crowd of Markham's officers had assembled. The Managing Director's daughter performed a ceremony and gave her her name and number. We were surprised at this action. It is customary for the owner, namely Admiralty, to select someone to perform this rather special ceremony. Perhaps somebody up top somewhere agreed to this, but it took us by surprise. But our immediate concern was the safety of the craft at her first immersion. Coles was aboard, as soon as she floated, to check around inside, and to ensure that all valves were correctly shut, and that there were no leaks. All was well. The builders' representatives departed, and the Navy escort came alongside, took our overnight bags, and stood by while motor and engine were tested.

The fuel lines had to be vented of air, lubricating oil level checked, and a dozen other details attended to. I got into my Ursula suit, the submariners' alternative to oilskins, and my seaboots, and gave my first order as Commanding Officer.

"Engine clutch out, tail clutch in. Ready ahead, group down." We were to start our journey to Kames Bay, on motor, until clear of the crane barge. My orders were repeated from ERA Coles, seated at the steering position, forward in the control room. S/Lt Brooks was at the motor, engine and pumping controls, aft. He had already checked all of the batteries and electrical circuits at Markhams. I got up onto the casing, shut the hatch, and stood by the multi-purpose engine air induction trunk, voicepipe and guardrail, and conned her out into clear water. Carefully, taking time to check everything, the engine was started and we were underway on our first voyage, following our escort. We were all anxious lest something was not correct, but all was well. As *X22* entered the Clyde at the Tail of the Bank and proceeded south toward Bute, confidence gradually built up in this small vessel crammed with gear, pushing her first bow wave along one of the world's most famous waterways.

There followed, in the next weeks, the customary trials to prove the craft. She performed better than we would have dared hope. Every submarine had some defects on commissioning, but not this one. Our programme of trials was soon completed and exercises for crew training commenced. This was a repeat of what we had already been through in *X5 - 10*, and were also progressing well. It was the bane of Commander "Boy" Brown's life to have one craft after another report defects that put her out of action for days or even weeks. He was the Operations Officer, and had to get all craft through every phase in the given time. He was long-suffering, and took these frustrations well. He had a speech peculiarity, causing his "r"s to sound as "w"s, and a habit of calling each of us X-craft hands 'Colonel'. Joe Brooks did a water colour of him in a typical dilemma, having just been advised by one of us skippers, by phone, of a disabling defect. "Oh, you misewable Colonel. You have wuined my whole pwogwamme. Weport to me after coffee."

A group of senior Russian officers visited mother ship *HMS Titania (Tights)*, to examine X-craft, presumably with a view to building their own. I met them as they assembled aboard a small pontoon to which *X22* was moored They asked plenty of questions of me, then went to Joe with the same, and returned to me if the two answers differed at all. Three of them asked to be taken on a simulated attack. They made quite a crowd in the tiny control room as we ran out to a point one mile distant, dived, and set course for the centre of *Titania*. They asked endless questions as Joe adjusted the trim and I took periscope bearings and modified course accordingly.

We had half a mile to run when one of our visitors, an engineer, asked me about the arrangement of our tanks. I told him, pointing out their positions, and had another look at *Titania*. We would have had to go deep within minutes, to be sure of passing clear underneath. But the Russian was not satisfied, so I took the chart from the chart table, turned to the back, and, as quickly as I could, sketched a sectional view of the craft with the tanks. Then, raising the periscope again, I was alarmed to see the steel plates and rivets of *Titania's* side almost at our bow.

"Stop. Flood Q. Half astern. Forty feet." Air hissed from Q tank as the motor increased speed astern. THUMP went *"Tight's"* bottom against the periscope guards, where the upper deck compass was mounted.

"Stop. Slow ahead. Blow Q." and all was under control again as the ship passed quietly above us. But the looks of suspicion on the faces of the Russians could not be ignored. There was no light-hearted remark to ease the tension. Reassuring smiles on their faces were as absent as those of the Party officials atop Lenin's tomb during a May Day Parade in Red Square.

It was in *X22* that I made my first passage through Crinan Canal, from Ardrishaig on Loch Fyne to Crinan on the Sound of Jura. Thence our route led us past many of the islands of the Hebrides. We were to undergo this type of navigation exercise several times as it was closer to operational experience than traversing the calm waters of the Firth of Clyde. I will describe it in more detail on a subsequent occasion, but this was our first, and by the time the circuit was completed, and *X22* re-entered the sea-lock at Crinan, every crew member was tired. It takes several days at sea to adapt to sea routine and short periods of sleep. This exercise was too short for us to have gained our sea legs.

As we proceeded through the fourteen locks, and were in the last long reach, fatigue was upon us all. Joe was busy with his electrical maintenance routines in the control room, while Ginger Coles was steering and manning motor and engine controls from the after position. As there was nobody at the forward steering position where the voicepipe was located, telephones were in use between the upper deck and the helmsman.

I was on deck, conning *X22* along this long, narrow stretch of canal. At one point, I had called for five degrees of port rudder, but there was no reply. A little louder into the phone. "Port five!" Silence. *X22* was swinging slowly toward the right-hand bank.

"Stop!" very loud. The engine continued to run at half speed. *X22* reached the overhanging branches of a tree on the bank, and I was swept back along the casing at four knots. If she did not hit the bank soon, I would be pushed over the stern into the canal.

THUMP! She hit the bank and stopped, engine still driving ahead.

I burrowed forward again, through the leaves, twigs and branches, until I came to the hatch, forced it part way open against the foliage, and squeezed through into the W&D. Ginge was at his post and quickly stopped the engine in response to my signal. He was still wearing the telephone headset, unaware that the plug had become disconnected. He plugged in again, I returned to the casing, and with a few motor movements, X22 was in mid-canal, resuming her passage to Ardrishaig, none the worse for her run ashore.

Admiralty were concerned lest Germany should retaliate against units of the home fleet in Scapa, using weapons similar to our now successfully proven X-craft. All three entrances to Scapa were defended with nets, loops and hydrophone equipped patrol vessels, and it was considered prudent to make realistic tests. In January 1944, "Digger" McFarlane, who had commissioned X24, alias *Expeditious*, was selected to tow up to Pentland Firth, the strait between the Orkney islands and the Scottish coast, there to slip, dive, and to attempt to enter Scapa Flow undetected. X24 had numerous defects, and the exercise was put back a few days. When ready, X24 took the tow from *Syrtis*, who, in the process, got the tow around her propeller, causing further delay. That remedied, more defects occurred in X24. To cap it all, Digger confided to me that he had a pain in his lower gut, and suspected appendicitis. "Don't say anything," he said, "This exercise has been delayed long enough already." No doubt he was keen to achieve a success to compensate for the loss of X8. Not that he was in any way to blame for that misfortune, but, like the rest of us, he needed to complete something to contribute to the progress of the war.

Capt S12 made a decision to avoid further delays, and ordered McFarlane to take over X22, and me to take X24. So, the crews changed ships, and off went X22, under tow by *Syrtis*, while my crew started work repairing X24, which went on for weeks. No sooner was one crop of faults remedied than another sprang up. There were leaks in the HP air system, leaks from glands and hull joints. Valves stuck, the induction trunk jammed, and so on. The main hull joint aft started leaking. There were three sections to the hull, one forward of the W&D, the parallel control room, and a tapered section aft containing the engine and motor. The sections were joined by bolts through two inch wide end flanges. To fix this leak, *X24* was taken up on Varbel's slipway at Ardmaleish Point, two miles across Kames Bay to the north. Here, the after section was unbolted and moved away from the main section. The flanges were found to have distorted during construction, and the resulting gaps to have been filled with putty; not good submarine practice. Ginger Coles and our second ERA, Fred Stanton, spent the daylight hours of the following weeks hand filing the two inch flanges over their entire length, until they were true.

The interior of the slipway shed was dark, cold and cheerless. Notwithstanding the miserable conditions, these two men, assisted by the stoker in our towing crew, persevered with this considerable task and many others, until *X24* was virtually rebuilt. Both ERA's had been proficient tradesmen before enlistment, a factor leading to the ultimate reliability of *X24*. As a testimony to their thorough work, she now stands on concrete blocks as part of the Submarine Museum at *HMS Dolphin*, Gosport, England. She has been unbolted at that same flange, to allow visitors to see inside. Whenever I visit her, I reflect on the feat of workmanship that converted failure into success.

On Thursday, 17th February 1944, while we were still refitting *X24*, *Syrtis* towed *X22* into Pentland Firth and a raging storm. The officer of the watch was washed from the conning tower as waves built up in this turbulent tideway. Something could be seen floating in *Syrtis'* wake as she turned to retrace her track. In the rough sea it was taken to be the man overboard. She moved slowly toward to pick him up when the shock of a collision told them the worst. They had struck and sunk *X22*. No one was recovered.

On completion of her self-refit, her operational crew took *X24* to Loch Goil for two lots of trials, the first over the sound detection range at Loch Goilhead, to be followed by a deep dive to the designed depth of three hundred feet. The sound trials were most interesting. With the craft secured fore and aft between buoys, I came ashore into the laboratory to watch the instruments indicating noise levels received by hydrophones suspended from buoys out on the loch. I spoke by phone to Joe, who was in command aboard *X24*, instructing him to run one component at a time; main motor, pump, periscope hoist, HP air valves, and so on. Scientists recorded the noise levels and commented on their values and whether these were normal. I learned which auxiliaries to avoid using within certain range of a patrol vessel. Then the craft surfaced, cast off from the buoys, and proceeded up and down the loch on engine, then submerged on motor, at various speeds. The hydrophones told us that the HP air manifold shrieked when a certain valve was opened. Later, Coles and Stanton investigated, and found a drilling error which was causing the organ pipe effect, and rectified it.

That night, as was the custom, the X-craft and escorting drifter crews stopped off, on their walk ashore, at the Loch Goilhead Hotel. The village of Loch-goilhead had adopted the submarine service and contributed generously to their entertainment and comfort. Hospitality at the hotel was always warm and generous. There was the occasion during winter, when the beer drawing equipment suffered freezing of some part that resulted in drinking water steadily diluting the beer. It took a long time to be noticed, and was probably a good thing in the long run.

But, this night, nothing was diluted. I could not keep up with the glasses of whisky that were lining up in front of me, treats by local men who had watched our endeavours in the loch. At a late stage I called a halt, and made my way toward the residence of Mrs Thomas, with whom I had stayed on a previous occasion. Her house overlooked the loch, one and a half miles from the pub. I was not at all sure of my bearings. It was the cold air, I thought. Stumbling up the steep road, I came past two men leaning on a gate, and asked if they knew where Mrs Thomas lived. They did not. Further on, I saw two more men, and asked them.

"We already told you, we don't know." Next thing I recall was being awakened by Joe. I was, miraculously, in my bed at Mrs Thomas' house.

"How do you feel?" asked Joe.

"Terrible," I answered.

"Well, wait till you see Ginge."

I got up and went into the next room. There was Ginge, sitting up in bed, with a blood-red bandage covering his head. It all had a good explanation as you would expect: Ginge had left on his homeward way when the party broke up. Climbing the steep road, he heard calls for help from the still loch. Responsible fellow that he was, he rushed to give assistance, clearing the parapet wall at a bound and landing on his head on the beach fifteen feet below. Help in the first instance was called for by sailors, from our drifter, who had jumped into the first boat they found on the beach, shoved off only to find there were no oars. Help was now needed by Ginge more than they. This he got in the form of three stitches from a local doctor, so he was on the mend by the time I saw him.

For the deep dive, we rendezvoused with a boom vessel at the junction of Loch Goil and Loch Long, where there was sufficient water depth. *X24* stopped under the lifting horns, and shackled on the heavy wire sling and cable with which she would be lowered and, if necessary, hauled back to the surface. A telephone was connected, and down we went, vertically. At three hundred feet we phoned to say "low enough" and examined every fitting for leaks. There was a ticking sound coming from the periscope dome, where three small circular windows were fitted. The top one of these had a crack across one of the three layers of glass. As I looked, another crack flicked across the glass. There was a brass cover outside the window, operated from a spindle which was mounted through the hull. I tried to swing the cover over, but the water pressure was too much. Joe fetched our ensign staff, placing it under the spindle so we could both lift. The spindle rose, I swung the brass cover across to cover the glass as all three layers cracked and fell into the control room. I looked at the other two windows. It was pitch dark outside, but no leaks or cracks were in evidence. After writing a list of leaks from various joints and glands, I phoned the boom vessel and asked to be hauled up. This was safer than blowing main ballast, which could bring us up underneath her. That went well. On the surface we came to full buoyancy, unshackled, thanked the crew above us, and set off for the Gairloch again, this time for de-perming and degaussing adjustment as explained below.

Here, we went into a space between two timber jetties. Once moored in position, a loop of electric cable with inflatable buoyancy, floated up from the depths to surround us. A diesel generator on one jetty was started, and current passed through the cable. Then a "Boffin" came aboard and operated the degaussing control panel on the port side of the control room. He switched so that the amps flowed one way through *X24*'s coils in the keel, then the other way, reduced the amps and kept repeating this procedure till he had reduced the amps to zero.

"What are you doing?" I asked him.

"Cycling down the PLM," he answered. Ask a silly question, and you will get a silly answer, so they say. In fact, it was not a silly answer. He was reducing the permanent magnetism running lengthwise in the hull, but it sounded like touring by bicycle.

The proof of all this amp juggling came next day, when we moved a few miles south to Largs Bay, where Admiralty had laid test loops. We ran south and then north, over these, and then left for Kames Bay, our tour of special tests completed. I was impressed with the thoroughness of all this treatment of *X24* to make her as undetectable as possible, and felt confident that she would live up to her name and be expeditious when next entering and leaving an enemy harbour.

Testing of the Scapa defences was now considered urgent. I was ordered to hoist *X24* aboard *Bonaventure* for transit to Scapa, and to make a submerged approach through each entrance. Fortunately, by continued working on the part of my crew, *X24* was defect free, for the present anyway. We hoisted and proceeded north. The arrival at Scapa was exciting. The weather was good as we entered from the south and saw units of the Home Fleet at their moorings, including battleship *HMS Anson*. A Navy escort was provided and the first run was made next day. One reason for our mandatory escort was to make clear to all that the small submarine was "one of ours" and not to be fired on, rammed, or otherwise maltreated. It was also useful in case of defects arising, though I cannot recall ever having to be towed home. We had practised and were becoming proficient in self-refit.

The three submerged runs through the entrances went without hitch from our point of view. Knowing that we could reliably cut through an A/S net, these were opened for us, rather than having to repair them afterwards. I had learned, from my days in *Bluebell*, the conditions which affected asdic and hydrophones adversely, and made the best of this experience then, keeping speed down, using auxiliary machinery sparingly, steering through the wake of other vessels, keeping close to the bottom, and other techniques. Once through, we would surface, signal by aldis to our escort, and be led back to *Bonaventure*. I noticed as we passed *Anson*, a growing number of officers accumulating at the quarterdeck guardrail to get a glimpse of this unusual craft flying the white ensign, conned by a solitary figure who seemed to be gliding on water. In heavy seas, the casing was frequently invisible.

Joe and I decided that next day we would observe the Naval custom of "sounding off" to *HMS Anson*, she being the senior ship. Upon surfacing after completing penetration of the defences of the second entrance, I flashed to our escort "Please pass close astern of *Anson*." She acknowledged and altered course accordingly. As we approached, I saw officers gathering, and called Joe up onto the casing. We were dressed in uniform, with caps, as we should be. Joe had a bosun's call, the silver whistle used for commands and ceremonies. At our closest point, Joe sounded "Still" on the call. I saluted to the quarterdeck. The battleship's quartermaster sounded "Still". Every one of the forty or so officers stood at attention, returning my salute. *Anson* sounded "Carry on", and Joe did the same. Everybody carried on, and *X24* did likewise, toward *Bonaventure*. We reckoned that forty salutes in return for one, was good value.

Next day, we were returning from the third and last trial entry, and noticed that Admiral Sir Bruce Fraser's flagship, battleship *Duke of York* was at her mooring. It was rough, waves breaking over the casing. I was wearing wet weather gear, and in no mood for ceremonials. Without any request, our escort led us astern of the *Duke of York*. I called Joe up to have a look at the Flagship. He took one look, aimed the aldis lamp at her signal bridge, and flashed "What a big bastard." She answered "T". That was all. I said to Joe, "You shouldn't have said that. It officially will be delivered to the admiral and the captain. It does not matter to me, I am not a career officer, but you are."

"No," said Joe, "I suppose I shouldn't." But it was done. I could have made another signal saying that my former signal was OOW to OOD, and referred to the size and power of the ship, but hoped that it would be taken in the spirit in which it was sent, one of admiration, and left it at that.

I did see the Admiral's Flag Lieut next day, and expressed my hope that the signal got no further than the signal bridge. He looked knowingly, smiled, and winked.

"Don't you worry," he said, but nothing else. The admiral visited *Bonaventure*. We were lined up on the quarterdeck to receive him.

"Were you on deck crossing the Flow yesterday, Shean?" he asked.

"Yes, Sir."

"It must have been a bit wet!" In the Navy, 'wet' can mean dumb or stupid. Was he getting one back? Next night, he had Joe and me aboard *Duke of York* for dinner.

The day of the dinner, I had been to a discussion on the exercise, chaired by Fraser. There were officers responsible for boom defence (nets) loops, hydrophones and visual patrols, giving reports on their success. Each reported with seeming confidence that they would have no difficulty in detecting and preventing entry if an enemy midget submarine should attack. After the meeting concluded, each came to me, saying that if I did this or that, I could enter undetected.

Navigation was an important skill to be learned and exercised by all commanding officers, both operational and passage. *X24* was sent on her first, and her crew's second, ocean cruise from Kames Bay, west through the Kyles of Bute, up Loch Fyne to Ardrishaig, through Crinan Canal into the Sound of Jura, then around the Islands of Mull, Muck, Eigg, Rhum and Canna, returning by the Sound of Jura and the outward route (map at end of chapter 16). This was good fun for the most part, all on the surface at full speed. It included one night at sea, thus exercising watchkeeping in two watches, Joe being in charge of one watch with Ginge, and I of the other with Sub Lt Frank Ogden.

The OOW would be on deck most of the time, and the second man in the forward control position where he could steer, operate the diving and surfacing valves, and communicate via the voicepipe with the OOW. If the order to dive were received, he would call the "watch below" (men off watch). He could still dive the craft without delay if it were necessary, anticipating the arrival of the planesman at the after control position by the time the craft submerged, otherwise she would go under with the engine running, but this was not likely, because nobody had far to go to reach his station.

It was winter, and the small islands looked beautiful with snow on their hills. The sea was usually rough once the shelter of Mull was left astern, and so it was. For the first time, I experienced long high seas breaking over the deck, as I clung to the safety rail on the induction trunk. Frequently the whole casing would be covered with foaming water, the only visible objects being the trunk and me. It was the nearest I would ever get to walking on water. We had the customary drifter escort, where the OOW was a sub lieut, less experienced than we were. It was night by the time we reached the Firth of Lorne, south of Mull, approaching the Island of Fladda, with its lighthouse which marked the entrance to the Sound of Jura, through which we were to return. Joe was on watch and I asleep in the control room bunk. It was very rough. We were ahead of schedule and proceeding at half speed. The drifter OOW must have got himself lost and signalled Joe "Steer north." I would have told him, literally, where to go, but Joe obliged, only to observe a few minutes later, ocean swell breaking on the rocky shore of the Ross of Mull right ahead of us, so he resumed the former, correct, course. During these course alterations, *X24* was rolling through wide angles until there was a bang, which Ginge reported to Joe, up the voicepipe, with his joyful chuckle,

"The kettle has been rolled out of its bracket and hit the skipper on the head." The skipper must have been deep in sleep because I had no recollection of anything unusual which, I suppose, it wasn't.

When I came on watch, Joe told me about the signal. He said that the drifter had made further signals on the same theme, but as we had kept to our course, it did the same. Dawn was coming. I looked for Fladda light, and saw it on the expected bearing. I flashed the drifter, "See you at the lighthouse," increased to full speed and set course to leave Fladda to starboard. This island was composed of slate which, over many years, had been quarried until the only thing left standing was the lighthouse. We soon passed it, well ahead of the drifter, and steered to the east of the Sound of Jura. South of Fladda are the islands of Scaba and Jura. Between them is the famous Gulf of Corryvrecken and its mighty whirlpool, and I gave it a respectfully wide berth. I could hear the roar of the waters as we passed.

Arriving at Crinan, we entered the sea-lock and secured, awaiting the drifter, which, it seemed, we were now escorting. Presently, she secured beside us, the gates shut, and water flooded in through the sluices. In ten minutes we reached the level of the basin, opened the top gates, and moved X24 ahead on the motor to a vacant berth alongside the masonry wharf. Here were fishing boats of various sizes and, on the wharf, fisher and other folk, all curious to have a close look at this unusual craft. The pressure hull was barely visible as we were now floating in fresh water at a lower level than usual. Also, it was covered full length by the casing, which was really just a deck to walk on and locker space for cutters and ropes, and had metal cut away at regular intervals to prevent air from being trapped when diving. This puzzled one young lass, who exclaimed with disgust, "Och, it's full o' holes. You must get awfu' wet."

Near the sea-lock stood the Crinan Hotel. While waiting for the next lock-gates to open, all the crew went ashore to the hotel, where we bought a half-pint of beer each. I phoned through to a canalside inn near Ardrishaig to book an evening meal. We sat on the seat outside the hotel to drink our beer, and saw the next lock-gates opening. Quickly draining our mugs, we hurried back to *X24* and got underway.

Steering in the canal was an art which must be quickly acquired, otherwise the craft would keep running into one bank or other. Steering a fishing boat would not be difficult because the helmsman could see where he was heading. Even so, a sharp turn near Crinan was known as "Propeller Bend" because of the number knocked off when sterns swung too close to the outer bank. Conning a submarine, where the OOW can see but not steer, calls for more care. Along the straights we kept to the centre, but on the bends, steered a little toward the outer bank. This caused a wave to build up between craft and shore and kept her from striking the bank.

On arrival near the Ardrishaig end, I stopped her alongside the left-hand bank, made fast to bollards, and called the crew up to go ashore to the inn for a lovely meal of bacon and eggs, fresh from nearby farms. Then it was off to the final lock and Loch Fyne, which led us back to Bute.

Following this successful exercise, the Passage crew were sent in charge of *X24* around the Mull of Kintyre, and north to Crinan. Somehow, they had navigation difficulties and put into West Loch Tarbet instead. Now, when one is in one loch while thinking he is in another, the chart may look as though it fits, but there are bound to be differences, and one was the presence of rocks where deep water was expected. As *X24* approached this hazard, a nearby trawler hoisted international signal flag "U", meaning "You are running into danger." Willie called to Frank down the voicepipe to ask the meaning of the signal, but Frank did not know either, so *X24* ran on the rocks. She came off without serious damage, but other defects had occurred. Willie did not know which Loch they were in, and all were exhausted, so they moored her, went ashore, telephoned *Varbel*, and asked for help.

Joe, Ginge, and I went by boat to West Loch Tarbet while the others were returning to base. We worked on the defects, one relating to the engine clutch which would not remain engaged. To get us home, we made temporary repairs and left for Crinan. On arrival in the basin, we found it frozen over, but the ice was thin and *X24* seemed to enjoy breaking it into small pieces as she moved onto the next lock.

We were becoming accustomed, by now, to transiting Crinan Canal, and all went well until we had locked out at Ardrishaig and were running south in Loch Fyne. Here our temporary clutch repair tossed it in, and while the engine still ran sweetly, the propeller did not. We stopped the engine and I wriggled aft and put a large lashing around the shaft to hold the clutch in the engaged position. Off we went again, secure in the knowledge that a stout length of rope was more reliable than intricate links and levers, just so long as we did not have to stop in a hurry, because the engine did not like being run backwards and there was no quick way of declutching it. Fortunately, we had an uninterrupted run, having to stop only upon arrival at the mooring at *Varbel*. I still could not go astern to get the way off her, so leaped onto the mooring buoy with the rope and carried on into the water on the other side, but not for long. I was out and back on the buoy almost before I was wet.

X24 passing battleship Duke of York in Scapa; Joe Brooks with signalling lamp: "What a big bastard." No reply from Duke of York.

Max Shean in X24 demonstrating attack technique to Russian flag officers, who diverted his attention during approach, hence delay in going deep and damage to the upper deck compass.

CHAPTER TWENTY ONE

BERGEN

Crippling *Tirpitz* had been clearly a worthy mission for X-craft. There were not many suitable targets, when the cost of mounting an attack was reckoned. One consideration was whether it would be a more effective use of resources to employ a big submarine and an X-craft for a month attacking any selected target in a harbour, or to send the big submarine on patrol to sink whatever came within range. Such decisions were made at the level of the Flag Officer Submarines, no doubt in consultation with his flotilla captains like Captains Banks and Fell. We only knew about targets once approved.

One use was for gathering intelligence prior to the invasion of Europe which, as we all know now, started in June 1944. It was late 1943 before *X24* was ready for action, though defects did still occur, but at less frequent intervals. A group of Army and Navy personnel came to Varbel, exercising with X-craft to evaluate their suitability for landing and retrieving intelligence gatherers. These trials took place in Etterick Bay, on the south side of Bute, at night. It took some time for the Army and Navy to get to know each other's requirement. The rubs that occurred were similar to those prior to the *Tirpitz* operation, when the Charioteers joined our crews. Having put soldiers, dressed in lightweight waterproof suits, into the sea, off a featureless beach at night, it took time to locate them two hours later, especially when the sea was rough. They would want us to venture closer in than we considered safe. To save them a long swim, we risked running aground. On a falling tide, this could prove fatal.

On the lighter side, Joe was somewhat put out when one of the swimmers, having regained *X24*, came aft in the control room and sat, dripping, on the gyro compass. On another occasion, *X24* was returning from a similar exercise and approaching the drifter, where Ginge was waiting.   Suddenly he saw dense black smoke billow from the engine exhaust outlet.   Fearing a serious engine malfunction, he lost no time in boarding as soon as we berthed, and made straight for the engine. What he found was soon remedied. The swimmer had draped his wet clothes over the engine to dry them, and his underpants had slipped and been drawn into the air intake, thus starving the engine of air.

Each crew member in turn lost enthusiasm for the reconnaissance role.   Nevertheless, the ruffled feathers, or should I say scales, were smoothed by Willie Banks and *X24* was allocated to other duties, much to Ginger's delight. He was now able to resume his rightful place in the operational crew, having previously to make space for the swimmers.

It was Ken Hudspeth who eventually took these courageous men to the French coast to survey the selected beaches. *X24* had run aground during one exercise, and, although she came off quickly after pumping water overboard from the compensating tank, there was a minor confrontation between the parties.   As Willie Banks explained to the Army Officer involved, "These X-craft crews are good chaps, but they do become Prima Donnas." I agree with this statement, in fact it is one of the results of intensive training to become single minded. Lt Cdr Boy Brown sent for me one day to discuss a confidential report which he was making on X-craft officers. This was a routine matter in which one rule was that anything derogatory had to be read to the officer concerned. After a very reassuring introduction to the subject, our Operations Officer said, "While you are here, Maxie, you might just be interested in what I have said about you."   There were the usual words like skilful, courageous, determined, reliable, dedicated and so on, finishing with, "This officer has, to a certain extent, overcome a tendency to be pig-headed." Fair enough.

The job which was given to *X24* was a real challenge, right down our alley, we believed. Germany was using Bergen, as well as other Norwegian harbours, as a U-boat base. In the Laksvaag industrial area, two miles south of the city centre, there was a large floating dock, and several small ones without pumps. These, with U-boat contained, could be floated into the large dock which would pump itself up to full buoyancy, allowing draining of the small dock, which would then be refloated. U-boats could be dry docked in this manner without occupying the large dock for more than an hour or two. On completion of maintenance or repair work, the U-boat could be refloated by simply flooding the small dock. It was important to the battle of the Atlantic, from the Allies' point of view, to destroy the floating dock, and that was my job.

The obstacles to be reckoned with on this operation were the 40 mile approach from the open sea, through confined waterways patrolled by German "E" boats (like our MLs, fitted with echo detection and depth charges), two declared minefields, possibly loops, anti-torpedo nets, and the busy ship and boat traffic (map at end of chapter). In every reconnaissance photo, boats were to be seen, hurrying about the waters, close to the dock.

A net was laid close to the Kames Bay floating dock to simulate the Laksvaag arrangement. We practised attacks on this dock until we could find it every time, even without using the periscope in the final half mile of the approach. The technique of attack had been thoroughly discussed between Captains Banks and Fell, Boy Brown, Joe and myself. Banks considered that we should remain at periscope depth until inside the anti-torpedo net, which had a narrow opening close to the adjacent land-backed coal wharf, where ships were frequently berthed. I was concerned that if we stayed so long, and approached that close at periscope depth, when the casing was only eight feet below the surface, there was a high risk of sighting or collision. I considered that we could safely use the periscope, even in calm conditions, to within half a mile of the dock. At that point, a compass bearing on the end of the net would give a clear approach course. Once past the net and before reaching the coal wharf, an alteration of course to port would bring us under the dock which could be seen, in outline at least, through the upper window, or scuttle as it was called. The point at which to alter course to port would be indicated by the water depth. If we approached at that depth and slow speed, the turning position would be as soon as we touched bottom. The dock could be recognised by her fore and aft orientation, which was nearly at right angles to that of the nearby coal ships. On the charts and reconnaissance photos there was no large berth on the same fore and aft compass bearing as the dock.

The captains left the details of the approach to me. It was, after all, a matter of judgement. With their method, there would be no doubt about getting under the right target, though there was a greater risk of detection before we got that far, and the increased probability of being sunk by collision. That minefields were there, we were assured by Norwegians who came to brief us, but so were the safe channels, which they identified on our charts. There were lookout posts along the shores of West Byfjord which led into the harbour. There were no A/S nets, though patrol craft were active over the whole of the forty mile approach. If we had to abandon ship and go ashore, contact people were available. Their names and addresses we had to remember. We were conscious of the terrible risks such people were taking, and resolved to take extreme care if it came to contacting them.

Further navigation exercises were carried out in one of the sea-lochs running east from Loch Cairnbawn and were reached by navigating the narrow tide-swept channels at Kylesku. This turbulent strait had to be traversed on the surface, but, as soon as the waters widened and deepened, X-craft would dive and remain so throughout their exercise, practising navigation up and down the loch while remaining invisible; not that there were many folk living in these mountainous, lonely parts.

One fine day, we had spent the forenoon stealthily traversing the depths of Loch Glencoul. I had observed through the periscope a farm at the head of the loch, which elsewhere had quite steep sides. We decided to manoeuvre the craft close to the shore, where we would be hidden from view of the farm folk by a headland, to surface and put two ashore to walk to the farm and buy some milk. This was done with great care, in accordance with the object of the exercise, to remain undetected. I went ashore with Joe and walked the mile or so. There was nobody in the field, so we went up to the front door and knocked. The farmer's wife, Mrs McLeod, came to the door and provided some rich fresh milk, but would take no payment. I suppose we should have expected that. We thanked her and retraced our steps along the lochside. She had made no remarks and asked no questions, even though we were probably the first Navy personnel in uniform who had ever appeared on her doorstep.

Joe and I felt that we should return her kindness in some way, however small, so, before next day's exercise in the same loch, we bought some chocolate from the ship's canteen. Repeating the same secret manoeuvre, Joe and I stalked along the steep bank again at lunchtime. This time, the farmer was stacking hay in a field near the water's edge. His little girl was sitting in the hay.

"Hello," he called to us as we approached. "We are surprised to see you. Wee Ishbel thought that it was a different submarine today."

HMS/M Sceptre, commanded by Lt McIntosh, was to tow us, a happy choice because we had got to know him before the *Tirpitz* Op, and besides, he was Australian. As there was to be no diving, we took S/Lt Frank Ogden as fourth man. Frank was capable of fulfilling any duty in the craft. S/Lt "Willie" Britnell was CO of the passage crew, although we decided, in view of the comparatively short distance, that the operational crew would do most of the outward bound tow, and the passage crew would bring her home. The code name for the operation was "Guidance".

My mother, in one of her letters, told me that her aged uncle Charlie had died, that he had been a seaman, in his youth, in square riggers, and that among his belongings was a caul. This is a membrane which covered a baby's head at birth and believed, by some, to be a lucky charm and preservative against drowning. She enclosed it in the envelope. This was the first I had heard of such a thing, so I showed it to my crew, who immediately advised that it should be carried aboard *X24*. We already had Mickey Mouse, a Tiki donated by Bernie Tonks, *Bonaventure's* RDF Officer from New Zealand, and a wish-bone from some unfortunate chicken. With such an array of good luck, who needed skill?

Willie Britnell deserves further mention at this stage. This large, good-humoured man was, among other things, *X24*'s stores officer. He drew food and other supplies from *Bonaventure's* store.

Now, this may sound like an automatic process, devoid of need for any initiative, but, not so. There are stores, and stores. The basic needs were automatic, if you like, but there were some perks for the getting, depending on the approach. Willie had the right approach. *X24* had tinned fruit, fruit juices and trimmings that other craft may not have known about. It was also Willie who convinced the stores officer that the Bergen Operation could not succeed without a flagon of rum. Besides skill in this important endeavour, Willie was also a competent passage commanding officer.

Ian MacIntosh and I had a good rapport. We had discussed all that we could think of. The feeling was one of confidence, even though no X-craft had, as yet, returned from a successful attack. From 0900 Sunday 9th April, 1944, the time we proceeded under tow from HHZ, things went as they should. There were defects cropping up from time to time, but nothing beyond one of the crew's ability to make good. Joe was always thorough in his supervision of electrical circuits, testing them with his Wee Megger every day, and, when dampness set in, drying them with his electric hair dryer. This improbable appliance proved to be excellent also for drying seaboots, which kept water in, as well as out. Ginge was always busy, when not steering and keeping depth simultaneously at the after control position, attending to some mechanical component which leaked or became inoperative. Frank did his share with watchkeeping and log writing. He did the position plotting during tricky navigation as when negotiating a minefield or attacking, and also his share of meal preparation. I kept the periscope lens clean.

The passage crew, S/Lt Willie Britnell, ERA Syd Rudkin, LTO "Lofty" Element, and Stoker Bill Gillard, were in charge of *X24* as we left HHZ and headed for Burra Firth in the Shetlands, escorted by *HMS Alecto* and Norwegian destroyer *Narvik*. Sea conditions were near calm, and remained that way. *X24* dived at 1006, and *Sceptre* at 1024, to adjust diving trim, then surfaced and proceeded on engines at eight knots. It was arranged to reduce to five knots to allow *X24* to surface and ventilate for ten minutes at 0700, 1300 and 1900 and at 2100 to recharge batteries and HP air.

Next day, at 1645, without warning, *Narvik* dropped a depth charge two and a half miles away. *X24* surfaced to find out what was going on, her phone having failed two hours earlier. There was no explanation, and *X24* remained on the surface as we entered Burra Firth and anchored for the night. The tow rope was found to be chafing at its after end, due to *X24* overriding it as *Sceptre* pitched in the swell. This was made good, and at noon, Tuesday 11th, we got underway with the Operational crew aboard *X24*.

At 0337 on the 12th, *Sceptre* dived. The phone was working satisfactorily. When *X24* surfaced to charge at 2100, there was trouble with the compressor, but we had enough air, so were not worried. Next day, at 1835, *Sceptre* saw, through her periscope, an outward bound U-boat on the surface, 800 yards away. This was satisfactory for torpedo attack, had it not been for the restraint in our sailing instruction. This was the second time I had felt like an obstacle in the way of a submarine captain!

That morning, *X24*'s bilge suction blocked. We always kept bilges dry, and while the amount of water to be removed was not so much as to endanger our safety, it was poor seamanship to have bilges half full. It was good for morale to have everything shipshape and Bristol fashion, or, as Scott would say, "Nothing, if not smart." Ginge had tried a spanner on the offending valve, but it resisted being taken apart. He was already doing a more important job, so he returned to that. Having nothing better to do at the time, I took his spanner and another long bar of metal, recalling another observation of Archimedes, "Give me a place to stand, and I will move the earth." He was speaking of the mechanical advantage provided by a lever. I found a place to stand, which was the first difficulty in such close quarters, and applied the bar as one lever, to the spanner, as another. The valve, out of respect to that learned Greek of yore, yielded, and I was able to remove the cover and the blocking debris already sucked up from the bilge. First, there was a scrap of insulating tape. This was clearly Joe's department, and he was duly apologetic for having let his waste material fall into the bilge. Next came to light a split pin, as used by the ERA to secure something onto a shaft. Ginger paused a moment from his important job to mumble an apology. Finally came a wad of periscope paper, as used by the skipper to clean the periscope lens. I had nothing to say except that I would take no disciplinary action against the others this time.

Meanwhile, *Sceptre* and *X24* were forging ahead at eight knots toward the Norwegian coast. The tendency to porpoise was always present, but, by close attention to depth, hull angle, and the careful use of hydroplanes, not to overcorrect and so to start the craft oscillating up and down, all went well. This type of oscillation was referred to in University as "simple harmonic motion". It helped to know the right words and also what others had learned about it; that it will go on indefinitely unless damped. This means to take some of the energy out of whatever is moving, at each cycle. This was what I did in *X6* on my first tow, and is what most humans do, instinctively, whenever they encounter it, though they probably don't use those terms. Joe was expert at depth keeping, and could maintain it accurately without loss of concentration, for hours. In brief, we had here a crew who were good at what was needed, to get a submarine from here to there, and back.

Our tow rope was manilla and held, with even a working telephone. On Thursday 13th, Mac called me to surface to look ahead where the island of Fedje, off the Norwegian coast, was visible.

"Keep a good lookout for aircraft, and dive immediately if you see one."

We surfaced by pumping No 2 main ballast to conserve HP air, and blew Nos 1 and 3 partly. The sea was calm so we would not need full buoyancy, only sufficient to keep her up if the W&D should fill while I was getting out. I got into this compartment, shut the lower doors, opened the main hatch, sprang up and shut it again quickly. It was uncanny to see *X24* moving ahead at five knots, silently and with no visible means of propulsion. *Sceptre* was submerged. There were no aircraft in sight. Presently, a periscope emerged from the water right ahead. It was like the arm, clad in white samite, mystic, wonderful, that caught King Arthur's Excalibur and drew it down into the lake. I waved at it. Further ahead, beyond my horizon, was a dim outline of mountainous land.

That night, as soon as twilight faded, at 2050, we reached the slipping position.

"I have brought you five miles closer to the land," said Mac over the phone. "This will give you a start. When you spot us tomorrow night, signal the letters 'MAC' and I'll know who it is. Good luck. Slip now."

We were already on the surface and could see nothing except, barely, *Sceptre's* dark outline. I called down the voicepipe "Ready ahead on engine. Slip the tow." I went forward, opened the door in the casing over the towing bolt, and unplugged the telephone cable. The heavy steel securing cam at the port end rotated slowly, the stout pin swung to starboard, and the tow bar, with six hundred feet of manilla, ran forward and sank. I reset the pin, came aft, and called below "Secure the towing slip," then "Slow ahead." A cloud of mist rose from the stern, the engine rumble started, and *X24* moved forward toward Norway again. Within minutes, we had increased to full speed into the darkness. We could have been anywhere for all I could see, but I had no doubt that, at the estimated time, Fedje Horden Light would appear. The Germans had, upon occupation, extinguished all navigation lights showing to seaward, but the shoreward sectored lights continued to show. Right on time, the light appeared on our port beam. We ran on for two miles, then turned to starboard to run through Fejeosen to Hjelte Fjord, inside the outer row of islands toward West Byfjord twenty five miles to the south. For the first time, we were in enemy defended waters. I had a tingling sensation in my legs. Not the shaking caused by fear eighteen months earlier, at *Dolphin*; this was excitement.

My feelings of elation were modified a little when Ginge called up the voicepipe, "We will have to stop the engine. Water is coming out of the cooling system."

"Very good. Stop engine." The engine stopped. Soon, Ginge was back.

"It's caused by the compressor. I have declutched it. You can run the engine now."

"Right. Thank you. Full ahead, on engine." The engine started and we were away again with our bow and stern waves making arrows on the black water. Soon, Ginge was back on the casing.

"We have got one full group of air, and two part full. I

don't know what is wrong with the compressor, and it is hot back there. The compressor is close to the exhaust, and that is damned hot."

"Allright Ginge. Tell No1 that we will carry on. We have enough air for three or four surfacings if we are careful. We can pump out No 2 main ballast, and that is nearly enough in calm water. Tell him not to use any air unnecessarily." Ginge went below and we pushed on. An hour later, he came up again.

"It was the third stage bush, leaking air into the cooling water jacket. I have removed it, and replaced the seals. The compressor is running, and seems OK."

"Well done Ginge; in that heat and space too. I bet that you are the first Tiffy who has replaced compressor seals within enemy waters."

There were no patrols to be seen but, as island after island slipped by to starboard, the loom of bright lights became visible on our starboard bow. They appeared to be static, if not permanent, so we kept on. The inshore system of navigation lights was great. Each showed a white sector along the navigable channel, a red sector to one side and green to the other. Heading toward or away from each light in turn, one had only to steer to keep within the white sector to be safe from natural hazards and, we observed, the declared minefields as well. So we were able to negotiate the first of these on the surface, in the dark, at full speed. Well before dawn we had proceeded as far as was advisable on engine. Its noise, and that of the propeller at full speed, could be detected by hydrophones miles off. The engine was stopped, and the motor run at speed for three knots. Buoyancy was reduced. I opened the hatch and stood in the W&D ready to dive quickly. At 0230, well before dawn started to break, we quietly dived to forty feet. For at least an hour there would not be enough light to see through the periscope. Our position was certain; clear of the first minefield, and in a waterway wide and deep.

An hour later, at periscope depth, I was able to take bearings on landmarks to verify our position. It seemed little different from being in Loch Striven. At 0550 we turned to port, into Byfjord, and entered the second minefield. Vessels of many kinds were doing the same. This was reassuring in that we must have been in the swept channel, but meant that we could not stay at periscope depth for fear of collision. Back to twenty five feet we went. Frank plotted our position and gave me the time to alter course. There was a dog-leg in the swept channel. It would have been good to have taken bearings at that point, but on balance, it seemed better to rely on dead reckoning, taking good care to keep on course, which Ginger was doing without any urging, and to keep accurate record of course, speed and times. After each of the two course alterations, I was relieved to hear the sound of propellers throbbing overhead. It was a busy channel. At our rate of progress, we should arrive by 0900, probably the busiest time in any field of activity.

When Frank's plot showed that we were clear of the second minefield, we altered course to starboard toward Laksvaag, and depth to ten feet. As soon as the periscope broke surface, there, right ahead, was a black patrol boat. Clearly visible were the swastika flag and a crew member relieving himself over the stern. Behind us, further away, was another, similar boat. I took a bearing on Laksvaag, noted the concrete submarine pens to the right, and went to twenty five feet. Then it was that we heard the 'ping...ping...ping' of an echo detector, sounding on our hull. This did not mean that we had been detected, but it was possible. I ordered a short period of increased revolutions on the motor, and altered course twenty degrees to port, then forty degrees to starboard, then back on course. Presently the 'ping' went silent, and we continued on. Another fifteen minutes, when our position should be within one mile of the target, we returned to periscope depth. Ginge was ready to flood Q tank in case we had to get down in a hurry. Joe came accurately to ten feet, and up went the periscope.

All was clear in our immediate vicinity, though there was some haze over the dock area. Checking our course, we continued on, taking peeps frequently. At 0800 I could see the dock 850 yards away, flooded down. To its right were two ships at coal berths. The one nearest to the dock had an old style counter stern which appeared to be overhanging the berth. It was difficult to be sure of the position of the end of the anti-torpedo net, so I estimated its position, reduced to one knot, set course to pass clear to the right, and ordered sixty feet.

At the expected time *X24* grounded gently. In the final approach, several propeller sounds had come and gone as the vessels passed overhead or close by. With rudder hard a'port, *X24* moved under reduced motor revolutions to enter the net protected area. An object darkened the top scuttle, then a second. No details were visible, but the draught could be that of either a dock flooded down or a ship. I could see the approximate bearing on which this second object lay, and it was the same as that of the dock, but it seemed to be too soon. The plot at this stage was not accurate because our speed fell to zero on touching bottom, and would take some time to pick up again. We continued on for about ten minutes without passing under anything else. I considered that we must have passed the dock, and ordered port rudder to retrace our track. Once again, the large shadow passed above.

"I am not sure if that shadow is the dock so we will go out to the middle of the harbour and take another bearing," I said. This we did, at slow speed so as not to make noise. I was torn between two courses of action, one to take time to make sure we had the right target and two, to get on with it before we were sighted, or rammed, and after all, our information revealed that there could be only one object lying on that heading, and that was the dock.

Back in the middle of the harbour, we turned to point at the estimated position of the entrance, and stopped. I asked Joe to bring her up to ten feet, stopped. This is difficult to do, but was within Joe's capabilities. *X24* came up and stopped at periscope depth. Perfect. I took the bearing, ordered sixty feet, slow ahead. Ginge asked, "What course?" I gave him the course calculated from the bearing. As before, *X24* grounded, course was altered to port, and at the same interval of time, a shadow appeared. We carried on past it with the same result as before, nothing else seen.

"That must be the dock," I said, "Port thirty. Steady on the reciprocal course. We will attack." I felt very dry in the mouth.

As soon as the shadow reappeared, we altered course to port and went astern, sat on the seabed, set four hours delay on the first (port) side cargo, and released it. It peeled away without a hitch. Joe pumped her back to diving trim, and we went ahead, dead slow, bringing up suddenly on a hard bottom. Rock spalls were visible to starboard. This was as I had expected, being the short rock pier leading to the shore end of the dock. We stopped the motor, sat on the bottom and released the starboard cargo with the same clock setting. It also peeled away correctly. I ordered slow astern with rudder hard a'port. *X24* moved astern and round to port.

"Stop: slow ahead." When the water outside the scuttle stopped moving toward our bow, I ordered "Midships. Starboard thirty." and then gave Ginge the course to clear the ship and the net. Once past these only obstruction, course was set for the entrance to the first swept channel, at forty feet and speed increased to two and a half knots. Joe turned around and gave me two hard thumps on my back.

Ginge said "Well done, Sir. Let's have a tot."

"Thanks Ginge, but let's get clear of enemy waters first," I replied.

Entering the channel was easy, but it was still busy with boats, and periscope fixes were inadvisable. Nevertheless, we had to have at least one reliable position to begin with, known as 'departure' position. I decided to take this at the end of the first minefield leg where we would be clear of the harbour traffic, and to keep to the starboard side of the swept channel. Frank told me when to come to ten feet. Just as we got there, a clang forward told us that we had indeed finished the first leg. I ordered "Stop".

"Do you want to go astern?" asked Joe.

"Yes. Full astern." As she slid off the rocks, I took a look through the short periscope. The bow was awash and right ahead there was a structure looking very much like an Army lookout post, but no men were apparent. Speed was reduced as soon as we were clear of the bottom, and we proceeded slow ahead, setting course for the second leg of the channel, awaiting a response to a possible sighting. All was quiet, apart from the regular sound of vessels passing nearby. At a time indicated from the plot, we altered course, at fifty feet, to negotiate the final leg of the channel. Frank and I estimated time to alter course again, once clear of the mines, and to pass the next visible mark, a buoy which we had seen on the way in.   When that was due to be close on our starboard bow, we returned to periscope depth and there it was.   We decided to go into two watches in the meantime, so that two could sleep.   We drew lots, and I was one of the lucky ones.   Joe remained on duty while I, in spite of the benzedrine dose taken three hours earlier, had the best hour's sleep of my life, tucked in, between pipes and motors, on the port side of the control room.   Ginge also got his head down.

An hour later, Joe woke me as he had been unable to spot the next buoy.   This soon came into view, so we were on track. The detonation time had now passed without us hearing a sound, and there was no unusual activity around.   We hoped that they did detonate.   The second minefield was nearly as easy by day as by night, and soon Joe and Frank were asleep.   It all seemed too easy to be true.   Here we were, still in enemy waters, having planted two-ton mines a few miles away, motoring quietly toward the open sea, half the crew asleep, and no X-craft defects.   There was some distance to go yet of course, but it seemed that the further we went, the less hazardous it should be.   We were already twenty miles from Bergen.

As daylight faded, the air was becoming heavy.   We felt nausea and heads were beginning to ache (it was later found that the Protosorb air purifier was not functioning).   All would be better when on the surface, with the diesel running to change the air, but that was two hours away, and we all had to be alert on surfacing. This is the most risky time for a submarine which has been blind during the twilight.   At the last daylight, the waters were clear of vessels of any kind.   We went deep and waited for darkness, still making economical speed for the open sea.

As the time drew near, I got into my Ursula suit and sea boots, and switched to red lighting.   This allows eyes to become sensitive to dim light.   Feeling rather tired and dull, at 2055 I shut myself into the W&D, having ordered "Surface. Blow main ballast." As she broke surface, I opened the hatch and looked all round. Ahead was the dark shape of a vessel.   I shut the hatch and re-opened the internal door.

"Dive. 40 feet," I called.   Down we went, levelling out at

that depth. Right away there was the sound of echo detection on the hull. Had we been heard surfacing? I altered course to port to run close to the rocky shore, a mile to the west. This would confuse an echo detector (now sonar) operator and, besides, we could risk bumping rocks more than he could. The sound faded. It would have been good to have been breathing fresh air by now, but we had to be patient. How long should we allow before surfacing again? Visibility was perhaps one mile for us to see him, but less than a quarter of a mile the other way round. After one and a half hours, I reckoned that the vessel should be far behind. Nothing had been heard, no ping, no propeller. If she were lying astern, stopped, looking and listening, we should be out of visible range.

Surfacing this time, knowing it to be calm, I pumped the No 2 main ballast and only partly blew Nos 1 and 3. My head was out of the hatch as soon as it broke surface. Nothing was in sight. I stood on the casing, shut the hatch and looked around twice, slowly, with binoculars. Still nothing. I felt sick.

"Stop. In engine clutch. Slow ahead." Presently, the familiar white plume of fog gathered above the engine exhaust, but no familiar rumble. The plume became a cloud, conspicuously white. Surely that could be seen miles off. Ginge called up "The engine won't start."

"Keep it turning. The air is bad. The engine will pump it out." Eventually the Gardner fired, and slowly, slowly picked up speed, with clouds of fog, which we were now leaving astern.

I was sick over the side. The crew below were similarly affected. We all had headaches. But Fetje light was ahead and soon we could turn to port and the North Atlantic. Joe came up to relieve me after an hour, while I went below to plot our position. We had to make an accurate rendezvous with *Sceptre*, and had to have a good departure. I had taken a bearing on two of the inshore lights before they became obscured. Down below, the crew were starting to feel better. The sound of the diesel, while deafening, was also reassuring. This was sea routine. We were moving at best speed and, as far as they knew, in the right direction, but I was not as sure. However, Frank plotted the bearings and put us on the chart. He then laid out the course to steer and the time to alter course for the pick-up position. I reached for the "RG" receiver and switched it on. This was an infra red receiver. *Sceptre* would be transmitting an invisible infra red beam toward the shore and we would search for it on the reciprocal bearing. Therefore, we had to be in the right place to start with.

It was hard to be patient and to wait until we were within receiver range. The power of the beam had to be restricted lest *Sceptre* should give her own position away to the enemy. They too knew about infra red. I returned on deck as Joe was thinking of heading back to Scotland independently. Then at 2300, there it was; a point of green glowing in the receiver, right ahead. I flashed "MAC" and waited. "MAC" came back. I stopped engine and proceeded on motor close to *Sceptre's* port side.

Mac called out "Follow in my wake." Presently, she swung to port and headed seaward on engine at five knots. We re-started the diesel and followed, watching from time to time for the glimmer in our RG receiver. After an hour and a half he stopped. I stopped and closed *Sceptre* on motor. Mac called from the conning tower. "We will use the dinghy." I acknowleged, and manoeuvred to his stern to take the tow. Presently the inflated dinghy with Willy and another crewman aboard floated toward us. We lifted the end of the tow and threaded the auxiliary towing pendant through it and back onto the towing slip. Two were called up and boarded the dinghy as I made a brief repor to Willie, The dinghy was hauled back to *Sceptre* and after another round trip, the changeover was completed and we were underway. Our main concern was possible detection by the enemy in the change-over process, so the quicker the better. Shortly after 0300, *X24* dived, and towing routine was resumed.

Once in *Sceptre's* wardroom, I gave Mac a verbal report on our movements since we had parted the previous evening. All seemed to have gone according to plan. Next evening, when well clear of the target area, he sent a signal to FOS reporting that the operation had been completed. A reply came several hours later, "Well done, especially as the one concerned does not know what hit him." Mac thought that this sounded rather oblique, but I was satisfied. The tow home also went to plan. By 0635 on Tuesday 18th April, when we entered Eddrachilis Bay via Burra Firth, the four of us had caught up on sleep, we had celebrated Ginger's birthday on 16th, and I had written a Patrol Report. As *Sceptre* moored, one of *Bonaventure's* boats came and transferred us to the mother ship, while Willie cast off the tow and secured *X24* in a berth alongside.

Joe and I went with Captain Fell to his cabin. He had welcomed us at the gangway with the warmth that was typical of him. He sat us down around a coffee table, with coffee as well, and listened carefully to our account of the operation and the tow each way. He was particularly interested in details of our final approach to the target. I went over every part a second time. After hearing us out, he said that aerial reconnaissance showed the dock still floating, and a German coal ship *Barenfels* sunk at her berth close by. The horrible reality struck me immediately, aided by the doubts which I had felt at the time. Joe took longer to accept what had happened. He had done his job perfectly, so had Ginge and Frank. I had been misled in target identification.

"Tiny" Fell was kind to me, probably more kind than I would have been had I been him. He said that one thing which helped to ease the disappointment was that, in the planning stages, he had met the former manager of the dock, who did not know the British intentions. This charming Norwegian was so interested and enthusiastic in his pride and joy, it was good, in one way, that it was still intact. I asked to be allowed to go back and finish the job, but it was not that easy. It would take some time to get a submarine for a repeat run and the days were getting too long for night passage and charging. I broke the sad news to the rest of the crew. All of them had performed splendidly.

There was a long session analysing my Report, and all other related documents. Close examination of the recent aerial photographs showed that, subsequent to the printing of the chart with which I had been issued, an additional berth had been constructed across the end of the existing land backed coal berths. The orientation for a ship at this new berth would be the same as that of the dock. It was an unfortunate thing that none of the pre-operational photographs showed a ship at this berth. The first evidence was when I sank a ship that was. Another unfortunate coincidence was that the dock was flooded down during my approach. Had she been in full buoyancy, I would have known that the "shadow's" draft was excessive, and would have persevered until I found another object with the expected draft of ten feet or so.

A composite report was compiled as *Bonaventure*, with *X24* aboard, steamed back to Kames Bay. There were further conferences with both captains and then with Admiral Barry. Finally, I was summoned to meet them. I was informed that, all things considered, the operation was a success and that I was to be congratulated, along with my crews. This was the first time in the history of the Royal Navy that such an attack, resulting in the sinking of an enemy ship at her berth, had been completed without loss. The flotilla needed a success such as this. There would be a dinner to which every officer in the flotilla would be invited, to make it clear to them what had been done, and their part in it.

This made me feel a little better. It certainly let me off the hook officially, and congratulations abounded. I still blamed myself, out of date and incomplete intelligence notwithstanding. I should have heeded that horse-sense coming from within that was saying "This is not the target. It is too soon. Go on further." But I heeded my rationalising other self that said, "You have taken the bearing twice, and come to the same object twice. You have gone beyond it, and have found nothing. This has to be it." It was not until after the war, when Ginge called into Fremantle Harbour and we were standing on Victoria Quay, that he said, "Do you remember when we came to periscope depth with a stopped trim, and, for the second time, you took a bearing on the dock? You ordered Joe to run the motor ahead without giving me a course, until I asked you for one. When you gave it, I had to turn to port to bring the ship's head onto it. Would that have displaced our track to starboard?" I recalled the incident as soon as he triggered my memory. Yes, that would have been a factor, but the main one was that my strategy for attack was based on incorrect information. In fact, our sailing orders nominated the dock as prime target and any German ship as second target.

The *Varbel* dinner was a great occasion. All the complimentary and encouraging things were said. I spoke to each section of the flotilla personnel, telling them of the importance of their contribution to the success of this operation, and that we would expect the same high standard in the future. I was acting the part of a successful commanding officer, while feeling the opposite. Joe said to me afterwards, "How can you say all those nice things about the base staff, when you know that some of them are just there for the ride?"

"Well, Joe," I replied, "there are some as you describe, but most of them work for the cause as we do. They deserve to be complimented and encouraged, and it won't do the others any harm either. The flotilla needs a boost, and we can help give it one." I'm not sure that Joe was convinced.

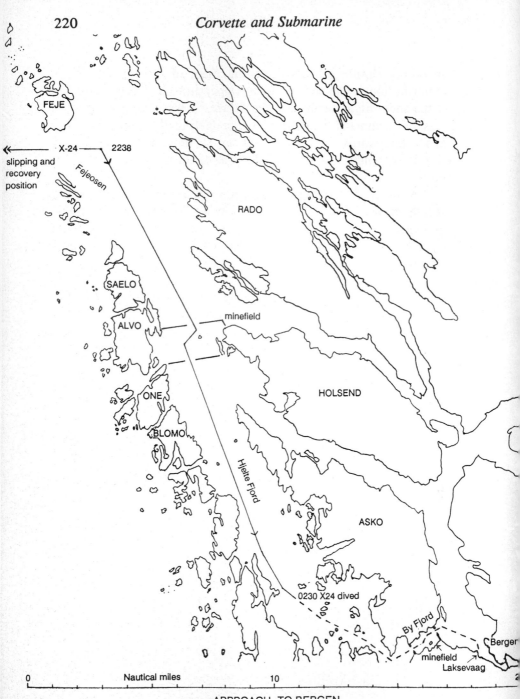

FEJE

X-24 ——— 2238

slipping and
recovery
position

Fejeosen

RADO

SAELO

ALVO   minefield

ONE

BLOMO

HOLSEND

Hjelte Fjord

ASKO

0230 X24 dived

By Fjord

Berger

minefield
Laksevaag

0   Nautical miles   10

APPROACH TO BERGEN

2

X 24

1

*-oyal Air Force reconnaissance of Laksevaag, Bergen in July 1944 shows, at figure 1, Barenfels partly sunk by X24 in April
-d the floating dock close to the south. Note the busy marine traffic which impeded X24 on her approach and at figure 2 to
-e north west, U-boat bomb-proof pens under construction.*

X24 in HHZ on return from sinking Barenfels. CO "Willie" Brinell of the passage crew, having brought his X-craft and crew safely home, stands by the "Jolly Roger", customarily flown by submarines returning from patrol, with one white bar for each enemy ship sunk, one in this case. X24 was mounted post war at the Royal Naval Submarine Museum at Gosport, near Portsmouth, England.

CHAPTER TWENTY TWO

BACK TO SCAPA

In the process of being debriefed, Joe and I went to London, reporting to Northways, the building where FOS had his headquarters. That took only a day, so Joe invited me to his home in Lowestoft. During my few days enjoying his mother's hospitality, one of the highlights was his twenty-first birthday, for which Mrs Brooks had gathered a fleet of sailing dinghies to be crewed on the day by guests at the celebration. I was skipper of one, with Fanella Royson as crew. It was certainly a novel party. We spent the day racing and obstacle racing on Oulton Broad. Fanella was a capable sailor. We made a tour of the waterways after the races were over, sat on the bank for a while, and spoke about everything in general, and nothing in particular, just what I needed to unwind.

After those wonderful few days, I took trains to Aberfeldy to make plans for my marriage to Mary on 14th June. All of the arranging had been started, and was completed by Mary and her parents. All I had to do was to find somewhere to spend a honeymoon. Every place was booked out, but I wrote to three hotels on the banks of the River Thames, and hoped that one of them could oblige, at least for part of the time. Before my leave was up, I received a phone call from *Bonaventure*. It was not a serious matter, but I was required to return forthwith, and could complete my leave in a fortnight. One did not ask questions over the phone; everything was secret, so I said goodbye to Mary and her folks, and returned to Bute and *Bonaventure*.

His Majesty, King George VI, was to visit the Home Fleet in Scapa Flow, and he had specifically requested that *Bonaventure*, her Charioteers and X-craft crews be aboard. That would be a

Royal Command I should think. *X24* was still on deck. We got busy shining her up and gave her a new coat of a smart shade of black paint. We were not sure whether His Majesty would descend the W&D and slide feet first into the control room, but smartened it up just in case. This entailed much work because the interior surfaces were covered with equipment of all kinds, and painting between and behind each item took an age. On arrival at a mooring in Scapa, there spread an epidemic of activity. *Bonaventure* herself had to be painted. This was no extravagance: every ship during wartime needed painting; there was never time to keep up with the rust streaks. Some crews were proud of their rust stained ships because they spoke of sea-time. But there is a time and place for everything, and the time for us to paint was before King George came aboard. *Bonaventure* had so much grey surface it could not all be covered in the time available, so her No 1 walked the upper deck with his note book, noting which side of what His Majesty would see on his inspection.

There was also a rehearsal for the Royal visit. We were all lined up on deck with a human torpedo well to the fore, and *X24* on her chocks behind. The quartermaster sounded "Still", Captain Fell and the first lieutenant at the head of the gangway saluted, and up the steps and onto the quarterdeck came *Bonaventure's* RDF and Cipher Officer, Bernie Tonks, a rather small man with spectacles, smiling broadly as he acknowledged the salute given him by his Captain. It was too much for the Ship's Company, who could not stop laughing. Captain Fell also saw the funny side of this and thought that it gave KG VI a hard act to follow.

The real visit was a wonderful experience for all. The King was a short man. I am sure that he and Bernie could have worn each other's jackets, though Bernie would have had to develop his arm muscles to be able to lift all that gold braid. I had the honour of showing the King over *X24*. He declined to go below, for which I did not blame him. He would have covered his expensive jacket with wet paint, braid and all. On return to the Flagship, *Bonaventure* received a signal: "NAVAL MESSAGE. To: *Bonaventure*, From: Commander in Chief Home Fleet. 121912B May 1944. Following message from HM the King. Begins - I am very interested to have had the opportunity of inspecting the Officers and men of your Flotilla. I am impressed by their work and keenness, and wish them good luck. 'SPLICE THE MAINBRACE'."

The following day I was invited to represent X-craft crews at a dinner, aboard *HMS Duke of York*, given by Admiral Sir Bruce Fraser, in honour of His Majesty. There were guests from other ships in company, and all were briefed on how to address the King when he entered the wardroom, by bowing our heads a little, giving our names and name of ship. I sat next to Tiny Fell and opposite Captain Russell of the *Duke of York*. He asked many questions about X-craft, how many crew, engine horse-power, speed, and so on. Having informed him on details of the smallest ship represented, I asked "How many horse power does *Duke of York* develop, Sir?" He thought for a while because I expect he would not know much about the "Plumber's" department.

"Well, Shean, I have never counted, but I go up onto the bridge early in the morning and order 'Half ahead together (four engines)', then go down to my cabin for breakfast. By the time I have returned to the bridge, she is just beginning to move, don't you know!" This last was a favourite expression of his. Following the dinner, a ship's concert party entertained us with a splendid show of topical humour, some of which was directed at the 'Don't you know' man, so I expect that some sailors got some extra duties the next day.

Bonaventure returned to Kames Bay, but I did not ask for the remainder of my interrupted leave as I was to clear my entitlement commencing 13th June, to be married the following day. I received disappointing replies from two of my hotel accommodation applications, but at the last minute, The Compleat Angler at Marlow, on the Thames, advised that they could accommodate us for a week. This was a relief because a honeymoon with nowhere to go would not impress my bride. Helen Howland, third officer WRNS, cypher officer in Varbel, had already helped us enormously, and had offered to use her best endeavours to get us in at the Bells of Ousley, near Marlow, if all else had failed.

Preparations for an Allied landing were consuming the country's every resource. As May wore on, all leave and train travel was stopped, except for important Service requirements. I was doubtful as to whether Mary and I would keep our date. Joe Brooks had left the flotilla by this time and was at sea, retraining in a big submarine. He was to be our best man. If Winston Churchill had only consulted me first, we could have arranged another month for the invasion. The date and place were secret, of course, but we knew that Hudspeth and Honour were on the south coast with *X20* and *X23*, ready to precede the invasion fleet by a few days, and to station themselves at the extremities of a landing beach and to make guiding signals, so D-Day was imminent.

We all now know that the invasion started on the 6th June. Notwithstanding that the biggest combined service manoeuvre in history was in full swing, Joe's submarine put into port long enough to let him ashore; Helen, Joe and I were given leave and travel permits to go to Aberfeldy on the 13th. What is more, Captains Fell and Banks happened to call at Aberfeldy on the 14th, on their way from HHZ to Bute, and attended the wedding. It may have been coincidental, but on the previous day, Buckingham Palace announced the award of the Distinguished Service Medal to ERA Vernon Coles, the Distinguished Service Cross to S/Lt Joe Brooks, and the Distinguished Service Order to Lt Max Shean.

It was half-day trading in Aberfeldy on 14th June. In addition to Mary's popularity, the unprecedented Naval presence and the news of the decorations made a hit, and the church was full to the gallery. Commander "Mopsy" Myers, Commander (S) at Varbel, had insisted on Joe and me wearing swords, so that is what we did. I had been drilled by the same commander that I would not look around at my bride as she approached the altar: it showed impatience and lack of discipline he said.

Mrs Howland had made the cake, the fruit and other ingredients having been sent from Perth, Australia, by my mother, and Mr Howland a London hotelier had magically produced six bottles of Australian champagne. Reverend Lewis, Chaplain to the RAF, married us, and the reception was held at the Weem Hotel not far from Menzies Castle, across the River Tay from Aberfeldy.

The story goes that the former Prime Minister of Australia, Sir Robert Menzies, was in London and wished to visit his ancestral home. He asked at Euston Station for a ticket to Weem. The ticket officer said that he could not take the train to Weem.

"I am Robert Menzies, Prime Minister of Australia. Menzies Castle, in Weem, is the home of my ancestors and that is where I am going. Please sell me a ticket."

The officer, a Scot as it now became clear, answered. "You may be Prime Minister of Australia, but your name is 'MINGIS' (pronounced that way), and you want a ticket to Aberfeldy. From there you go across the river to Weem."

Mary, Anne Scott her bridesmaid, Joe and I, were piped to the reception where, at the door, I was both honoured and horrified to see Mary presented, by Captain Fell, with a framed photo of His Majesty and me standing on *X24*'s casing. I had never said a word to any of Mary's folk about submarines! But it was an act of great kindness, especially as the picture was signed by many of my *Bonaventure* shipmates. The wedding breakfast was lovely, in spite of the severe rationing that had been in force for over four years. Having so many Navy there boosted me no end.

Joe was to read the telegrams; to arrange all Navy messages of doubtful propriety last, not to be read. He arranged them in the desired order, but forgot to stop, resulting in a climactic finish, much appreciated I might say, by most of the guests. One particularly apt message from *Bonaventure* read, "Awards are out for this operation, but be expeditious."

After the reception, Mary and I were driven to Pitlochry and took the night train to London. She had not been there before and, as there had been no bombing for months, I had booked two nights at the Overseas League, and seats at the Coliseum, Charing Cross, for "The Quaker Girl", to be followed by a week in Marlow. First night, after the show, the air-raid sirens sounded.

"Don't worry," said the man-of-the-world, "that will be a false alarm." Presently, there was the sound of a not so distant explosion. This was the first of Hitler's 'buzz-bombs'. There were several explosions during the night. Mary's confidence in me probably started to decline from that time, and has never recovered.

Next day, we met Ken Hudspeth with Audrey, his future bride, and enjoyed a pleasant lunch, at which they gave us a present of two prints. These still grace our walls.

The Compleat Angler was also the complete retreat, a lovely location on the river bank, no doubt with Moles, Water Rats and Toads thereabouts. The first night, there were sirens again, and more explosions, more distant this time. We later learned that the first of these was a bomb on the Bells of Ousley.

The weather was fine. We spent afternoons lying on the river bank, watching the RAF towing gliders, packed with soldiers, across to France. I felt uneasy that I should be enjoying peace while these men were flying into the thick of war. I hired a sailing dinghy from Henley, and gave my reluctant bride her first taste of my favoured pastime. In the narrow river, with its busy traffic of tugs and barges, we were frequently sailing into the rushes and holding on until the wash subsided. There was a good fresh breeze, and three times gear broke, causing moments of instability. I enjoyed it all, and my bride put on a brave face out of duty, saving her comments till after the honeymoon. We trained back to Aberfeldy, and I returned to Bute to resume international hostilities. They had not yet started with Mary.

Back in *Varbel*, preparations were being made for a second attack on the dock. Lt Pat Westmacott, RN, was to command *X24*. I was disappointed not to be given another chance, but had to accept that each CO deserved a share of the action. I was to stand by one of the new design X-craft intended for Pacific Ocean operation. Pat and I spent some time together handing over the craft and briefing him on all that I had observed on our run to Bergen.

Updated charts were supplied, so as to simplify his approach. *Barenfels* was still lying on the harbour bed and would make an excellent navigation mark. Also, it seemed from intelligence, that *X24* had not been reported, and probably not detected, by the Germans. Our evasive action when detection seemed imminent must have been completely successful. Therefore, Pat should have an even better chance of success. The interval between the two attacks would be six months, long enough for any additional vigilance to have subsided. *X24* was in excellent condition. The initial defects had been corrected and she was not yet old enough to have worn any component to a noticeable degree.

The second attack on the floating dock by *X24* took place in September 1944, *HMS/M Sceptre* again doing the towing. All went as for the earlier operation and the dock was destroyed. In fact, the time from slipping the tow to recovery was within minutes of the same. There was, however, one tragic episode. Sub Lieut David Purdy RNZNVR, the fourth crew member, went up onto the casing when on the surface at night to ditch gash (dispose of rubbish). The craft had insufficient buoyancy. A wave swept over the casing, filled the W&D and she submerged. David Purdy was lost.

The Brown gyro compass design had been modified, so a group of us went to their works, west of London, to have further instruction. All officers had been there in the course of their initial training. The modifications were to the electronic 'follow-up' system which caused repeaters at three other locations to follow the master gyro without imposing any force on it, as might influence its accuracy. The modifications were soon learned, and, as we were now well experienced with the compass, we had time to spare. In the training room was a large wooden box of components, more than a complete set. We got to work to assemble parts, not expecting to make a complete compass because some of these parts had been well handled and were rather shop soiled. Nevertheless, we did manage to complete the assembly and requested a power supply to test-run it. Power was supplied, and the compass started. It took fifteen minutes for this model to reach speed and three hours to settle down, pointing north. We had long known how to accelerate this process, and to have a compass correctly orientated within thirty minutes. This was an important advantage when a craft suffered rapid movement as in very heavy weather or when striking the seabed. Once having settled down, our reconstructed gyro performed exactly as it should. This was more than a bit of fun. It was typical of X-crafts crew's attitude to their craft. The more they knew about it, the better their chances of success and survival. That night I took a long walk to the 'Bells of Ousley' and saw for myself what I had heard in June, the destruction of part of the building. I had a drink at the bar, to our good fortune.

There was time to fill in before the next six craft would be ready in November. The fact that more were being built was due to the now known success of the *Tirpitz* attack, and the complete success of the Bergen and Normandy Beach operations. Ken Hudspeth left the flotilla to seek a change. He had been in from the inception, and was due for a shift. A normal Naval appointment was two years. I decided to stay on because I felt that I had something to contribute, liked submarines, and the war was progressing definitely toward a conclusion in Europe. Our flotilla was to be sent to the Pacific, which would satisfy any Australian who had been restless since Japan had entered the war.

Mary came to Bute twice for a week, and once to Dunoon for a few days, so we were able to enjoy short periods of married life, and she met all of my shipmates. She also saw X-craft exercising from the shores of Kames Bay. Captain and Audrey Banks had us to dinner, and presented us with a pair of silver serviette rings engraved with our names. We use these every day.

I had long been impressed by our flotilla captains. Not only were they splendid leaders in the official sense, carrying out all flotilla management requirements efficiently, but they also cared for the personnel and acted accordingly. I endeavour to emulate them whenever I have responsibility for people. Their policy seemed to be one of fairness and honesty. They were all for the job, not themselves. Surely, when appointed to a position of command of men and women who look to you for leadership, it would be a deception to do other than your level best to that end. It does not always happen, as we all know, but would be better for all if it did. It is an application of the Golden Rule - to treat others as you would want to be treated. My crew showed confidence in me. What a deceiver I would be not to do my best. You can see that I had an idealistic expectation of the Navy. I was not often disappointed.

THE TRIALS OF A JIMMY

Here Joe Brooks is expressing his frustration as a first lieutenant (Jimmy). He has actually controlled the submarine to a correct periscope depth. The CO has not raised the periscope to full height. He has only to press the "Raise" switch to take it up so that it will see above the sea surface. Without thinking, however, he blames his first lieutenant and expects him to bring the submarine to a shallower depth. The "Jimmy", while doing so, responds with an expressive hand sign.

"What's the depth No 1?"
"Nine and a half feet."
"Well, keep nine feet Damn you."

CHAPTER TWENTY THREE

EXCITER, XE-4

O n 15th November, 1944, I was appointed CO of J.3012, the contract number for *XE4*'s construction by Vickers Armstrong of Barrow-in-Furness. Joe, as I have mentioned, had left the flotilla, so our successful crew was robbed of its key member, which was a disadvantage, but not a disappointment. It was good to see Joe receiving greater responsibility.. In his place, S/Lt "Ben" Kelly joined Ginge, Willie and myself. Two new officers were attached, S/Lt Ken Briggs from Glen Innes, Queensland and S/Lt Adam Bergius of Glasgow. Stoker Gillard continued as additional, and several more joined our total establishment. Policy was to provide two passage crews for operations in the Pacific, so we ended up with ten people in *XE4*'s full complement. Ken and Adam were trained as divers, and very proficient they were. ERA Sheppard, Leading Seaman Rhodes, and Stoker Butters were our other new acquisitions.

The craft had several modifications. It was a tribute to the original designers that no major change had been found necessary, only developments in detail. The hull was lengthened eighteen inches, and the casing profile was made straight for the full length, to replace the step-down forward of the main hatch, and was made of aluminium to save weight. Side charges were replaced by limpets, two hundred pounds of explosives in each, of which six were carried each side. These were to be fixed to targets by divers, and held magnetically. Three 'antennae' were fitted to the casing, these being steel tubes three feet long, which were raised so that the craft, rising under a target ship, would be held clear, and allow the diver access from and to the main hatch. Air conditioning was fitted, serving to cool and dehumidify the internal air which always became moist, affecting crew and electrical equipment alike. The engine and main motor were mounted on a sprung frame to reduce noise transmitted through the hull. One powerful trim pump replaced the two smaller pumps, and its control was simplified. Main vent valves were operated by levers instead of handwheels, ensuring rapid action. Ben, Ginge and I went to Barrow to stand by our new craft. This was a good opportunity for Mary to come down and live in digs for a week. Vickers were very proficient and there were no problems with the construction.

As before, a name was chosen from the 'ex' section of the dictionary. I selected *"Exciter"* as being appropriate in the general sense that excitement goes with action, and in the technical sense that in electric power generation, an exciter is a small generator mounted at the end of a massive alternating current generator to energise its rotor; a small item central to its whole function. For an emblem we chose a sea-horse with trident prodding a whale. Cecil Broad, one of Vicker's design staff, and a good artist, drew a beautiful design on this theme. A badge should have been carved, preferably in oak, but we progressed only as far as cutting two sea-horses from sheet brass and mounting them to the periscope standards. A schoolmaster whom we came to know in Barrow, gave us a Latin motto "Tridenti stimulabimus hostem" which, as you would guess, means "With trident, stimulate the enemy." Stimulation is near enough to excitement.

Mary spent her days shopping in Barrow, where she bought a very thick exercise book for recipes. She was, and is, a born housewife in the best Scottish tradition. That book is now fully written up, and bulging with cuttings. Many a good meal it has specified. Our kind landlady was Mrs Hetherington, and her small dog, 'You two'. Every time she called her dog, we sprang to the summons.

When we took our special train to Faslane, Mary went direct to Bute. A launching had been arranged for Monday 4th December 1944, at the Ardmaleish slipway, where J.3012 was hauled up on a cradle. Mary broke a bottle of Australian champagne saved from the wedding, over the bow, saying "I name this ship *Exciter, XE4*. May God bless her and all who sail in her." *XE4* rolled down the slipway, with Ben Kelly, Ginger Coles and me aboard, to commence her trials and crew training exercises, the pattern of which were now familiar.

Exercising in Loch Striven always required that the X-craft signalled the 'tower' at Varbel, her intention to dive and her estimated surfacing time. Upon resurfacing on conclusion of the day's work, she would make her number. By this time, we knew all the lovely WRNS signallers, or 'Bunts' as they were called. They were a bright lot, and ever ready for a little morse code repartee. It got to such a stage that, before surfacing, we had to have some remark to add to the official report, to get in first, you might say. On New Year's Eve, 1944, we composed some doggerel that went like this:

"Oh beautiful Bunts, in your tower so high
Who watch us e'er with flashing eye
And call us home with words of cheer,
We wish for you a guid New Year."

On this round of Loch Goil, and other test areas, Mrs Thomas gave me two crystal condiment dishes and spoons, for a wedding present, typical of the interest and caring that the Scottish people had developed towards members of the submarine service. We had no bother falling over walls or with broken windows at three hundred feet. At the degaussing establishment in the Gairloch, we decided to ask for a bunk for the night from a US Navy tank landing ship, *LST 373*, moored nearby, instead of going ashore to the rather spartan RN accommodation. The Americans readily agreed, issuing each of us with new blankets from the ship's store. They also gave us dinner, more than we could eat, and asked if it were not uncomfortable aboard such a small submarine.

We described the conditions which led them to the point of their interest. They said that some extra supplies might help ease any discomfort. Their ship was on the point of being taken over by the Royal Navy. There were certain stores that were not included in the transfer, and might be useful to us. If we liked to look below in the vehicle hold, they would be found, stacked, starboard side. In those days of rationing and shortage, what we found was magical. There were large tins of preserved fruit, bags of sugar and cans of butter, nearly half a ton altogether. We left one crew in the hold, sent one down into *XE4*, while the other two removed a hatch cover above the hoard, and lowered a rope. It took an hour to haul up the treasure, lower it over the side and to stow it in *XE4*'s battery compartment and control room. We celebrated with a game of football in the hold, and turned in feeling like kids on Christmas night. Next morning, when we returned our blankets to the ship's store, we were told to keep them, and did not need a second telling.

Fortunately, we were not required to dive during the loop trials later at Largs Bay. With that load aboard, Ben would have taken a while to catch his trim. Back at Varbel, there was a distribution of the spoils among the rest of the crew, not forgetting certain senior officers, who enjoy windfalls like everybody else. I traded some of my share of food for blankets which the single men did not want. I was planning for setting up house in Australia next year, or the year after.

Kames Bay had become a busy waterway over the months preceding and following the Normandy landing. Assault craft of all sizes could be seen travelling to and from the adjoining Kyles of Bute. Many of these would be carrying commandos in training on Loch Fyne a few miles to the west. The exercise area for X-craft was close by this busy channel, so good care had to be taken while submerged, to keep within our allotted area.

One afternoon, I was in *Varbel*, looking north across this stretch of water, when I saw *XE4* surface in the wake of a tank landing ship. Her aldis lamp flashed to the signal tower, "Run down by landing craft. Periscope bent." I could read this, as could anybody looking in that direction, and one other who was, happened to be Captain S12, W E Banks, RN. We met on the stairs.

"Bergius is out exercising in *XE4*, Sir, and has had a minor accident."

"Yes, I read his message. What was he doing outside the exercise area, Shean?"

"I don't know, Sir, but he has some inexperienced crew under training. Possibly he has been kept down with a bad trim, and overran his area. I will talk to him as soon as he berths, and let you know. I apologise for this setback to the programme, and the damage caused."

"Right, Shean. I will leave that to you. Tell him that I am bloody annoyed."

"Aye, aye, Sir."

That was all we heard from Capt S. It indicated that he had trust in the crew, though this incident would have put a doubt in his mind. All the same, I was pleased that he left it to me to sort out, because Adam Bergius was a first class seaman and navigator, and it would have been counter productive to have taken any serious action. The periscope was replaced, and *XE4* was as good as new. Adam, of course, was suitably humbled. I tried to convey the Captain's displeasure without overdoing it. A suitable summary comment, which did not occur to me until I heard it from another, could have been "One of these days, Adam, we may laugh about this incident, but not today."

1945 brought preparations for *Bonaventure's* departure for the Pacific. Captain Banks had left the flotilla, leaving Captain Fell as Capt S14, to lead the X-craft initiative. It was still January when I said goodbye to Mary on Glasgow railway station. This was the first serious goodbye, she returning to her parent's home to await world peace, and I sailing to participate in the war in the Pacific. It was a bleak prospect, and Glasgow was not the most cheering of cities. *Bonaventure* was soon on her way with *XE's 1 - 6* on board, heading for Panama Canal, and San Diego near Los Angeles.

On 17th February, while *Bonaventure* was proceeding to join the Pacific war, *Bluebell* was in the Barents Sea within the Arctic Circle, defending Convoy RA64 returning from Murmansk. There were six U-boats awaiting the convoy as it formed up off Kola Inlet. *U711* hit her with a torpedo in the magazine and she blew up in a sheet of orange flame. Petty Officer Albert Holmes was the only survivor. I cannot be sure how many of those lost had served in her before I left, but Commanding Officer Geoffrey Walker, Stoker PO WF Nunn and Leading Steward G Lightowler were three who had been aboard since her commissioning. Another of those lost was Lieutenant W W Twiss, Royal Australian Naval Volunteer Reserve.

Bluebell has become more deeply engraved in my memory as the years have passed. She was one of the first corvettes to be commissioned, and the third last to be sunk, having escorted many ships throughout the war. To me she typifies the small escort, manned by ordinary men, who persevered in their duties without individual recognition. There were thousands of them. Whenever I hear Aaron Copeland's "Fanfare for the Common Man", I think of *Bluebell's* men.

Our stay in the USA was short in the extreme. Admiralty maintained secrecy on anything concerning our flotilla. We were not allowed ashore, in spite of attractive invitations from Americans to visit Hollywood and all the rest. Morale sank for a few days, but as soon as we were at sea again, all returned to normal. As Nelson said, "Harbours rot good ships and good men." Pearl Harbour was another thing. This was a naval base and leave was granted. US officials cleared one of their Servicemen's Rest and Recreation Camps at Scotland Bay, on the other side of Oahu, so that *Bonaventure's* crew could relax without security risk, a most generous act. One of the attractions, apart from the girls, was the Service Canteen at Pearl Harbour. It was like Christmas again. All kinds of good quality articles at low prices. Not that we were in need of any essentials, but it was a taste of pre-war plenty, unknown for five years.

Bonaventure crossed the Equator on Ginger's birthday, 16th April 1945, in longitude 174° 24' west. We were far from the areas of action, so a 'crossing the line' ceremony was arranged. A canvas swimming pool was rigged on deck amidships, and important figures recruited to represent King Neptune, his Queen Amphitrite, Clerk of the Court, Barber, Physician and attendant Bears. Captain Fell was, of course, King, and everybody who could not produce a certificate to prove he had already been initiated into the Comradeship of the Deep was summoned to the Royal presence, tried, found guilty, given a shave, a soap pill, and a good ducking by the Bears who, having been carefully selected for their strength, could not be resisted for long. Although all South Africans, New Zealanders and Australians had obviously crossed the Line at least once, we went through the process regardless. One of the most difficult to dunk was Ken Briggs of *XE4*, a powerful man who held the Bears, and a team of willing helpers, at bay for five minutes, at the end of which he had his soap pill like everyone else.

But it was worth the taste of soap, which has now faded, and I have regained my breath from the long submersion without my submarine, because I now have a splendid Certificate testifying to the fact that I have been so initiated, and imploring all sharks and other sea creatures to abstain from harming my person if ever I should fall overboard, or find myself in the ocean for any other reason. This document was drawn by one of *Bonaventure's* navigation staff, beautifully adorned with colour drawings of sea creatures, including one lovely mermaid. It was reproduced in Brisbane and my copy graces the main bulkhead of my yacht *Bluebell* and, to date, has been completely effective.

Next stop was Brisbane, where I went ashore and phoned my parents. I was surprised at the sound of my mother's voice, but not at her delight at our arrival in Australia, albeit on the other side of it. Captain Fell flew to Sydney and Melbourne for briefing, and returned with tidings which were something of a letdown. It seemed that the Pacific was an American sphere of influence. It was difficult for any other nation to take any worthwhile initiative. Nevertheless, there was one task for us. He had been asked whether his midget submarines could locate and cut submarine telegraph cables. He said that they certainly could, and was told the importance of this being done promptly. It was connected with the planned re-occupation of Singapore. The Allies had cracked the Japanese codes, and could therefore know the content of all their radio traffic. However, there were submarine telegraph cables from Singapore, running via Saigon and Hong Kong, to Japan. All the traffic sent by cable was secure from Japan's viewpoint, as all these terminals were in Japanese hands. It was important to cut these cables before any landing on Singapore. A cable ship, escorted by destroyers was a possible method of doing this, but was likely to lead to a naval action on a large scale close to Japanese held airfields. The losses could be heavy, without any guarantee of success.

By some miracle, *Bonaventure's* Pilot (navigator) produced charts from his library showing the exact position of these cables at Saigon and Hong Kong. A Cable and Wireless Ltd engineer flew up with the Captain to discuss details with us. He said that if a cable ship were to do this job, she would drag in deep water with a large grapnel (like an anchor), haul the cable to the surface with a powerful winch, and cut it. Our cutters would do this last act, but it would be out of the question for a midget submarine to locate the cable in deep water, and for our divers to work at that depth. He recommended that we consider grappling for the cables in thirty feet depth, although they would possibly be deep in moving sand so close to shore. If unsuccessful, further grappling should be tried in progressively deeper water. We should get the cables where bottom sediments do not normally move, at fifty to one hundred feet.

This information gave us a chance, though one hundred feet was too deep. The next thing was to learn about grappling. This is like ploughing. Shallow ploughing of the seabed would be no trouble, but X-craft would not have the power to penetrate the seabed more than about six inches. We looked up books on grapnels and had our own favoured designs under production in *Bonaventure's* workshop as she steamed out to the Whitsunday Islands to commence trials. As soon as she came to anchor in Cid Harbour, the ship's crew laid a wire hawser on the harbour bed for us to practise on.

We had most success with what our book called a 'Flat Fish' grapnel. This comprised a diamond shaped steel plate, three feet long, with fins shaped like halves of a crescent moon welded top and bottom. The diamond was towed by chain, and lay flat on the seabed while the lower fin dug into it. The second fin dug if it lay the other side up. This experimenting went on all day and nearly every day, during May, till we had it worked out.

But, all work and no play makes Jack Tar a dull boy, so early in June, *Exciter* took her entire crew for a few days to Hazelwood Island, where we camped on the beach, living off the land, or sea as it turned out. Oysters in plenty were there. I caught an enormous crayfish, stranded in a rock pool.

While all of us were walking across the shallows of the flat area behind a coral reef, Adam trod on a stingray which stung him on the ankle, causing great pain. We helped him back to the beach. The pain worsened so I decided to return him to *Bonaventure* straight away. Ginge, Ben and I took him out by inflatable dingy, and *XE4* set off into the gathering dusk. It was soon quite dark and there were no navigation lights. But we were used to this, navigating in the dark, and managed to keep to the deep water till *Bonaventure* showed up ahead. I signalled by lamp, "Bergius stung by stingray. Coming to starboard gangway." As we came to the landing and stopped, stretcher bearers were there waiting. Adam came on deck and walked up to the quarterdeck. He must have been in considerable pain, but determination will triumph over adversity. He was going to show them what stuff Scots were made of. His ankle recovered in due course, and next day I took *Exciter* back to Hazelwood Island to recover her crew who, after two days doing for themselves on an island paradise, were glad enough to return to the Navy.

As a last trial, we shifted to Hervey Bay where there was a disused telegraph cable in depths down to fifty feet, over a distance of a mile. Each craft crossed and re-crossed this cable, submerged, with its diver following like the ploughman, observing the grapnel's performance. Adam and Ken took turns at this and reported good results. All was not so well with other craft. During this phase, Bruce Enzer was drowned, followed soon after by David Carey. This was a shock, two of our most experienced divers. Bruce had been Ken Hudspeth's First Lieutenant on the *Tirpitz* operation. David was a Midshipman at Dartmouth Naval College with Joe Brooks. It was unthinkable that these two athletic men should be lost under the ideal training conditions of Hervey Bay.

Apart from this tragedy, all was satisfactory, and *Bonaventure* sailed northward. Two other jobs in our normal line of business now came to the flotilla. Two Japanese cruisers, *Takao* and *Myoko*, were berthed close to shore in Johore Strait, a narrow, not very deep waterway between Singapore and Johore. These had to be reckoned with before the Singapore invasion. Attack by X-craft was required. In the allocation of jobs, Lt "Tich" Fraser, RNR, in *XE3*, and Lt Jack Smart, RNR, in *XE1*, were to go for the cruisers, while Pat Westmacott, in *XE5*, and I were to cut cables at Hong Kong and Saigon respectively. *Bonaventure* steamed to Subic Bay in the Philippines where *XE5* and her crews and supplies were off-loaded. The hydraulically powered cutters, designed for nets, had to be adapted to deal with the much larger cables. This was competently done for both *XE4* and *XE5* by CERA Ron Fisher, aboard *Bonaventure*.

While we were at Subic Bay, Admiral Lockwood, USN, inspected *XE4* and asked to be given a demonstration. We took him

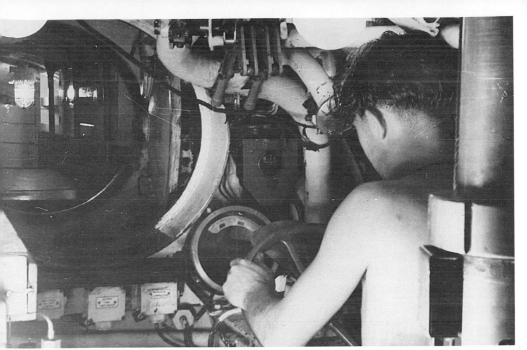

oking forward from the control room in XE4. Stoker Bill Gillard is in the helmsman's seat on the right; in front of him the
cular door through a bulkhead, leading to the W&D compartment from which the diver emerged and re-entered. This
npartment contained the WC. Further forward through the second watertight door is the battery compartment where the
w sleep, in some discomfort.

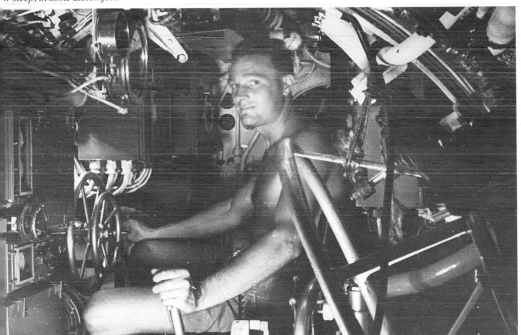

oking contentedly at home in the claustrophobic conditions in XE4, Leading Seaman Rhodes holds the trim control and the
droplane handwheel. He has the depth gauges before him and the side cargo release handwheel at his left shoulder.
usty" Rhodes had survived the sinking of S/M Tempest to be repatriated from Italian POW camp and volunteer for X-craft.
was mentioned in dispatches for his part in the passage crew on cable cutting operation.

XE4 being hoisted out of Bonaventure in Brunei harbour ready for the operation at Saigon to cut cables and sever Japanese communication with Singapore. On Bonaventure's port side, out of the picture waits Lt Cdr Youngman in Spearhead to tow us there and back. The side cargoes which give XE4 a pregnant look, hold twelve

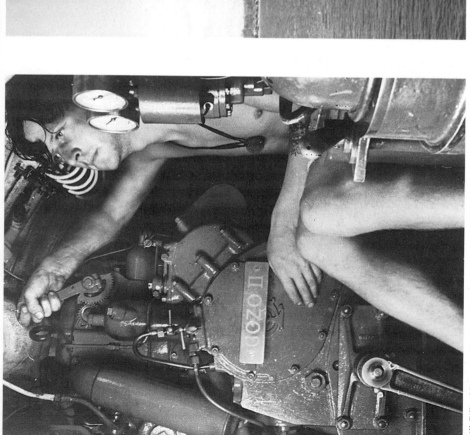

Bill Gillard has moved aft to indicate the decompression (hand start) lever on the diesel. On his left is the master gyro compass. The inclined cylinder top left is the air intake where the reconnaissance swimmer nearly lost his underpants.

for a run on the surface on engine, and dived quickly, sometimes referred to as 'crash dive', though this term had little relevance. We always dived quickly, wasting no time, to practise the crew. On this occasion, Ben said to me, "I forgot to shut the engine exhaust and muffler valves till we were well down." I nodded to him, saying nothing more, in order not to draw the Admiral's attention to a mistake. The engine was probably full of sea water, but, as long as we did not try to run it, no harm would be done for an hour or so. Ben was not to be put off. He told me again.

"Allright, Ben, I heard you. Just carry on," I said, but the Admiral had become aware that something was amiss.

Notwithstanding our flooded engine, we continued with a simulated attack on *Bonaventure* and returned our appreciative guest to the ship, where Ginge got busy pumping water from the crankcase, turning GOZO II by hand frequently. I was on the lower bridge when there sounded a pipe:

"Do you hear there? A cyclone is approaching. All *XE*-craft must leave their moorings and lay off immediately." I dived into the ocean and swam to *XE4* at her berth at the starboard after boom. Ben was also on board, so we got away on motor, stood off half a mile, and dived, sitting her gently on the harbour bed. Here, Ginge was able to continue with his pumping without further interruption while the wind screamed up top.

By the time Ginge had completed de-watering GOZO II, and given him an oil change, we reckoned that the worst of the wind may have passed, and came to periscope depth. The waves were only moderate, so we surfaced. I told Ginger that he could run his engine when he was ready, and soon the reassuring slow throb emanated from back aft. After GOZO II had time to warm up, and all looked in order, we went for a slow run on engine, around the harbour, to get rid of the last traces of water. The sump had already been flushed with fresh water and the run dried that out, so we were confident that all was well again, and so it was. Captain Fell was pleased to hear that no lasting harm had been done. The Admiral had seen and understood exactly what had happened. He had been a submariner himself, and no doubt had experienced a blunder or two in his time.

On 25th July, *Bonaventure* returned south to Brunei Bay in

Borneo, whence the other three operations were to start. Three S class submarines, fitted for towing, arrived, and final preparation were made. *XE4* was to be towed by *Spearhead*, commanded by Lt Cdr R E Youngman, RNR. We would take two divers because there were two cables to cut, one south to Singapore, and the other north to Hong Kong. Willie Britnell would again command the craft on tow, with ERA George Sheppard, Acting Petty Officer Victor "Dusty" Rhodes, and Stoker Percy Butters, as crew.

Operation "Sabre" had a secondary object, to destroy enemy shipping if present, and commenced at 0740 on 27th July, when *XE4*, under the command of Willie Britnell, secured the tow from *Spearhead* and proceeded toward what was then called French Indo China - now Vietnam.

Within an hour, she dived, which caused intermittent failure of the telephone, though it did remain sufficiently effective for our purpose. There was no need for chatter, and with a well established routine, most of the time the phone was not in use. Initially, the time between ventilations was six hours, but air became stale before the end of this period, so the interval was shortened to five hours. We tended not to use the air-conditioning plant because of the power it consumed and the consequent need for longer recharging periods on the surface at reduced towing speed.

Some of the crew were less experienced than others, as must happen with the flotilla in its third year, the movement of experienced men to other appointments, and new men joining. This was something all COs had to accept, a frequent replacement of older hands, by men with good potential which took time to develop to the full. Willie was experienced in towing, but the others had yet to become accustomed to the sensation, and to become skilled in depthkeeping at ten knots.

Ocean conditions were calm to moderate, making for reasonable comfort during the four-hour charge on the surface. It may seem odd that a submarine which had used power sparingly on lighting, gyro and occasional pumping, for twenty hours, should need four hours to recharge. The reason was that 'topping up' batteries to their full capacity was a slow process, requiring a long period at low current. It was necessary to have batteries near fully charged at all times to be ready for unforeseen circumstances. A nearly expended, or 'flat' battery, could accept a fast rate of charge, but to allow it to be in such a condition was risky. One could never be sure how long it would be and how much power would be needed before the next chance to remain on the surface to recharge. It may seem to non-submariners that a submarine had the advantage at all times, but its strategic advantage applied only so long as it remained undetected. Once located, it could only evade. It could not defend itself. Therefore, it must always be prepared to remain dived for as long as necessary for any threat to go away.

The three day tow was competently handled by the passage crew, without incident. At 0400 on the fourth day, crews changed over by bringing *XE4* close astern of *Spearhead*, making fast with a short line and running the motor astern to prevent contact. We stepped from one to the other. Sea and swell were low, enabling the changeover to be completed quickly and easily. The engine was run for half an hour to ventilate, following which we dived, and towed at ten knots. The craft was in excellent condition. At 1100 hours we surfaced to ventilate. I went up onto the casing to keep a lookout for aircraft as *Spearhead* had dived three hours earlier, and we were nearing Japanese held territory.

All that I saw of note was a sea snake quite close to port. These creatures abound in tropical waters and, while quite venomous, have small mouths capable of biting one's finger but nothing large. No doubt somebody will refute this, because snake stories also abound, in the tropics and everywhere else. We ventilated again at 1600. At 1900, *Spearhead* phoned to suggest that I might like to surface to have a look at Cape St Jacques lighthouse to the east north east, seventeen miles away. This was to be our principal landmark for the task ahead, when accurate position finding would be essential. I surfaced, took a quick look, went below, and dived the craft. We surfaced finally at 2100 hours, and having said our farewells, slipped the tow, and proceeded at half speed on engine toward Cape St Jacques. The night was quite dark, the lighthouse was not operating, and I could not yet distinguish its outline as we closed the shore. The only other landmark was a range of mountains called Nui Baria, to the north. Mountains are not the best for navigation because they are distant from the coast. Unless a bearing is absolutely accurate, the error in plotting a position increases with distance.   Nevertheless, they were very conspicuous and were useful as a rough check.

The wind was rising while we were running in to make a landfall on the lighthouse, setting up a short sea in the comparatively shallow water over the Formosa Bank. Spray swept over the casing, misting up the binocular lenses till they were useless. Several times I had to go below to clean them. To get back up on the casing in a choppy sea, one had to open the hatch and quickly leap up to sit on the casing, swing legs out of the hatchway, and over the side, and shut the hatch before a wave broke over the casing and down the hatch.

One time I did all this just as a larger wave than usual broke over the craft and swept me into the water. *XE4* was going slow ahead on engine, and by the time I got my head above water, I was back level with the rudder. I took several swift strokes, and grabbed at the jumping wire which ran from the periscope guard to the rudder. At this speed of about two knots, it was not difficult to pull myself hand over hand, forward along the wire, and regain the casing, even with the binoculars hanging on their lanyard around my neck.

I had to go below again to reclean the lenses and to inform the crew of my swim. They were not aware that anything was wrong. If I had missed that wire, which we had rigged for that very purpose, *XE4* would have continued on until maybe a quarter of an hour had passed before the crew noticed the absence of any communication from the upper deck. Then they would have discovered my absence and turned around to search, though a recovery would have been unlikely. But, I had caught the wire, after swimming the fastest few strokes of my life, so all was well. Next time on deck, I spotted the outline of the lighthouse.

Having established our position from our own observation and found, as expected, that it confirmed that given to us by *Spearhead* we stopped, and commenced standing charge of air and batteries. I rigged the grapnel in readiness for the day's work. The heavy steel 'Flat Fish' was already shackled to twenty feet of chain, and thirty feet of three and a half inch circumference sisal rope. This was spliced to a bridle which surrounded the hull, and was attached to the towing slip. The bridle ensured that the whole rig would be pulled from a point below the keel, near the seabed. The grapnel would be just aft of the propeller. The rope and chain had to be long enough so as not to lift the grapnel off the seabed if the submarine should rise, but not so long that the cutter with its hose would not reach. The towing slip was used as the point of attachment in order that the whole rig could be released from within, in case of necessity.

Once the grapnel was streamed, we had to take care not to get out of position. There were several abandoned cables radiating from the terminal station ashore. All but two had been abandoned over the years due to wave damage. We had to be sure of cutting those two cables which were in use, identifiable only by their positions. We were in the correct place to start grappling, and had to remain there until daylight. At the last moment, we would stream the grapnel and dive.

At 0330, I sighted two junks under sail, making for the mouth of the Mekong River and Saigon. They were heading for us. Not wanting to get out of position, I dived *XE4* and sat on the seabed until 0600. Just as dawn was near, we surfaced to ventilate and stream the grapnel. Three junks were close by, one heading in our direction, so I dived the boat earlier than I would have wished, and proceeded at slow speed toward shore, coming to periscope depth from time to time as daylight increased. There were several junks, under sail, as was the case throughout the day. I did not want to alter course for fear of getting off track and picking up the wrong cable, so went deep to let the junks pass overhead. Unlike the traffic near Bergen, there were no propeller noises to indicate the movement and proximity of passing traffic. Although the junks were not likely to sink us in a collision, they would damage the periscope with the slightest contact, and that would be a serious impediment to further navigation.

Here let me quote from my patrol report ...

"0748: Fixed position as NW edge of Formosa Bank. A/C (altered course) to 090 degrees and commenced first run, keeping depth 10 ft clear of the bottom.

My plan of operation was as follows -

First try to pick up Singapore cable on Formosa Bank where the water was shallow and divers could work longer and with ease. Failing that, to sweep further to seaward though the depth of water increases steadily to seaward and as all personnel were a little fatigued, working divers in deep water was not desirable. Having located and cut the Singapore cable, then proceed to sweep for the Hong Kong cable on the same line of soundings. Sweeping for the cables inside of Formosa Bank was considered inadvisable in view of the convergence of two unused cables and the presence of old pieces of cable in that vicinity. Formosa Bank seemed to be coarse sand and the grapnel dragged heavily. With average revolutions for two and a half knots, we made good 1.3 knots with .5 to 1 knot of tide in our favour.

0812: Altered course to 085 degrees, that is, toward wreck of cable ship (sunk on rock 1935) which was reported to be visible. The wreck was not visible though our navigation for once was correct for at...

0900: Struck rock/wreck, swung to starboard and concluded that we had completed the first run without success....."

The next run was started after turning to starboard and setting course to cross the cable's recorded position in slightly deeper water. There was nothing for the divers and me to do but to have patience. Ben was keeping depth as best he could with the ever changing pull of the rig, while Ginge was keeping her on course. I lay for a few minutes on the small bunk next to the chart table, feeling depressed. I knew that we could not expect to contact the cable first time. All the same, after all our trials, preparation and the activity of the previous twenty-four hours with little sleep, we had arrived at an anticlimax. What if we could not find the cable? How deep was it in the alluvial deposit from the Mekong River, the mouths being just a short distance away?

On the other hand, all was well with *XE4*. This was only the second run on the first morning. There was no deadline, we could carry on dragging for a long time yet. There did not seem to be any Japanese patrol vessels around, though among the junks there could be sympathetic or opportunistic observers, ready to report anything suspicious. We must not break surface, however difficult it was to control the craft's depth while pulling a sea plough.

At 1000, I came to periscope depth and took bearing on the lighthouse and mountains. We had passed the line of the cable for the second time. The Cable and Wireless company engineer had assured us that the positions as shown on the chart would be accurate to within fifty feet. We had ploughed across it twice, so it must be too deep in the sand. The next run must be in deeper water, where finer sand, or silt, could be expected. I turned to port and set course for run number three. The depth now exceeded forty feet. At 1027 the craft suddenly stopped. I increased motor speed. We remained in position until full speed, then moved forward. I turned to recross the same position, at reduced speed. She stopped again. This could be it, though there was a doubt. During trials, when a cable was caught, the grapnel did not let go. But the only way to be sure was to have a look. The motor was stopped, and water pumped into the compensating tank to hold the craft in position on the seabed. Water was flowing past the scuttles at about half a knot.

Ken Briggs dressed and went through the W&D. Depth showing on the gauge was forty feet, indicating a bottom depth of fifty feet. Ken must not remain there for more than fifteen minutes. The understanding between us was that the diver should attach himself to the cutter hose. Then, if he were overdue, we would surface, pull him aboard, dive immediately, revive him, and await any reaction from the Japanese. But nothing went wrong, except that Ken returned within five minutes to report there was no cable, only a patch of hard clay. We continued the third run, feeling rather disappointed.

Within ten minutes she stopped. Again, to quote the Patrol Report:

"1205: Craft brought up suddenly. At full ahead grouped up, she lurched and swung to port. Stopped motor and craft swung to tide - ship's head 220 deg. Tide appeared to be .5 to 1 knot. At full astern grouped up craft did not move. Stopped, and bottomed in 44ft (on gauge).

1229: Diver out (S/Lt Briggs, RANVR).

1236: Diver cut Saigon-Singapore cable.

1242:   Diver in with short length of cable as evidence."
First success. Well done Ken. Communications severed. But, to be doubly sure, the northbound cable should also be cut. We proceeded again at slow speed, coming round onto course 075 degrees and up to periscope depth for bearings to fix our position.
"1313:   A/C to 040 deg to cross cable at right angles.
1326:   Craft brought up suddenly. Depth of water 45 ft (on gauge). Ship's head 180 deg. Tide now much weaker.
1402:   Diver out (S/Lt A K Bergius, RNVR).
1407:   Diver cut Saigon-Hong Kong cable.
1414:   Diver in. Reported cable cut twice, but cutter not working efficiently, and cable had not parted.
1441:   Diver out (S/Lt Bergius). Cut cable again with second cutter.
1452:   Diver in with piece of cable. Due to the four cuts, cable had fallen apart and several pieces of armouring were lost in the mud. However, the diver had about one foot of the core as evidence."

The principal objective of Operation Sabre had been achieved, that is, assuming that they were the correct cables, which was not really in doubt, as bearings on the lighthouse had confirmed. We had intended to make another cut of this cable where it crossed a shallow patch, but when we arrived at that position, the water depth was sixty feet, so we called it a day, so far as cutting was concerned. The next move was to shift further from shore, away from the possibility of observation.

In the very early days of X-craft training, we had tried raising the engine air induction trunk when going slow at periscope depth, and opening the hull valve, keeping careful watch on the depth gauge. Water already in the pipe drained into the bilge. The engine was then started at slow speed ahead. The planesman had to be careful not to go below eight feet. When, occasionally, he did, the helmsman had to shut the air inlet valve immediately, to stop an inrush of water when the top of the induction trunk dipped below the surface. The engine continued to burn the air in the craft, causing the air pressure to fall steadily, and the depth gauges to read progressively a deeper than true depth. As soon as the trunk resurfaced, the air valve was opened, air rushed in, forcing a pipeful of water before it and restoring normal pressure. This sequence was repeated until the planesman got the hang of it, by which time the crew were rather tired of having their ears popped with falling and rising air pressure. With practice, crews became quite proficient, though they had to be on their toes every time depth increased. Failure to shut the air valve could result in flooding and sinking to the bottom.

We had reported this discovery to our superiors, who did not approve, as it was not considered to be good submarine practice. I agree that there was a risk involved. On the other hand, it enabled distance to be covered, and ventilation, in areas where the submarine could not be safely surfaced without being seen. There was a risk of radar detection, sighting the wake, and engine noise being picked up on hydrophones, so the use of this technique would have to be subject to discretion. At about that time, U-boats were fitted with a similar trunk for the same purpose, called a snorkel. They made effective use of it, though they experienced the same air pressure fluctuations as we did, and resulting nausea among the crew.

The situation off Saigon was conducive to a little snorkelling, and as the air in *XE4* was becoming stale, we ran the engine for 40 minutes at half speed, covering three miles without ill effect. This practice did impose a back pressure on the engine exhaust, but as long as all gaskets were tight, and only half power was developed, no harm was done. It certainly improved conditions in the craft, and nobody was sick, then or later. The periscope did vibrate a little, while the engine was running, so it would be inadvisable to employ this method before an attack, lest the periscope should develop a leak, one of the main difficulties in the *Tirpitz* operation.

There remained the secondary objective of an attack on ships in the Mekong River, for which we carried a full cargo of limpets. However, our divers had had enough for one day, so we sat *XE4* on the seabed to allow the crew to rest, and to wait for darkness. At 2132 we surfaced and commenced a standing charge at the maximum rate, to get the batteries up fast. After an hour, the HP air groups were fully replenished, so we proceeded with a running charge to the recovery position. At 2340, *Spearhead's* infra red beacon was sighted, and by 0100 on 1st August, we were close to her starboard side. I had a brief conference with her captain. I told him that the cables were cut. He told me that aerial reconnaissance showed that there were no ships at Saigon. We agreed that the job was finished, and proceeded to secure the tow. Again, the sea was calm enough for this to be done in close company, followed immediately by the changeover of crews. Within an hour the tow home was underway. The telephone cable, damaged in the act of securing the tow, was repaired next morning and worked all the way home. We reached *Bonaventure* in less than three days, with no defects.

This operation did not seem to have been as hazardous as those carried out in heavily defended harbours, like Bergen. No Japanese Naval vessels had been seen, though some of the junks could have been armed, or at least have been maintaining visual patrol, and Japanese Navy patrol vessels would be standing by in Saigon Harbours to hunt and destroy if a sighting report were received. The greatest risks were taken by the divers. Working depths down to thirty feet was reasonably safe, despite the fact that three had been drowned when no deeper than this. Cutting the cables at the depths encountered did involve a real risk of loss of consciousness. Ken and Adam were aware of this, and worked accordingly.

Technique was important. It could mean the difference between success and failure. Both men had worked with care and skill. Each had had to make two exits in order to complete the job, and would have been near the limit of his endurance by the time of his re-entry, when shutting the main hatch required the maximum strength that he could muster. That each of them completed the whole evolution twice, without delay, is a tribute to their expertise and determination. It is said that an expert makes the difficult look easy.

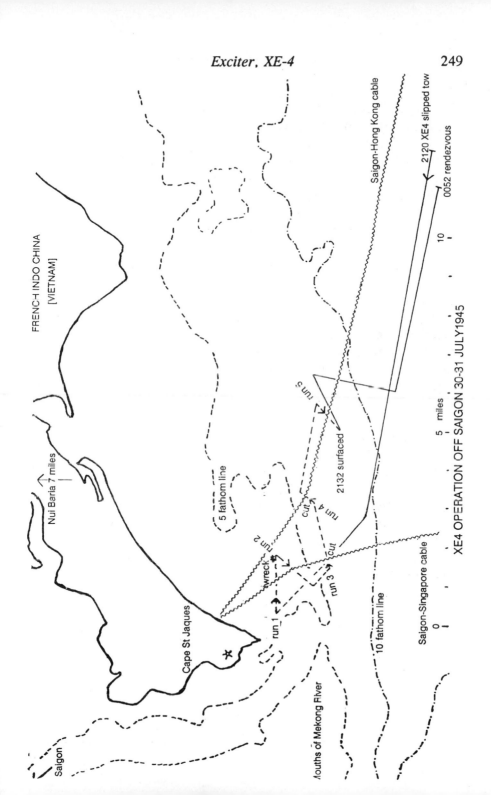

FRENCH INDO CHINA
[VIETNAM]

Nui Baria 7 miles

5 fathom line

Saigon-Hong Kong cable

2120 XE4 slipped tow

0052 rendezvous

10

run 5

2132 surfaced

Cut
run 4

run 2

wreck

Cape St Jaques

run 1

Cut
run 3

10 fathom line

Saigon-Singapore cable

Mouths of Mekong River

Saigon

5   miles

0

XE4 OPERATION OFF SAIGON 30-31 JULY1945

CHAPTER TWENTY FOUR

FINAL OPERATION

All craft returned in good order. Pat Westmacott had persevered in his cable cutting at Hong Kong, though the job was made difficult by the depth of mud and his diver injured his finger in the cutter. Tich Fraser had also managed an effective attack on his cruiser, in spite of very little space between her bottom and the seabed. His diver showed great tenacity in getting limpets into place. Jack Smart was unable to reach his cruiser, which was further up the Strait. That all craft were in good condition was ample indication of the progress made in combating the difficulties encountered in the *Tirpitz* operation only twenty two months before.

It was considered important to cripple the second cruiser *Myoko*. Tich and I were called into Captain Fell's cabin and told that we were to prepare for the attack. What action! We were only days after returning from one sortie and were into the next. This was stimulating, and I felt encouraged that our flotilla was proving so valuable, compared with initial indications upon our arrival in the Pacific a few months earlier. I told my crews of our mission, and the urgency of preparation. There was instant activity.

I studied the geography of the Johore Strait, and started to plan our attack. One of the obvious difficulties was that if Jack could not make the distance, how would we? Johore Strait was a narrow waterway, not wide enough to allow an X-craft to traverse on the surface undetected, even at night, yet too long, from entrance to target, to allow submerged approach, attack and withdrawal within the daylight hours. It seemed that we would have to spend one night within the Strait. This meant entering past the net defences early on the first day, finding as remote a place as possible where we could surface and charge overnight, attack early next morning and withdraw. By the time we could have reached the defences again, our charges would have detonated and all defence operators once again alerted to the presence of an attacker. This would be similar to the situation around *Tirpitz* on 22nd September 1943. There would be no big guns, as we would be many miles from the cruiser, but patrol vessels would be on the lookout for anything that moved. I thought over this at length, and talked with Tich. We could think of no plan to avoid these two risks; that of being caught while charging at night within defended waters, and that of detection on the way out. It would be about a month after the first attack, and the resultant activity and attention would hardly have subsided. I was a little apprehensive as to our chances of remaining undetected.

There was a difference between emergency escape briefing for the Norway operations and for the Japanese held areas. In the former case, as long as we were in uniform, even if apprehended while trying to get back to Allied held territory, the worst that was likely to happen was capture, interrogation, and imprisonment in some PoW camp. With the Japanese, we could expect to be decapitated or, if we were lucky, retained under starvation conditions in sub-standard camps. Whereas escape from PoW camps in Germany could sometimes be successful, from a Japanese PoW camp, it seldom was. We were advised not to try.

Notwithstanding these concerns, we completed our preparation, including a towing exercise with *HMS Spark*, and the eve of departure arrived. Reaction from our Saigon operation was now showing among crew members. We all felt the customary depression, but Willie Britnell's crew felt it most. They had been subjected to more rigorous conditions than my crew. I have described the constant feelings of anxiety when on tow. I had been exhausted on my first tow of one day; they endured it for six, and were about to go through it again, before they had recovered from the first lot. Willie and I had difficulty in reassuring his crew. In fact, the passage should be no worse than the recent one, and that had gone well. But as I said earlier, rationalising may satisfy the conscious mind, but sub-consciously, uneasiness may prevail, and it did then in all of us, though some kept it to themselves. I tried to reassure all members that we all felt the same, deep down, that the passage crew had shown themselves more than capable for such a task, and that it would be a short, conclusive operation. Nobody opted out, but there were still some very unsure people.

At this time another factor, with the opposite effect, arose. The daily news sheet which appeared on *Bonaventure's* notice boards, reported that two 'atomatic' bombs had been dropped on two Japanese cities. I had no knowledge of any such weapon, though from my university studies, I was well aware of the theoretical possibilities of nuclear energy. Reading this news release, it struck me that nuclear energy had been developed in this surprising form, and that the message surely should read 'atomic'. The subject was well discussed in the wardroom, as it must have been discussed everywhere else. Further details on the extent of the devastation soon followed. We all felt a sense of tremendous relief. Our operation was still on, but we considered that, following such an attack, with the probability of more to follow, Japan, who was already on the run, with their own military resources declining, while ours were mounting, must capitulate, unless they were led by a maniac of Hitler's class.

Rumours of a surrender circulated. That night, the gun's crew of one of our S class towing submarines, lying alongside *Bonaventure*, manned their gun and commenced firing starshell. It was a lovely sight. The immediate response was a signal from the senior ship in Brunei Bay.

"Cease pyrotechnic display. The war is not over yet." The next outcome was a signal to *XE3* and *XE4*,

"Sailing delayed until further notice."

"This," I thought, "is our reprieve." I lost no time in informing my crews. I had mixed feelings, of anticlimax due to the challenging operation for which we were prepared, now being unlikely to proceed, and intense relief in the knowledge that my crew and I would be spared the risk of extinction. We were saved by the bombs. Nobody expressed outrage that this was an unfair way to treat such an enemy.

Bonaventure called at Subic Bay to hoist *XE5* aboard and set off for Sydney. There were celebrations, of course, as soon as the surrender was announced. I had already thought carefully about my future. While in Brisbane, earlier in the year, I had taken the opportunity to discuss what I should do, with an experienced professional engineer who, with his family, had entertained several of my crew. I was unsure whether I would resume studies after the cessation of hostilities, or join the workforce, which was fully employed at the time, and become rich more quickly. He left me in no doubt. Return to university and qualify, then do what I would. I had heard that before, from the recruiting officer at Fremantle, in 1940. Subconsciously, that was my compulsion, but I needed to test it with one who was unaffected by the influences of five years of distracting activity. I had written to Professor Blakey, Dean of the Faculty of Engineering at the University of W A, asking if I would be re-admitted, and received an encouraging reply.

As *Bonaventure* approached the Australian coast, there was a suggestion from her Staff Officer that, in order to show what our flotilla could do, a mock attack could be mounted on Sydney Harbour, and that I should lead it. I replied that the war was over; I did not consider such an exercise, where there would be a real danger of collision, was worth the risk. The idea was dropped. But the press did come aboard and interviewed many of us. I received more than a fair share of attention, being an Australian. The ABC asked me to record a talk, and all sorts of other involvements crowded in. I began to appreciate additional advantages of top secrecy. It was a remarkable thing to read all about *X*-craft in the Sydney Morning Herald.

Tiny Fell sent for me several days after our arrival in Sydney Harbour, and advised that he was to fly to Melbourne next morning, and would like me to go with him, then on to W A, on leave, and to demobilisation, if that could be arranged. He knew of my university's letter to me, and the disposal of personnel was now one of his urgent responsibilities. I thanked him, accepted, and hurried to pack and to hand over the care of *XE4* to Ben. Then there were the crew farewells and 'sippers' (of rum) in the ERA's mess, mainly from Ginge.

In the plane to Melbourne, I scribbled notes for the ABC,

and called at their studio on arrival. I was sat at a desk before a microphone, and got on with my first public revelation of formerly top secret material. When, five minutes later, it was finished, I found, at my elbow, a cheque for five pounds. That was my first peacetime earning from my wartime experience. It was also my last. Next, at the Navy Office, I tendered my university letter, informed them that third term was about to start, and was given two weeks' leave while my discharge application was being processed.

So, it was a quick farewell to Tiny Fell, and we parted in Melbourne without more ado. My rehabilitation had begun. The RAAF would fly me home the next day. I boarded the Dakota at Essendon airport, and sat among a full complement of servicemen and women. There were two long seats, each occupying the full length of the cabin, against the sides. At Cook, the crew brought an urn of coffee for us passengers, a very kind action. During the next hop to Perth airport, the wireless operator came to me with a welcome home message from Rom Moran, one of "R" class, now a flight controller at Perth. My family and friends were at the airport of course, sister Yvonne in her WRANS uniform. My mother had spent hour upon hour gazing, in solitude I believe, out to sea, during the last five years, and now it was allright; her family was together again. Many a mother was still searching.

That was a Friday. Monday morning I went to University and called on Professor Blakey, Dean of the Faculty. He welcomed me with more compliments than I deserved, and advised where I would slot back into the somewhat altered course. I attended lectures the same morning, wondering whether the early wartime predictions of "never settling down" would become an insuperable obstacle. I admit that I did feel out of place among this class of youth, five years younger than I. This was felt by them as well, and took a matter of days to dispel. Those undergraduates are now among my closest associates. A bogy had evaporated.

Mary arrived by ship to Sydney in November, and, after several welcoming parties by family representatives quite unknown to her, was put aboard the train for Perth, passing Kalgoorlie in 104° of heat. The day she came home to my parents' house in Suburban Road, South Perth, there came a knock on the door.

Yvonne answered to find a navy lieutenant with a slight limp.

"Come in," she said, without any enquiry. It was a day when, whatever happened, it was allright. Peter Philip introduced himself. Mary hugged him, the only other person she knew on this side of the continent. Peter was bound for his home in Cape Town, aboard a ship which called at Fremantle; a more opportune coincidence I could not have wished.

Before the expiry of my leave, I was summoned to *HMAS Leeuwin*, as the Fremantle Naval Depot was called, to be formally discharged. The officer involved mentioned that the press would like to meet me. I replied that the Navy and hostilities were now behind me. I had a degree to study for, and anyhow, did not want to become an "old sailor" who could do nothing but recall glories of the past, not that they were all that glorious. He gave me a little advice. The services must continue to maintain a certain strength, even in peacetime. This meant obtaining an adequate annual budget allocation in Federal Parliament. The degree of success depended largely on the whole population's appreciation of the need for an adequate Force. Publicity was needed to keep the people informed. I had a naval story to tell. It was my duty to the service to take every opportunity to do so. This I had to accept, and have done, as best I could, ever since.

On 18th November, 1945, Admiralty announced that the King had been graciously pleased to give orders for the following appointment to the Distinguished Service Order, and to approve the following Honours and Awards:

Bar to D S O, Lt Maxwell Henry Shean, DSO, RANVR.
The Distinguished Service Cross:
Sub-Lt Adam Kennedy Bergius, RNVR.
Sub- Lt Kenneth Maxwell Briggs, RANVR.
Mention in Despatches:
Sub-Lt John Britnell, RNVR.
Sub-Lt Bernard Alexander Niall Kelly, RNVR.
ERA Vernon Coles.
ERA George Maldon Sheppard.
P O Victor Douglas Rhodes.
Sto Percy William Butters.

The President of the United States awarded me the Bronze Star.

   People ask me, "What is it like to be depth charged?" I feel that I am disappointing them when I tell them that I never had that experience. A submarine's only defence was to remain undetected. We had neither the guns with which to fight back, nor speed sufficient to run away. The object was to reach the target, place explosives with detonation time-delay, and to withdraw to the open sea, without the enemy knowing that we had been there. Far from feeling that I had let my audiences down, I take some satisfaction in the fact that no submarine in my command was ever detected. Otherwise, I would probably not now be telling you about it.
   What of those five years? War is, of course, a folly, peculiar to humans, who nevertheless describe it as 'inhuman'. For the individual faced with it, as we all were, it was a fact to be reckoned with. Anyone with a social conscience could not ignore it. We ex-servicemen are frequently accused of glorifying war. Our accusers apparently cannot understand why people defend what is threatened and why the survivors honour those who died in the process, and their dependents.
   Having said that, what of *Bluebell's* and the *X*-craft's contribution? As for *Bluebell*, she probably sank one U-boat, forced another to submerge and prevented any attack on OG77. She escorted many other merchant ships safely to their destination; ninety five percent of them, and she rescued many of the crews of the five percent which were torpedoed.
   Of *X*-craft, the crippling of the *Tirpitz* alone made it worth their existence, and all other operations added to that success. They were fully operational at the end of the war, ready for whatever work, in their own line, that needed doing.
   For myself, I take some satisfaction from *Bluebell's* success and survival during the 14 months of my appointment, for the engineering contribution I was able to make to *X*-craft operation and maintenance and, above all, the maintenance of their crews. That no one was lost while under my command was, no doubt, largely due to the seamanship and efficiency of our whole crew with, perhaps, some contribution by way of good fortune from our caul,

wishbone, Tiki, Mickey Mouse, and the thoughts, prayers and good wishes of our friends and loved ones.

Having introduced several characters in detail, it would be as well to report on their subsequent progress. Peter Taylor returned to university and completed a Bachelor of Science in Engineering degree, married Charlotte, and entered the field of commercial engineering in Sydney. They had two children and led a happy life until Peter suffered a nervous breakdown and died a few years later. In support of Charlotte's application for a war widow's pension, I made a declaration in which I quoted Peter's account of an action he experienced in a cruiser; "Only the laundry and I knew how frightened I was." The success of the application gave me the immense satisfaction of having been able to help my shipmate's widow in the spirit of Legacy.

Wilfred Stiff pursued his musical career to become manager of the Royal Liverpool Philharmonic Orchestra. He married Susan and also had two children. Wilf became a musical entrepreneur, and when I asked him if he had been able to assist any of his clients to reach the heights, he replied, "Well, there was Janet Baker."

Robert E Sherwood won a DSO in *Tay* and survived the war to return to the sea. I wrote to tell him of our reported success in sinking *U208*, of which he was unaware. He and Wilf kept up their friendship and I did see him make a convincing statement on convoy defence action in a television series on the war at sea, and noticed that he had put on a little weight.

Naturally I have maintained closer touch with those with whom I sailed in submarines, later in the war. Joe Brooks, on completion of his commission in the RN set up an engineering business, specialising in underwater work, carrying out many difficult projects around the British Isles connected with oil and gas production. He married Eileen and had two daughters and a son. He lost both feet in a diving accident while still in the RN, and succeeded in the tremendous task of learning to carry on with tin legs. This triumph over adversity was consistent .with his performance in *X*-craft.

Ginger Coles served on for many years in submarines and later was appointed engineer in charge of the USA base at

Greenham Common. He Married Marie, has three children and coordinates gatherings of the X-craft personnel with particular emphasis on *X24* and *XE4* crews. Whenever I visit the UK, I look forward to the first meeting with Joe and Ginge. On the last occasion we discussed a list of questions concerning these writings, while I made notes and a tape record. It took a while for the three of us to ignore the recorder, but those tapes are among my treasured souvenirs, to be played whenever I need the comradeship of my former shipmates.

Adam Bergius married Fiona, and raised a thoroughly Scottish family of five. He became Director of William Teacher and Son, whisky distillers, and the owner of a succession of fine yachts. He is an "old world" sailor who shuns modern aids like electronic instruments and manages quite well with his thorough seamanship. He and Fiona are excellent hosts, and many a happy hour have Mary and I spent in their company, though we have yet to visit their new home on the west coast of the Mull of Kintyre.

Willie Britnell married Joan, a *Varbel* Wren, and has been brewing in Canada. Indeed he is, so busy we have met but once in all these years, though we do correspond, at Christmas.

Ben Kelly did not marry, continuing to live in Edinburgh. Although his health deteriorated in recent years, he did attend gatherings of flotilla veterans, and died but recently.

Ken Briggs married Doris, has a daughter and worked for some years in Perth, for the British United Shoe Machinery Company, who, you may recall, had manufactured a component for *Bluebell's* gyro-stabilised hedgehog control. Ken returned to Queensland and inspired his nephew to follow a naval career, a recent appointment being Naval Officer Commanding, Western Australia.

Ginge keeps the ERAs in touch, and through him I have met Syd Rudkin, Eddy Goddard of *X7*, "Tubby" Fishleigh of *X10*, and many others. Regrettably I have lost contact with Bill Gillard, Ivor Rock, Percy Butters and other shipmates, but Brace (Lofty) Element lately declared his happy settlement in Australia.

Mary presented me with daughters Heather, who qualified in Occupational Therapy and teaches violin at Scotch College, and

Ruth, a qualified teacher, now Chief Executive Officer of the Cerebrol Palsey Association, providing therapy to its clients.

Captains Banks and Fell I contacted from time to time. Being senior to me in years, as well as rank, they have long since anchored in the "port of many ships", so I will tell of our last encounters. In 1979, I had sailed my yacht *Bluebell* from Fremantle to UK, to compete in a race to celebrate the 150th year since settlement of the State of Western Australia. The race was from Plymouth via Cape Town to Fremantle, in the track of the ship Parmelia, which had been chartered to bring the first settlers.

I had advised each of my former captains of my intentions. Willie Banks arranged to meet Mary and me at Fortingall, near Aberfeldy, for dinner, while Tiny Fell, living in Wellington, New Zealand, instructed me to report, in writing, at each stage of the voyage. The dinner with Audrey and Willie was a delight. Willie presented me with an *IIMS Dolphin* tie, which I wear on every appropriate occasion. He also arranged for a Major Sillitoe, Royal Marines, to dine us in his barracks in Plymouth, another enjoyable evening. Meanwhile, I had written to Tiny recounting progress in our navigation of the Indian Ocean, Red Sea, Suez Canal, Mediterranean, French inland waterways, and the English Channel. The next report was of the fifty seven day passage to Cape Town, and finally our arrival at Fremantle on the specified day, 25th November, to win the Open Division.

Tiny, now in his advancing years, was obviously pleased. Thinking back to my first meeting with him, he a four-ringed captain, I a "wavy navy" sub lieutenant, I, too, was pleased that the gap in our ranks, had been bridged by a caring and lasting friendship between a flotilla captain and one of his submariners. It was deeply satisfying to have brought him such pleasure in his latter days as to have him reply, "You splendid man."

GLOSSARY

A/S.	Anti submarine.
aft.	Towards stern of ship.
asdic.	Anti-submarine detector. (Initials of Anti-submarine Detection Committee)
blow main ballast.	Admit air into ballast or buoyancy tank of submarine to displace water and cause submarine to surface.
Cdr.	Commander.
CinCWA.	Commander in Chief Western Approaches (to UK).
CO.	Commanding officer.
davit.	Crane for hoisting boat or depth charge, for example.
dhobying.	Washing clothes.
drifter.	Boat used in fishing with drift nets.
DSEA.	Oxygen breathing equipment used when escaping from a submarine. (Initials of Davis Submarine Escape Apparatus)
ersatz.	Immitation; artificial. (from German)
falls.	Tackle comprising rope and blocks for hoisting boat.
FOCNA	Flag Officer Commanding North Atlantic
FOS	Flag Officer Submarines
gash.	Naval for surplus or rubbish.
Grey Funnel Line	Colloquial for Royal Navy.
HG.	Convoy homeward bound from Gibraltar to UK.
heads.	Toilets.
hydroplane.	Horizontal rudder for depth control.
Lt. or Lieut.	Lieutenant.
log.	Instrument for measuring speed or distance travelled through water; ship's diary.
loom.	Of oars, the rounded section for the oarsman's hands.
main ballast tank.	Submarine's buoyancy tank.
main vent.	Air release valve at top of ballast tank.
mess.	Section of ship's company taking meals together.
No 1.	First lieutenant of a ship; executive officer.
OG.	Convoy outward bound from UK to Gibraltar.
OOD.	Officer of the day, in harbour.
OOW.	Officer of the watch, at sea.
PAC.	Anti-aircraft rocket with wire suspended by parachutes.
periscope.	Tall optical instrument enabling submariners to see above the surface when dived.

plot.	Graphical representation of ship's progress.
PO.	Petty officer.
port.	Left hand side of ship looking forward.
Protosorb.	Chemical used to remove carbon dioxide from air or oxygen.
Q.	Quick diving tank which is filled with sea water to add weight to submarine when diving.
RANVR.	Royal Australian Naval Volunteer Reserve.
RDF.	Radio direction finder; code name for radar when newly invented, to preserve secrecy.
RLB.	Royal Liver Building in Liverpool, housing RN administration.
side cargo.	Midget submarine explosive weapon secured each side.
slip.	Device for releasing tow line etc; to let go.
S/Lt.	Sub-lieutenant; rank below lieutenant.
S/M.	Submarine.
SO.	Senior officer of a flotilla.
splice the main brace.	
	Issue a tot of rum, initially to seamen on completion of a difficult job of rejoining a broken rope on a large sail of a square rigged ship.
starboard.	Right hand side of ship looking forward.
telegraph.	Communication system between wheelhouse and engineroom.
trawler.	Vessel used in fishing with trawl nets, larger than a drifter.
U-boat.	German submarine.
W&D.	Exit chamber for diver in midget submarine. (Wet and Dry)
WRNS.	Women's Royal Naval Service.
X-craft.	RN midget submarine of about 30 tons displacement.
1000.	10.00 am; in RN practice a four figure number up to 2400 usually means time. A capital letter following defines time zone; eg 1000Z [Zulu] means 10.00 am Greenwich Mean Time, not South African time as some might think.

BIBLIOGRAPHY

Axis Submarine Successes. *Jurgen Rowher* (Ian Allen)
British Vessels Lost at Sea 1939-45. *British Official Statements* (Patrick Stephens)
Embleme, Wappen, Malings deutscher U-boote. *Hogel* (Hogel Munich 1984)
German Naval History. U-boat War in the Atlantic. *Hessler* (HMSO)
Nightmare Convoy. *Lund and Ludlam* (Foulsham)
Oxford Illustrated Dictionary. (Clarendon Press)
Royal Australian Navy 1939-1942 and 1942-1945. *G Herman Gill* (Australian War Memorial)
Sink the Tirpitz. *Peillard* (Jonathan Cape)
Supplement to the Goverment Gazette of 10th February 1948. (HMSO)
The Mystery of X-5. *Walker and Mellor* (William Kimber)
The War at Sea. *Roskill* (HMSO)
U-boats. A Pictorial History. *Edwin Hoyt* (McGraw Hill)
U-boat Ace. The Story of Wolfgang Lüth. *Jordan Vause*
U-boats Under the Swastika. *Showell* (Ian Allen)
U-333: The Story of a U-boat Ace. *Cremer* (Bradley Head)
Very Special Intelligence. *Patrick Beasley* (Hamish Hamilton)

APPENDICES

SUMMARY OF BLUEBELL'S CONVOYS: JULY 1941 TO SEPTEMBER 1942

Convoy Number	Depart	Arrive	Ships Lost	U-boats hunting convoy
OG68	12 July	26 July	nil	nil
SL81	28 July	9 Aug	*Belgravian, Swiftpool, Cape Rodney, Harlingen Kumasian*	*U46, 74, 75, 83, 97, 204, 205, 372, 401*, 481, 558, 559, 565*
OG71	13 Aug	23 Aug	*Alva, Aguila, Ciscar. Empire Oak, Clonlara, Zinnia, Aldergrove, Stork, Bath*	*U75, 83, 106, 201, 204, 372+, 559, 564*
HG72	5 Sep	17 Sep	*Daru*(bombed)	nil
OG 75	27 Sep	14 Oct	nil	*U71, 83, 205, 432, 563 564.*
HG 75	22 Oct	3 Nov	*Cossack, Carsbreck, Alhama, Ariosto, Ulea [Ariguani, torpedoed but not sunk]*	*U71, 83, 204+, 205, 563, 564*
OG 77	28 Nov	13 Dec	nil	*U43, 67, 208*, 434+*
HG 77	31 Dec	12 Jan	nil	nil
OG 79	26 Jan	7 Feb	nil	nil
HG 79	22 Feb	6 Mar	nil	nil
OG81	17 Mar	29 Mar	nil	nil
HG81	5 Apr	15 Apr	nil	nil

Note: U-boats marked * were sunk by convoy escorts. Those marked + were sunk by other ships during this period.

Date : 11-12th December, 1941.

Weather: Fine, Cloudy, Visibility 6.
    Wind S.E. Force 1
    Sea and Swell: OO
Asdic Conditions: Fair. Contact very weak at 1200 yards.

     Report commences from time of R.D.F.contact - 2343 Convoy Q.Q.77.
Course 208°. Speed 8 kts.
BLUEBELL in position line of bearing 170°, 5 miles from convoy. Course 208°,
Speed 12 kts. Zig-Zag.

————————

2343   R.D.F. contact bearing 095 degrees, 5000 yds. Altered course to
      bring contact ahead. R.D.F. were ordered to report when range
      closed to 3000 yds.

2345   R.D.F. range 3000 yds. At same time submarine bow wave and stern wash
      observed ahead. Commenced Asdic transmission. Submarine's inclination
      about 050 degrees left, proceeding at high speed. Course altered
      40 degrees to port to intercept, and speed increased to Full.

2346   Asdic reported H.E. and torpedo was heard to pass down starboard side.

2347   Asdic reported H.E.loud. Submarine appeared to increase speed.

2348   Target appeared to grow smaller. Assumed that sub. was attempting
      to dive, but was unsuccessful.

2349   Further attempt was made to dive without success.
      Submarine was by this time ahead and on the same course, range closing
      very slowly.

2353   Submarine not being visible from gun platform, decided to fire one
      starshell and attempt to fire direct action in the light of the star.
      Unfortunately the starshell did not burst. D.A. was however, fired
      but no hit was observed. Further starshell was fired and again did
      not burst. It was found that the flash from the gun blinded the Bridge
      personnel, so decided to abandon the idea of shelling.

2354   Asdic obtained contact at 1100 yds, brg. 000°, moving rapidly left, marked
      opening. The enemy had apparently turned about 90° to port. Owing to the
      blindness by gun flash, he was not observed until bearing Red 60°. Asdic
      reported torpedo fired. Helm was put hard aport to comb the spread, and
      contact again brought right ahead.

2354-5. Enemy dived on course of about 320°. R.D.F. lost contact, range 800 yds,
      having held it all this time.

2355   Asdic range 700 yds.

2357   Fired light pattern set to 100 ft. on moderately good contact. The wake
      of submarine was clearly visible and the charges appeared to explode at
      correct distance ahead of the diving swirl.

0001   Regained contact, range 900 yds. Opened range to 1200 yds, and turned to
      attack. Target drawing slowly right. No doppler. Clear, sharp echo.

0004   Fired second pattern, set to 150 ft. On run out after firing, contact was
      regained and held to 700 yds. At this range it was lost and not regained;
      it is impossible to understand why. Continued to search in area.

0018   Asdic bearing tell-tale light and recorder failed. Continued search for
      further 25 minutes, by aid of torch on bearing mirror. No a very successful
      method, so, as nothing was found, returned to convoy.

                    R.E. Sherwood
                      Lt.Cdr. R.N.R.
                      Commanding Officer.

From : The Commanding Officer, H.M.S. Zest.

Date : 26th February 1945.   Ref. R. 14.

To : Captain (D), Second Destroyer Flotilla.

                    Sinking of H.M.S. BLUEBELL.

            The following account of the above is forwarded.

            About 1522A, 17th February 1945 whilst "Zest" was moving from
the port beam, position P on Close Screen, to the port quarter of the convoy,
Extended Screen, my attention was called by the Midshipman of the Watch to
the above ship, approximately in position P, by the remark that she appeared
to be increasing speed and altering course. I agreed but thought nothing of
it until about half a minute later I saw her blow up.

        2.   It immediately occurred to me that the ship must have already
been in contact with and was actually moving out to attack the U-boat at the
moment when the latter sank her.   It seemed therefore that there was a good
chance of detecting the killer and I ordered the relevant information to be
passed to D.17.   No trace of this signal can be found in "Zest's" R/T Log
and it seems regrettably certain that it was never passed, probably due to
the fact that T.B.S. Watch whilst leaving harbour and forming up the Convoy
had been kept in the W/T Office and was being turned over to Bridge Control
at the moment when the signal should have gone.   A rather similar signal was,
however, passed to "OPPORTUNE" at 1547.

        3.   "Zest" reached the scene of the sinking about 1536 when cries
were heard from about a dozen men who could just be discerned in the failing
light.   Although various floats and rafts from the sunk ship were drifting
in the vicinity, none was near enough to be of use and I therefore dropped
more, though it seems certain that none of the few survivors had the strength
even to reach them. If I could have stopped then it might have been possible
to rescue the majority of these men but instead I regretfully continued my
course to carry out an "Observant" in the hopes of detecting the U-boat.

        4.   The course to start this from the Datum Point was 300°, the course
to which H.M.S. BLUEBELL appeared to have altered immediately prior to being
sunk.   Whilst on the second leg of the search "Zest" was joined by "OPPORTUNE"
and on the latter's orders I returned to the sinking to pick up survivors.
The whaler was lowered at 1553 at which time there were still 3 or 4 voices to
be heard, but from scattered sources.   I shouted encouragement to them but it
was not possible to pick up more than one at a time.   Three were actually
recovered in an unconscious state, but only one revived, although artificial
respiration was continued for nearly 5 hours on the other two.

        5.   The whaler was hoisted at 1630 and "OPPORTUNE" and "ZEST" then
proceeded to rejoin the screen.

        6.   I spoke to this survivor, A/P.O. A.E.G. HOLMES, Official Number
P/JX.217490 next morning, who had been standing on the starboard side by
the Engine Room when the ship was struck.   He agreed that the ship was
increasing speed and said that he had just been sent for by the Captain,
possibly to pipe Action Stations (he was Chief Boatswain's Mate).   He retained
consciousness throughout, was with his Captain afterwards in the water, but did
not remember being picked up.

        7.   As reported in my 180905, the two dead men, Able Seaman W.H.BUTCHER
Official Number not known and another, now believed to have been Chief Mechanici
Edwards, Official Number not known, were buried next morning with due honours.
The sum of £13. -. 6d. was found on the former and taken on charge in the
Contingent Account.   The latter had an unusual cigarette-lighter from which
Petty Officer HOLMES later deduced his identity.

                                        Lieutenant Commander R.N.
                                        Commanding Officer.

THE TIMES SATURDAY MARCH 17 1945

THE ROLL OF HONOUR

H.M.S. BLUEBELL

The Board of Admiralty regrets to announce the following casualties sustained in H.M. corvette Bluebell, the loss of which has already been announced. Next-of-kin have been notified:—

OFFICERS

MISSING, PRESUMED KILLED

Walker, Lt. G. H., D.S.C., R.N.V.R. (in command); Fahy, T/A/Sub-Lt. A. M., R.N.V.R.; Hill, T/Sub-Lt. D. R., R.N.R.; Mackie, T/Sub-Lt. I., R.N.V.R.; Twiss, T/Lt. W. W., R.A.N.V.R.; Walton, T/Lt. A., R.N.V.R.

RATINGS

MISSING, PRESUMED KILLED

Allan, D., A.B.; Atkinson, R., Sto. 1; Baillie, S. McL., Tel.; Baxter, R. L., Sto. 1; Bellingham, T. J., A.B.; Brooks, J., Ord. Tel.; Brown, G., A/Sto. 1; Burgess, H., Cdr.; Butcher, W. H., A.B.; Carpenter, G. J., A.B.; Cheal, L. H., A.B.; Chopping, H. H., Ord. Sigmn.; Cooke, A. T., A.B.; Coombes, C., A.B.; Cooper, J. A. L., A.B.; Cox, E. B., A.B.; Crouch, H. G., P.O., R.F.R.; Cunliffe, J., A.B.; Davies, H. H., Sto. P.O.; Day, A. C., A.B.; Edwards, I. W. R., A/Ldg. Sto. (ly.); Edwards, W. K., Ch. Mechn.; Elling, P. H., Tel.; Erikson, C. E., Ldg. Supp. Asst.; Ferrier, R. K., A/E.R.A. 4; Flander, W. T., A/A.B.; Foster, E. W. G., Sto. 1; Gardner, R. F. A., Sto. 1; Gaul, S. G., Ordn. Mech. 5; Gentle, R. W., Ord. Smn.; Goodwill, W. E., Ldg. Sto.; Graham, W., A.B.; Greenslade, C. J., A.B.; Guest, A., A.B.; Hatchman, H. O., Sto. 1; Herrington, H. L., Tel.; Hill, J., Sigmn.; Howey, T., A.B.; Jones, S. V., A.B.; Kendall, D. P., Asst. Stwrd.; Kilgour-Miller, J. W., Sto. P.O.; Kilvert, R. W., Sigmn.; Lacey, J. H., Ldg. Tel.; Lambert, J., A.B.; Lawrence, J. E., Ord. Tel.; Lee, A., A.B.; Lee, D. S., Sto. 2; Lightowler, G., Ldg. Stwrd.; Loakes, S., Sto. 2; McBridge, J.P., A.B.; McGhee, W., A/A.B.; McGrath, D. D., A.B.; McNish, C., A.B.; McPhee, H., Sto. 1; Marchant, J. E., Cdr.; Marshall, E., Sto. 2; Martin, J. H., Ldg. Smn.; Masson, J. S. B., A/Sto. 1; Mears, A. A., A/A.B.; Mitchell, B. E. J., Ldg. Radio Mech.; Morgan, W., Sto. 2; Morris, J. A., S.B. Attend.; Nunn, W. F., Sto. P.O.; Owen, W., A.B.; Perkins, M. S., Ord. Sigmn.; Phillips, D. A. J., A/A.B.; Potter, R. E. W., A.B.; Reade, G. F., A/A.B.; Saunders, F., A.B.; Scott, L. G., Cdr.; Shaw, K., A/A.B.; Sherburn, R., A.B.; Shute, D. T., A/Ldg. Sto.; Staves, E., A.B.; Stockwell W. S., P.O.; Swan, J., A.B.; Thompson, R. L., Sto. 1; Thwaites, H. A., Ldg. Ck. (O); Townsend, E. W., A/Ldg. Sigmn. (Ty.); Unwin, C., Ldg. Ck. (S); Usher, D. A. E., A.B.; West, H. F. W., A.B.; Whitby, N., A/Ldg. Smn.; Whittington, J. A., Sto. 1.

H.M.S. BLUEBELL

Summary of Service 1940 – 1945.

H.M.S. BLUEBELL, a Flower Class Corvette of 900 tons, completed on 19th July 1940, was built and engined by Fleming and Ferguson, Ltd., Paisley. She was allocated to Western Approaches, Northern Escort Force, based at Rosyth.

In 1940 she was engaged on all the duties for which corvettes are responsible, escorting convoys, searching for and attacking U-boats which had sunk ships in the convoys and rescuing survivors. In the last four months of this year she was involved in the rescue of survivors from five incidents, including those from seven ships in convoy SC7 from Canada to U.K., which had been attacked by U-boats between 16th and 19th October. On the latter date she reported that she had 203 survivors from five ships on board and was rejoining the convoy. Two days earlier she had assisted in the hunt for one of the U-boats which had attacked the convoy, but without result, after rescuing survivors of two ships sunk in the earlier stages of the U-boat attack. In November 1940 she was allocated to the Fifth Escort Group, Western Approaches, based at Liverpool. On the 6th she was ordered to assist in rounding up Convoy HX 84 (Halifax to U.K.) which had been scattered after being attacked by the German "pocket" battleship ADMIRAL SCHEER on the 5th November, sinking the armed merchant cruiser the JERVIS BAY.

In the first days of 1941 the BLUEBELL was again hunting a U-boat, with H.M.S. WESTCOTT, CANDYTUFT, SCIMITAR and SKATE. Later in January she was detailed to escort convoy OGC 51 (U.K. to Gibraltar), but was in collision with, and damaged, the WESTCOTT, and escorted her to Londonderry. In March, when convoy HX 112 was attacked by U-boats between the Shetlands and Faroes, the BLUEBELL escorted to Greenock one ship which had been damaged and later landed 67 survivors from two ships which had been sunk. Two of the attacking submarines were however destroyed by the WALKER and VANOC. The BLUEBELL sailed to Gibraltar in July with four other corvettes and returned to U.K., escorting H.M.S. BRECONSHIRE. In August she was allocated to the 37th Escort Group, Western Approaches, still based at Liverpool. A further U-boat attack on a convoy took place in that month and again the BLUEBELL rescued survivors, on this occasion from two ships which had been torpedoed, and landed them at Greenock. She joined in an A/S sweep with the BOREAS later in the month after another convoy (OG71, U.K. to Gibraltar), had been attacked with the loss of ten ships. She was then recalled to Gibraltar to escort another convoy to U.K. On 12th October, C.-in-C., Western Approaches commended the BLUEBELL, among other ships, for her steaming performance during the past three months, saying it reflected great credit on all concerned. The remainder of the year was spent in escorting convoys to and from Gibraltar, including HG 75, which was shadowed and attacked for six days; but due to excellent work on the part of the escorts, only 4 ships were lost. On the night of 11th/12th December the BLUEBELL sighted and attacked a surfaced U-boat (U.67) off Cape St. Vincent but was only able to inflict slight damage.

The BLUEBELL continued to escort the Gibraltar convoys until the end of March 1942, when she went to the Tyne for a refit which lasted three months. Her next assignment was in September, as one of the four corvettes of the close escort for convoy PQ 18, a Russian convoy, which was attacked by aircraft and submarine torpedoes, and 13 of its 40 ships lost. About 43 enemy aircraft and 3 U-boats were however destroyed. In October the BLUEBELL was allocated to the 22nd Escort Group, still based at Liverpool. Between the end of September and December, no convoys sailed to Russia, but one made the return journey, QP 15, leaving Archangel on 17th November. The BLUEBELL was one of the ocean escorts of this convoy, which because it was severely buffeted by a succession of gales, and sailed in almost continuous darkness, became very scattered; but only two of the 30 allied merchantmen were lost.

During February 1943, the BLUEBELL again escorted a convoy. to North Russia, and in June she and the CAMELLIA were returned from the Kola Inlet, to the U.K. This was the second stage of an operation with a two-fold purpose, the first being to transport stores and reliefs for the force in Spitzbergen, and the second to pass out the two corvettes and to transport stores and reliefs for the British ships and establishments in North Russia. The whole operation was accomplished without enemy interference. H.M.S. BLUEBELL arrived in Bone on 9th July, being one of the escorts for one of the four assault convoys which sailed from the Clyde to take part in the invasion of Sicily. This successful operation secured Sicily as a base for future operations against Italy. The BLUEBELL was allocated to the 22nd Escort Group, Mediterranean Fleet, on 2nd August. In November she escorted a flight of 25 Landing Craft to the U.K., leaving Gibraltar on 5th November. In the early stages, she reported that she was being shadowed by enemy aircraft and on the 13th, heavy weather was experienced and the flight scattered in a N.W. gale. Four of the craft were lost but all the members of their crews were rescued with the exception of one rating, who was drowned. In December 1943, the BLUEBELL was allocated to the 23rd Escort Group, Western Approaches.

After a refit at Dunstaffnage in December 1943/January 1944, the BLUEBELL was again escorting Russian convoys, until April 1944, when preparations began for Operation "Neptune", the invasion of Normandy which began on 6th June 1944. She sailed with Convoy No. ECL1, as part of the escort for 31 L.S.T.s, on D + 1. By August she was again escorting convoys to and from Russia. She was allocated to the 8th Escort Group, Western Approaches, based at Greenock in September. In 1945 the BLUEBELL sailed with the Russian convoy JW 64 from Greenock on the 3rd February. The convoy was attacked on the 10th by two waves of torpedo-bombers. No ship was damaged and the attackers suffered substantial losses. The return convoy, RA 64, was not so fortunate. The Germans had assembled about six U-boats off the entrance to the Kola Inlet, and on the 17th February, H.M.S. LARK, which was sweeping ahead of the convoy, was torpedoed but safely towed into harbour; then a merchant ship was hit by the same U-boat and sank while being towed in. Before the day was over, at 1530, the BLUEBELL was torpedoed by U.711 and blew up. Only one survivor was picked up.

H.M.S. BLUEBELL was awarded the following Battle Honours:-

Atlantic	1940-4.
Arctic	1942-5.
Sicily	1943.
Normandy	1944.
Mediterranean	1944.

Her Commanding Officers were:

Lieut.-Cdr. R.E. Sherwood, R.N.R.,   May 1940.

Lieutenant G.H. Walker, D.S.C., R.N.V.R., 7th May 1942.

Naval Historical Branch
January 1969.

(Sta. 94/35)   ((GV445) W.t. 40584 D.8367. 50,000M. 12 45 B A S Lt. 91-78 2

S. 1420b.
(Established October, 1945

NAVAL MESSAGE.

To: FROM:

    S/H 14   COMSUBS SEVENTH FLEET

             RESTRICTED   PRIORITY.

         Upon release of the 14th Flotilla from
my command I again wish to express appreciation for
your co-operation and the fine spirit of willingness
in accomplishing assigned tasks. I have the greatest
admiration for the forthright sheer guts of you and
your personnel. May Divine Providence continue to
guide you and be with you in your future activities.

                  =190301=

1 - 7,13,21,27,32,41,48.
SEM   P/L   1420 i   DS   19/8/45

To the following I owe thanks for assistance in various forms:

Australian War Memorial for permission to reproduce the portrait
on the back cover.
Public Record Office, Kew, UK for access to official records.
Ministry of Defence, (Navy) Historical Section, UK for information
on U-boat movements.
Imperial War Museum and Admiralty for permission to reproduce
photographs.
Authors of books listed in the bibliography. These have been a
valuable source of data to augment and correct my recollections.
Wilfred Stiff, Bill Coates, Maurice Passingham, Ken Marcham,
Bernard Rhodes and Don Kirton, with whom I served in *Bluebell*,
for their recollections.
Joe Brooks for permission to reproduce his drawings.
Vernon Coles for his detailed and accurate accounts of much of the
X-craft story.
Ken Hudspeth, who graduated from *Rushcutter*, served in corvette
and X-craft and worked post-war as teacher and headmaster, thus
qualifying as the ideal proof reader.
Roy Hall another graduate from Rushcutter, Algra Clarke, Martin
Ridgwell, Eileen Mason and Harvey Morrish for proof reading.
Frank Walker, author of "HMAS Armidale: the ship that had to
die" (Kingfisher Press), for professional advice.
Michael Daube and his wife Ruth, for translation and having my
draft transfered to word processor.
Gus Britton of the RN Submarine Museum Archives for professional
assistance.
Murray Dare for corvette and submarine drawings.
Herta Simon and Otto Pelczar for translation of U-boat war diaries.

INDEX